WHEN MEN WALK DRY
Portuguese Messianism in Brazil

American Academy of Religion
Academy Series

edited by
Susan Thistlethwaite

Number 61
WHEN MEN WALK DRY
Portuguese Messianism in Brazil
by
Carole A. Myscofski

Carole A. Myscofski

WHEN MEN WALK DRY
Portuguese Messianism in Brazil

Scholars Press
Atlanta, Georgia

WHEN MEN WALK DRY
Portuguese Messianism in Brazil

by
Carole A. Myscofski

Library of Congress Cataloging in Publication Data
Myscofski, Carole A., 1954-
    When men walk dry.

    (American Academy of Religion academy series ;
no. 61)
    Bibliography: p.
    1. Brazil--Religious life and customs.
2. Portugal--Religious life and customs.
3. Messianism--History. I. Title. II. Series.
BL2590.B7M96   1988   291.2'3'0981   88-24015
ISBN 1-55540-256-9
ISBN 1-55540-257-7 (pbk.)

Printed in the United States of America
on acid-free paper

For my parents

Preface

In 1677, Eusébio de Mattos preached a dramatic sermon on the suffering of Jesus and warned his Brazilian congregation that the Day of Judgement was at hand. Taking his text from the Latin Bible (Lk. 21:26), Mattos proclaimed that "while men weep for their sins, while there are tears of penitence," the Last Days may be postponed, but "when men walk dry [of tears] the day of Judgement will infallibly arrive." (See below, p. 122).

Eusébio de Mattos was one of the preachers, missionaries, flagellants and saviors who continued the Portuguese messianic tradition in Brazil.

Table of Contents

Chapter 1

Introduction

Purpose

In the nineteenth century in Brazil, three messianic movements appeared in the Northeast region, beginning in the years 1817, 1838 and 1883. These three movements, of duration ranging from two to thirteen years, had a lasting impact on the religious and historical context of the Northeast, not only because of the historical and social role that they played in that time, but also because these represented dramatic expression of vital traditional religious beliefs in that part of Brazil. It is the hypothesis of the present endeavor, based on historical research, that these three messianic movements arose from a profound, dynamic Luso-Brazilian religious tradition of messianic beliefs and practices. This tradition, incorporating religious elements originally derived from the Portuguese religious complex, had been established in that region of Brazil from the early colonial period and, in its development over time, formed and continued a matrix of messianism and strategically related religious and legendary myths, ritual practices and social relation patterns. This Luso-Brazilian tradition was perpetuated by the representatives of the Roman Catholic Church in Brazil and by the Portuguese-descended residents of the Northeast as an integral part of their religious belief system and, as such, was the source for the beliefs, practices and forms of the later messianic movements themselves.

The purpose of this thesis will be to discover the beginnings of the Luso-Brazilian messianic tradition in its original locus in Portugal and to trace its structural development through colonial Brazil to the occurrence of the messianic movements of the nineteenth century. This study is undertaken for the explicit purpose of the testing of an appropriate historical model for the investigation of these religious phenomena, a model which would thus elicit the crucial religious

1

elements of the messianic movements under study from their religious historical background.

The positing of such a religious messianic tradition obviates the usual limited perspective for the study of messianic movements which designates these phenomena as epiphenomenal or isolated incidents. The present study will instead refer an understanding of the source and causation of messianic movements to religious precedents. Accordingly, the intent of this thesis is to introduce the possibility of the study of messianism as a dynamic religious tradition and to portray the development of such a tradition in a particular historical context, that is, between sixteenth-century Portugal and nineteenth-century Brazil. This study will attempt to show that this determinate, articulate tradition bore the seeds of and gave impetus to the radical religious activity of the three messianic movements of Northeastern Brazil. The specific task of this thesis is thus to establish the trends or motifs persistent in Luso-Brazilian messianism and the bond between them and to trace these, by means of empirical research, from Portugal to Brazil within the limits of this extensive time span.

The trajectory of this tradition will be followed in chronological progression from its determined beginnings to the manifestations of the Brazilian messianic movements. As Brazil was colonized and dominated by Portugal, and the participants of the nineteenth-century messianic movements were primarily of Portuguese descent, so this historical study will take as its starting point Portugal in the sixteenth century, the age of discovery. The elemental forms of the messianic tradition will be derived in that place and era; from that point the study will follow the transmission to the colony and thence through colonial and postcolonial Brazil, to 1899. For the purposes of this study, an empirical, historical approach will be assumed. Methods appropriate to text analysis for the consideration of messianic texts in this Luso-Brazilian history and for the sociological interpretation of group interaction will also be employed as necessary.

The historical data for this study has been obtained from archival records of participants, observers and historians of this religious phenomenon during the phases of its existence. Research was undertaken at the Joseph Regenstein Library of the University of Chicago, the Newberry Library of Chicago, and at principal libraries and archives in Brazil. These latter include the Bibliotecas de História e de Ciências Sociais of the Universidade de São Paulo, the Arquivo do Instituto dos Estudos Brasileiros (Universidade de São Paulo), the

Arquivo do Instituto Histórico e Geográfico de São Paulo, the Arquivo Público do Estado de São Paulo, the Biblioteca Municipal de São Paulo, the Archivo da Cúria Municipal de São Paulo; the Biblioteca Nacional, Arquivo Nacional, the Museu Nacional, the Biblioteca and Arquivo do Instituto Histórico e Geográfico Brasileiro, the Real Gabinete Português de Leitura, and the Biblioteca de Santo Inácio, in Rio de Janeiro; and the Biblioteca Pública Central do Estado da Bahia in Salvador, Bahia.

Definitions

The study of messianism, as the study of any other significant religious phenomenon, requires a preliminary statement which indicates or delimits the proper field of inquiry, that is, a definition. The problem of delimitation is complex, for criteria or definitional points may be derived from two different perspectives: on the one hand, a definitional base may be extrapolated from a small study of existent cults, generating broad characteristics from this limited beginning; or, on the other hand, a contrary method may generalize criteria so broad as to encompass as many varieties of cults as possible. Before proceeding, therefore, with the theoretical aspects and historical consideration of the Luso-Brazilian messianism under study in this thesis, a few categories and operational definitions will be discussed.

The study of messianism falls under the study of eschatology, that is, the study of the religious beliefs of a particular group or groups concerning "last things." The *eschaton*, from the Greek word for end or limit, refers specifically to the end of the world or cosmos and, correlatively, to established ages of the world and events leading to the often catastrophic end of all things. Judeo-Christian traditions include within this scope the Last Judgement, resurrection of the dead, the coming of the Messiah or the Second Coming of Jesus and related beliefs concerning the final millennium of history; other traditions focus on reversal of world order or destruction and renewal of this earth. Eschatology has primarily to do with the absolute end of historical time, and religious traditions lacking a concept of such an *eschaton* cannot be said to possess an eschatology.

Messianism is the belief in a messiah, that is, in the coming or return of a promised savior. This savior, chosen and extraordinarily endowed by the deity, will liberate humanity or a single part thereof from suffering and oppression, marking the end of this world and the beginning of a radically different existence. The term "messianism," again, derives specifically from the Judeo-Christian belief based on scriptural descriptions but has also been used to describe parallel beliefs in different contexts. General usage notwithstanding, messianism indicates the belief in a religious savior or savior-king, and it is in this sense that it will be used throughout the present work. Radical messianism, or better, radical eschatology, refers to the belief that the promised coming of the savior is imminent and demands suspension of ordinary or secular lifestyle in order to prepare for this event; deferred messianism, on the other hand, is the institutionalized belief such as has existed in the mainstream of Christian doctrine since the third century of this era which effectively postpones the advent of the savior until the indefinite "last days" in the distant future.

The terms "millennialism" and "millenarianism," now used interchangeably to indicate a staggering variety of religious movements, had originally specific and limited references. Millenarianism was thus the Christian belief that Jesus Christ will return to reign personally and visibly on this earth, surrounded by his saints and chosen righteous followers for a period of one thousand years, after which period the remainder of humanity would be resurrected and the world end for all time. Premillennial beliefs place the Second Coming of Jesus before the paradisial millennium; postmillennial beliefs place the deliverance by Jesus after an earthly millennium realized through human means. "Chiliasm," based on the Greek word for "one thousand," has understandably the same meaning as millenarianism.

Current usage of these terms has, however, removed the Christian specificity; these are now used to designate religious utopian movements of various cultures whose common belief is in the imminent advent of a golden age on earth in which the group will prosper or rule the world. Included in the structure of this belief is the perception of the world as imbalanced or evil, the expectation of a hero-figure to enact or initiate the change to the better existence and, often, detailed imagery of the terrestrial paradise to come. Religious movements or cults of this type have also been called crisis cults; for the purposes of this study, the referent will be as millenarian-type cults.

Under these rubrics, a wide variety of historical religious movements have been juxtaposed. Phenomena which may be classified as millenarian or millenarian-type cults include non-Western or dissenting religious movements such as African prophetic or revitalistic Christian groups, Brazilindian movements, Melanesian and New Guinean Cargo

Cults, and Amerindian Ghost Dance sects. Large-scale or widely based institutional religious belief systems, such as Judaism, Roman Catholicism and Protestantism, possess a belief in deferred messianism, and, although the presence of a true *eschaton* is controvertible, some Buddhist sects may also be said to hold a similar belief. Imminent messianism is related primarily to spontaneous and radical or dissenting religious groups; examples of these are medieval Christian messianic movements of Flanders and Germany, groups in medieval Judaism that gathered around a self-announced Messiah-figure, North American Protestant utopian movements, and the Brazilian Roman Catholic groups of the nineteenth century.[1]

This range of religious phenomena does not permit a single comprehensive definition; rather, the field must be divided, such that truly related religious movements are categorized under separate rubrics. The alternative would force such general and unusable referents as "crisis cults" or "utopian sects" with equally vague and untenable definitions.

For the purposes of the present study, one small portion of the vaster phenomenon will be circumscribed and defined. These are the messianic movements of nineteenth-century Brazil and comparable movements in the Judaic or Christian tradition of medieval Europe, with the following critical characteristics: (1) belief in the coming or return of a supernatural or other-world agent, a messiah who will (2) effect the cataclysmic end of the world and (3) initiate an age of religious triumph on this earth, (4) saving and exalting only the participants in the movement. This earthly salvation is (5) imminent, such that (6) all unrelated or diverting activities must be abandoned and all attention focused on preparation for the coming of the messiah. (7) The group does not, however, adopt a political plan in order to bring about the great transformation, but relies on prayers and religious rituals for the preparation of the group and depends on the messiah as the critical actor. Finally, (8) the beliefs and practices of the messianic movement,

---

1   Weston LaBarre, "Materials for a History of Studies of Crisis Cults: A Bibliographic Essay," *Current Anthropology* 12 (February 1979): 3-43, provides an excellent source, albeit now somewhat dated, for the study of the various types of messianic and millenarian movements. See also Sylvia Thrupp, ed., *Millennial Dreams in Action* (New York: Schocken Books, 1970).

although it is a dissent sect, derive from an established and contemporaneously acceptable religious eschatology, that is, from a religious tradition of messianism.

As part of historical religious traditions, messianic movements may best be understood in studies which proceed historically, following the persistence and development of key religious beliefs, activities and group organizations, and which integrate the elements of the eventual messianic movement within this tradition. The usual scholarly studies on messianic and similar movements, however, have taken alternate and less successful approaches; these will be considered in the following chapter. In the subsequent chapters the operative hypothesis of the present study will be considered at length and the historical discussion begun.

Chapter 2

Criticism

Messianic movements, variously defined, have continually been a source of great perplexity for the scholars who examine them, beginning with earliest historical accounts in the nineteenth century. These scholars, in their attempts to understand the development and characteristics of the cults, have produced studies ranging between the two extremes of ethnographic monographs—which overwhelm the reader in a flood of details on the historical particulars, peculiar participants and unusual characteristics of the movements under study—and vast encyclopedic and universalistic works—which draw comparative parallels between distinctly divergent types of messianic groups. These latter rely on common factors such as the critical historical circumstances in which the messianic movements occurred, the sociopolitical morphology of the messianic group and the dominant beliefs of the religious creeds in order to demonstrate the universality of the messianic impulse.

In the study of messianic movements, research has been dominated by historians and religious historians who have contributed primarily comparative works, by anthropologists who have produced admirably documented monographs, particularly on Cargo Cults, by psychologically oriented historians, and more recently by sociologists.

All of these theorists, even those who consciously limit their work to monographic treatment of a single outbreak, consider it an important part of their task to indicate the core meaning or significance of the messianic movement under scrutiny. All of these have inevitably concerned themselves with the causes of the messianic movements, that is, why they occurred, and the effects of such religious activity, that is, what the participants sought to gain through it. These are problems that no scholar can neglect because of the dynamic and unpredictable nature of messianic movements. Further, parallels have been repeatedly drawn between these religious movements and other social or political

7

movements, that is to say, secular movements. With the increasing importance in academic circles of the study of social structures and social behavior, greater emphasis has been placed on the parallels themselves, to the neglect of the unique features of religious activity in itself. This particular point will be explored below.

The theorists considered in this chapter certainly do not present the full range of theoretical possibilities in the study of messianic movements; that range is illimitable. However, they do represent important recent interpretations in this area, interpretations which have had a discernible impact on the ongoing understanding of messianism.

Scholars have employed various strategies in the explanation of messianic movements. Generally, in the process of explanation they have invoked a combination of factors rather than one key causal element. Yet each has placed considerable emphasis on one integral explanation of messianic movements to which the other factors are subordinate. Accordingly, their studies fall into two distinct categories as they emphasize (1) the situation in which the messianic movement took place, or (2) the psychological response of the participants of the group involved. These two categories may be further subdivided, as emphasis falls on the economic and political situation, or the social situation; on the psychological response of the groups as a whole, or the psychological response of the leader of the group.

The Situation

Explanations based on the *situations* in which messianic movements have appeared highlight the external pressures placed on the eventual participants. In general this view produces a rather mechanistic analysis of the relationship between a group's material condition, including global and local political configuration, social status, kinship structure and economic developments, and that group's self-initiated behavior. Independent or individual responses to the given situation are discounted, as are religious historical precedents or alternate behavioral responses.

Of particular interest here is change — sudden, inexplicable and irreversible change — from an accepted pattern to an unacceptable one, in the view of the group involved. This new situation is portrayed by the theorist as the ultimate source or motivation of the messianic movement. The same group of people in another setting, lacking the key external stimulant, would not coalesce into such religious activity.

As indicated above, this category may be subdivided into two distinct groups, those which emphasize the political and economic situation and those which stress the social structural situation.

Explanation Based on Politico-economic Situation

A small group of theorists, including Marxist historians, place preponderant emphasis on the political and/or economic situation as productive of messianic movements. These have characterized unstable governments, particularly at the local level, sudden change in governmental structures, and upheaval of the local economic system as significant events, or even causes, in the formation of messianic movements. Among those employing this method are Vittorio Lanternari, E. J. Hobsbawm, and Ralph Della Cava.[1]

Vittorio Lanternari, in his book, *Religions of the Oppressed*, places the weight of his explanatory argument on the situation of political oppression of one group by another—emphasizing the culture clash of colonization by Europeans. He includes in his comparative analysis the nativistic movements throughout Africa, the Peyote cult in North America, various sects in the Caribbean and Latin America, and Cargo Cults in Melanesia and Polynesia. That he is not only concerned with messianic movements *per se* is evident from his inclusion in the section on Brazil of Brazilindian revivalistic and *Santidade* sects, the spiritist groups of Candomblé and popular Roman Catholic movements, as well as the messianic groups. Instead, Lanternari blurs the distinction between these sects in an effort to isolate and characterize religious groups which evolve in reaction to poverty, oppressive conditions and, especially, colonization by a foreign power. He stipulates that the various groups all

> are equally an expression of the anguish of people seeking a way out of dangerous and oppressive situations in the hope of achieving liberty and freedom from all oppression.[2]

---

1 Vittorio Lanternari, *The Religions of the Oppressed*, trans. L. Sergio (London: MacGibbon and Kee, 1963); E. J. Hobsbawm, *Primitive Rebels* (New York: W. W. Norton and Co., Inc., 1959); and Ralph Della Cava, "Brazilian Messianism and National Institutions: A Reappraisal of Canudos and Joaseiro," *Hispanic American Historical Review* 48 (1968): 402-420, and *Miracle at Joaseiro* (New York: Columbia University Press, 1970).

2 Lanternari, *Religions of the Oppressed*, p. 195.

The conflict of the colonial situation in which a people lose their freedom, integrity of culture and possession of traditional lands results in a bursting forth of group protest by the oppressed. For Lanternari, then, the significance of the movements lies in their ultimate expression of protest, not in the religious configuration of that protest; he asserts that

> although these movements are primarily religious in character, they also demand and strive to secure for their followers certain riches without which life itself is scarcely worth living. These riches are freedom and salvation [from oppression].[3]

Interpretation of these movements in religious terms or as primarily religious phenomena would, for Lanternari, blunt the historical impact or moment they represent.

In his conclusions, Lanternari provides a distinction between sects which result from internal pressure, such as breakdown of the traditional culture, and from external pressure, such as colonization by a foreign power. The former, subject to endogenous pressure, would result in messianism which could be characterized as escapism; the latter would lead to revolutionary messianism.

His explanation, simply put, is that in the face of insupportable political oppression the oppressed peasants turn to messianic movements rather than to revolutionary or social reform movements in order to bring about favorable change and regain lost liberty. In this respect, Vittorio Lanternari's work forms part of that of a small group of universalist religious historians—following such theorists as Wilson D. Wallis and Rene Fülöp-Miller.[4] These, far from being critical scholars, instead introduce messianism as a function of human nature corresponding to a universal hope for a better life or the answer to the primal anxiety-dream of all humankind.

However, while Wallis and Fülöp-Miller devote their work to characterization of the messiahs or leaders as well as to the historical development of messianic movements, Lanternari has chosen instead to emphasize the oppressive situation. The information on the various cults described in his book, although detailed, is presented uncritically

---

3   Ibid., p. 301.
4   Wilson D. Wallis, *Messiahs: Christian and Pagan* (Boston: The Gorham Press, 1918); and Rene Fülöp-Miller, *Leaders, Dreamers and Rebels* (New York: Viking Press, 1935).

and with little regard as to the source. The treatment of the "natives" and their bizarre actions becomes at times reduced to the goggling found in nineteenth-century travel books. His presentation is continually hampered by the use of the distinctions "Christian" (us) and "pagan" (them) and by the extraordinary lengths to which the author goes in order to sympathize with the rebellious efforts and frustrations of the less fortunate.

The conclusions he reaches are vague at best: he describes malcontents seeking liberty by means of messianic movements and other unrelated religious sects. His definition of oppression is rather generous and extends to such a range of situations so as to render it meaningless and unusable. While he sympathizes with the protesters, Lanternari leaves unclear the viability and the result of most of the groups presented.

The reader is also left with the unfortunate supposition that religion can be assumed as a cover for political activity and is only used as a means or an expression of discontent. This theme finds an echo in each work discussed in this chapter. According to this supposition, political oppression, social upheaval, and psychological distress first propel the people into confused responses; they then turn, *in a secondary moment*, to religious modes to express their frustration, rebelliousness, etc.

E. J. Hobsbawm, in *Primitive Rebels*, presents a limited but influential treatment of millenarian movements in his classic typology of primitive social movements of the nineteenth and twentieth centuries.[5] He considers episodes and effects of social banditry, brotherhoods such as the Mafia, social rituals, and the Millenarian movements, including the Lazzarettists, and sects in Andalusia and Sicily. Characteristic of millenarian groups are (1) their deep dissatisfaction with contemporary political and economic conditions, (2) their millennial beliefs, especially related to Judeo-Christian radical eschatology and (3) their impractical or utopian vision of the means by which to achieve profound change for their group.

His explanation of the changing political and economic situation from which the millenarian sects emerge relies fundamentally on an arithmetic accumulation of factors. Of foremost importance is the general problem of the disruption of peasant society by externally imposed modern capitalism. Describing the conditions in Monte Amiata

---

5   Hobsbawm, *Primitive Rebels*, pp. 57-107.

during Davide Lazzaretti's influence, for example, Hobsbawm adds the introduction of land reforms and industrial crisis, harvest failure, impending European war, instability of ecclesiastical authority and the demands of new tax laws to the portrait of the disruption of the cultural integrity of the Monte Amiata area. As a primitive group, however, the peasants formed a messianic movement rather than a political revolution.

A significant part of the formulation of Hobsbawm's theory of these movements is a one-dimensional and nonanalytical understanding of the nature of peasants in peasant society. The reader is given to understand that the peasants, naïve in the face of economic reforms and lacking a political consciousness, fall headlong into acceptance of the impracticable dream of chiliastic ideology. Hobsbawm supposes that, when faced with the situation at Monte Amiata, "nothing would be more natural than for a peasant to pass through an intellectual and spiritual crisis."[6] The responses of the populace appear to be more or less automatic in the given historical conditions.

However, the impulse leading from the cited factors of the crisis to the specific elements of the millenarian movement is never elucidated. This lacuna becomes even more problematic as Hobsbawm turns to consider social anarchy and, then, communistic groups under the same rubric of millenarianism. These are clearly structurally different responses to apparently similar situations. The failure to map out the steps which lead from the stimuli of political stress to the response of millennial cult undercuts the entire analysis of social movements.

Also present in his work is an affirmation of the usefulness of the messianic belief as an ideology which is inherently adaptable to modernized political movements. Hobsbawm interprets the religious traditions of the groups to be a temporarily assumed belief pattern which may change into or be absorbed by the more progressive or advanced revolutionary movements. The messianic beliefs which crystallize the hopes of the followers and evoke their traditional perception of their own society are, through this theoretical study, characterized as superficial, enigmatic or, indeed, misguided expressions of political feelings, expressions which are easily abandoned.

Ralph Della Cava in his first contribution to the study of messianism (1968) offered a reappraisal of the messianic movement of Antônio

---

6   Ibid., p. 68.

Conselheiro at Canudos and the nonmessianic popular religious sect following Padre Cícero at Joaseiro. For this, he introduces the effects of national political history on the development of both groups. His purpose is

> to demonstrate that the popular religious movements [in Brazil] were from the outset...intimately tied into the national ecclesiastical and political power structures of imperial and republican Brazil; and that they were also enmeshed within a changing nationwide economy.[7]

Of critical importance in the situation that Della Cava presents is nineteenth-century reform of the ecclesiastical authority hierarchy in Northeastern Brazil and the change of government from the Empire of Brazil to the Republic in 1889, with the concomitant political reorganization at nearly every level of government and sweeping changes in tax laws. Also mentioned briefly is economic turmoil from 1877 on due to diminished agricultural production. Della Cava indicates the importance of each group on the national and state levels during the contemporary power struggles and insists that each event "reveals the interplay of the messianic movements and national structures."[8]

The argument throughout the essay is directed against earlier dualistic treatments of the Brazilian Northeast as a traditional, backward, conservative community fighting against the modernization forced upon it by the urban coastal government. Della Cava instead describes the section of Northeastern Brazil under discussion as an inseparable part of the national political scene and adds that the religious movements which occurred there were in reaction to change at that level.

Della Cava continues this approach in *Miracle at Joaseiro*. Although this later work deals with an essentially nonmessianic movement, the introductory explanation again stresses political history. The religious turmoil at Joaseiro was not merely an isolated rural phenomenon but, again, a reaction to crises of national, political and economic conjuncture. Understanding this sect from the point of view of political history serves to explain the persistence of the group as rigid religious theories cannot, in Della Cava's view. A "millenarian perspective" yields a bias similar to those of nineteenth-century interpretations which characterized messianism as the religious fanaticism of a backward people.[9]

7　Della Cava, "Reappraisal," p. 404.
8　Ibid., p. 414.
9　Della Cava, *Miracle at Joaseiro*, p. 3.

In both of these efforts, however, Della Cava fails to make any but the most tenuous connections between national politics and the messianic movements. Coincidence of events does not necessitate connection or causality. Further, while the political or religious elites may be involved in the effects of institutional change, the backlands community has not been exclusively dependent on the coastal urban community. The people of the communities near Canudos and Joaseiro maintain a more conservative religious outlook than the urban centers and in the past only occasionally became involved in political intrigues outside the region. Maria Isaura Pereira de Queiroz noted, by way of example of the relative isolation in that region, that currently in the Northeast one encounters the recitation of political leaders, from the most recent to the earliest, to be "Getúlio Vargas – Pedro II – Charlemagne."[10]

The analysis of economic conditions adds little to the explanation. Drought may have forced reduced agricultural production and the loss of a significant portion of the local labor force to the urban coast. However, the direct connection between these developments and the formation or persistence of the religious movements is never made.

In spite of the detailed historical account which these two works include, the religious movements are not clearly integrated into the pattern of political and economic events. The "origins and developments of messianism" are never drawn from the history itself,[11] and the assumption of the intimate connection is simply left inexplicit.

The theories which base their explanations on the critical politico-economic situation, however reasonable or well documented their argument of causation or characterization becomes, fail on two points. First, they are unable to elicit a concrete pattern of political events which inevitably leads to a messianic movement or to define the process of development of such a movement. Second, and more important, they cannot account for the essentially religious nature of the movement which they have chosen to portray as a response to political – i.e., secular – crises. Religion thereby becomes construed as an overlay or superficial aspect of a protest movement, and analysis of the religious

---

10   Maria Isaura Pereira de Queiroz, "Três sobrevivências portuguesas na civilização rústica brasileira," in *O campesinato brasileiro: ensaios sobre civilização e grupos rústicos no Brasil* (Petrópolis: Editora Vozes Ltda., 1976), p. 190.
11   Della Cava, "Reappraisal," p. 420.

beliefs and activities involved is either relegated to a distinctly secondary position or is simply omitted.

Explanation Based on Social Situation

This mode of explanation has gained considerable attention among scholars of messianic movements. Although the theories and schools of sociology vary from author to author, they consistently emphasize sudden critical change in social structures — both at the local and at the global level (e.g., nationally or in Western civilization) — in the strength of kinship ties, and in the assignment of social status in the explanations of the occurrence of messianic movements. Representative of this approach are Peter Worsley and Maria Isaura Pereira de Queiroz.[12]

Peter Worsley, in his treatment of New Guinean Cargo Cults, makes a clear effort to ground those religious activities in the colonial context from which they emerged. He generally characterizes millennial groups such as these as "embryonic nationalism" and considers the development from Cargo Cult to nationalistic political party to be a progression, though not necessarily chronological.[13]

Worsley begins his book with a weighty section on "Theoretical Considerations" in which he defends his sociological method and offers a characterization of the fate of most continuing millenarian groups.[14] These arguments are left behind as the historical and typological aspects of the Cargo Cults under study are considered.

Cargo Cults arose out of the profound disturbance of native society caused by the intrusion of European colonizers. The earliest Cargo groups formed before World War I: those in Tuka and the Fiji Islands began around 1885. The apparent causes of these influential, though short-lived, cults were the disruptive military conflicts in the area.

The majority of documented Cargo Cults took place during the British colonial rule of New Guinea. The native culture and social structure was shattered under the British by the process of

---

12 Peter Worsley, *The Trumpet Shall Sound* (New York: Schocken Books, 1968); and Maria Isaura Pereira de Queiroz, *O Messianismo: no Brasil e no mundo*, second ed., rev. (São Paulo: Alfa-Omega, 1976). See also Queiroz, "Classifications des messianismes brésiliens," *Archives de Sociologie des Réligions* 5 (1958): 111-120; and "O movimento messiânico do Contestado," *Revista brasileiro de estudos políticos* 9 (July 1960): 118-139.

13 Worsley, *Trumpet Shall Sound*, p. 178.

14 Ibid., pp. ix-lxix.

colonization – a situation exacerbated by the changes of European nationals and by the inherent instability of the British governing institutions and the missionary authorities. The new society which was to replace the traditional New Guinean social pattern appeared disorganized and unstable to the New Guineans. The new network of social relations which the New Guineans expected to form with the Europeans remained incomplete for two reasons. First, the Europeans, particularly the British, did not cooperate in the manner expected of them in order to form a new social whole; and, second, progressive growth in industry controlled by the government drew large numbers of villagers into the urban work force, causing further breakdown of the old social structure.

The Cargo Cults, in Worsley's view, expressed the resentment on the part of the participants faced with this social disruption. They also expressed the tensions derived from relations with European missionaries. In the traditional culture, religion had served as the source for knowledge, both for the New Guineans' understanding of themselves and for practical instructions for dealing with their environment. New Guineans came to associate both their lack of European manufactured possessions (cargo) and their inequality of status with the white colonizers with a lack of true knowledge. It was believed, therefore, that the missionaries had withheld crucial teachings. These difficulties were enhanced by the rivalry between the different mission groups for the loyalty of the natives.

The Cargo Cults, then, resulted from a state of confusion, from resentment of an unexpected lower social position, from frustration at the dissolution of traditional social status and social relations, and from the failure to achieve new, equal social relations with the Europeans.

In analyzing this emotionally charged colonial situation, Worsley focused on the relations between the oppressors and the oppressed in order to explain the emergence of Cargo Cults. Discussion of the religious configuration of the cults, beyond a rather sketchy outline, is not included. Cargo Cults emerged and flourished because they provided a unification point for diverse disinherited groups among the New Guineans. Worsley dwells on the achievement of this social solidarity, especially as a key step toward the development of nationalism and political alignments.

This account of the Cargo Cults, although rich in historical detail, does not provide a consistent explanation of the beginning nor of the continuation of these cults. Their role and structure as religious movements is uncertain, not, however, due to lack of information. For example, in his discussion of one of the earlier movements, Worsley notes that its leader was of a family of hereditary priests but does not go on to integrate that religious fact with either the man's function in the Cargo Cult or with the success of the cult's development.

The emphasis throughout this work falls on the role of Cargo Cults as unifying factors for the New Guinean people in the face of outside interference and on the further development of Cargo Cults into secular nationalistic parties. Because of the author's emphasis on the position of Cargo Cults as an intermediate stage of development, the reader cannot discover the reason that the Cargo Cults (rather than, say, politically revolutionary groups) formed at all, except owing to the folly of the natives. It is also unclear whether the social solidarity achieved by the cult members was actually the dominant impetus in the formation of each cult or simply a fortunate consequence.

Maria Isaura Pereira de Queiroz, the Brazilian sociologist, has written a number of studies of messianic movements, that is, on the general characteristics of messianic movements, on the specific aspects of Brazilian movements, including the Contestado movement which arose in Southern Brazil among the German-Protestant community, and a lengthy detailed analysis of Western messianism. This last book, *O Messianismo: no Brasil e no mundo*, offers description and classification of medieval Christian movements, North American Ghost Dance sects and Cargo Cults, as well as of Brazilindian, colonial and postcolonial religious groups. While Queiroz has now abandoned further research in this area, her efforts have had significant influence on Brazilian anthropologists and sociologists and on historians of the Brazilian Catholic Church.

The primary concern throughout these articles and books is to classify messianic movements according to the social situations in which they occurred. The definition of messianic movements is uncritically assumed and does not form a part of the process of classification. Accordingly, messianic movements share a definitional pattern of belief: that (1) the community has suddenly fallen into an evil historical period and that (2) change is desirable and imminent through (3) the agency of a saint or messiah who will (4) bring about a complete amelioration of conditions. The movements may also be defined according to their beliefs in the agent—the saint or messiah—who will bring about the hoped-for change, and according to the role and image of the leader.

Queiroz acknowledges that various factors—religious, cultural, economic or political—may be considered in the comparison of messianic movements. Classifications based on these factors, however, arise from the scholar's own perspective which is artificially imposed on the movements and not derived from the situation itself. The more valid explanation thus derives from the pattern of social structures during the development of messianic movements. The identity of the configurations of social structures at a time of structural crisis provides for Queiroz a simple classificatory schema. There are three basic structural situations which underlie the formation of messianic movements:[15] (1) *the formation of new global societies*, involving particularly the change from kinship-based social relations to economically based social relations, affecting movements such as those in medieval Flanders and Germany, and post-Reformation Portugal; (2) *change in the internal configuration of global societies* and resultant anomie, with the related movements in nineteenth-century North America, of the Brazilian Guaraní before the coming of the Europeans and those in postcolonial Brazil; and (3) *the formation of new societies, with change or anomie in the internal configuration of global societies*, related to movements such as those of the colonized people of Melanesia, Africa and Brazil. The crisis situations which fall into these categories may separately be understood as acceptance of or resistance to acculturation, social disorganization, political transformation or religious reconstruction.

The function of messianic movements is to provide a new framework for social relations during a period in which the old pattern of social relations is radically devalued and the new, apparently externally imposed pattern is either unacceptable or unattainable. The significant social relations are both internal to the messianic group, that is, between the leader and the followers, and external, that is, the relations of the leader, the followers and the whole of the group at once to the governmental and ecclesiastical authorities.

Queiroz' effort to produce a single schema for analysis results in a confused and overextended system of classification. The first two points in her schema, of crises in global societies and in the internal configuration of global societies, and the third point which combines the two remain at a highly abstracted level of analysis and do not serve

---

15   Queiroz, *O Messianismo*, p. 143.

to further our understanding either of the messianic movements so classified or of the crises themselves. The repetition of this classificatory system through the last one hundred pages of *O Messianismo* does not clarify the explanation, but rather complicates it.

Her treatment of the individual messianic movements, except in her specialized study of Contestado,[16] remains sketchy. Despite the generalized social-structural schema, her studies on messianism are merely descriptive and offer little valuable analysis.

Unanswered in her writings is the question of the development of religious movements from crises in social structures. The connection between social relations and religious beliefs or activities is not delineated. Although Queiroz suggests that one of the functions of messianic movements is the restoration of traditional ways, she admits in her final reflections[17] that many questions yet remain concerning the religious beliefs and movements involved.

In the explanations based on social situation, the theories involve a complex analysis of social relations, social structure and the problems of change on these levels. When a specific messianic movement is under consideration, the traditional or existent social situation is first discussed, followed by an examination of the crisis situation and the changes which the social situation undergoes. The conclusion of these discussions is that messianic movements begin and develop in direct relation to the stressful changes in the social situation. The operative hypothesis is that when an established social order is threatened, members of that order will attempt to form a new social order by means of a messianic movement or Cargo Cult. This process, from disruptive social situation to new cult, is historically proven by the various examples given, but it is not logically derived or derivable from the explanation itself. The explanation does not consider the reason for the formation of a religious cult when social solidarity or security is sought. Further, when, as in the theories of Queiroz, the social situation is indicated primarily as a characteristic of the described movements, generalizations based on comparison of these social situations entail a forced and incomprehensibly convoluted schema.

Explanations based on the political, economic and social situation from which the messianic cult emerges have described abysmally

16   Queiroz, "O Movimento messiânico do Contestado."
17   Queiroz, *O Messianismo*, p. 355.

chaotic, oppressive circumstances of the disintegration of acceptable ways of life, deprivation of economic independence and cultural integrity, disruption of valuative systems and interference by colonial powers. As the situation is constructed, the messianic movement arises as an integral and reactive part of the situation, a seemingly inevitable result.

It is here, however, that the primary difficulty lies. Messianism is *not* inevitable in any specific given situation. Innumerable examples may be cited of parallel political, economic and social crises in which no messianic ideas or activity appeared. Messianism is not the archetypal hope or anxiety-dream of all humanity when crisis occurs. Political disruption, economic devastation, social disorganization or any external crisis does not necessarily produce religious activity of such a particular and special nature.

Because no explanation is offered that could account for messianic activity in response to these described situations, messianism is unfailingly depicted as political or social rebellion under the guise or the folly of religious creeds and rituals. That is, messianism is understood to be *misdirected activity*, or merely an intermediate step on the road to true political and social movements.

This artificial conclusion occurs repeatedly when the religious beliefs and practices are not given serious consideration and the ulterior or supposed real motives of the participants are instead brought under analysis. This pattern of explanation, disallowing the role of religion in religious movements, recurs in theories based on psychological explanations.

The Psychological Response

In contrast with the approach presented above, a second group of theorists base their understanding of messianic movements on the psychology of the participants. These then utilize an internal approach to the conditions which significantly influence or actually precipitate messianic group activity.

After sufficiently outlining the related sociopolitical crisis, the scholars employing this explanation move to a different level of interpretation by exploring the *psychological response* of the individuals caught in that crisis. This psychological approach to messianism has characterized the emotional response as confusion, psychotic delusion, dream, fantasy, moral dilemma and anomie. While the situation may indeed be desperate, it is actually the emotional response of the participants which impels and fashions their messianism. Through this approach, human response to historical crisis is investigated and the posited emotional pattern then related to the religious cults.

This category of explanation will be considered in two groups: the first, of those placing emphasis on the participants or followers of the cults, and the second, on the leader alone.

Psychological Response of the Followers

In keeping with the significant influence of sociology and the study of social behavior, the majority of authors using this psychological approach focus on the collective psychological and emotional upheaval which sweeps a community into adherence to messianic beliefs and participation in messianic movements. Representative of these authors are Norman Cohn, Kenelm Burridge, Peter Lawrence and Michael Barkun.[18]

Norman Cohn's now-classic study of medieval messianic movements is impressive both in scope and in the depth of detail in which each group is considered. *The Pursuit of the Millennium* has been widely quoted and widely criticized.

Cohn investigates the medieval messianic movements against the backdrop of the struggle between lower and upper classes during the decline of feudalism. These movements continually drew on the mythic symbols and ritual behavior which formed part of Judeo-Christian eschatology and depended upon the European tradition of religious dissent.

Included in his study are cults in Flanders, Brittany and Bohemia of the twelfth through fifteenth centuries, the wave of flagellation cults of the thirteenth and later centuries in Southern and Northwestern Europe, and the heretical groups begun in the late medieval period. Cohn also discusses the Crusades as millennial activity, particularly the Crusades of the Poor in the twelfth and thirteenth centuries.

---

18   Norman Cohn, *The Pursuit of the Millennium*, second ed. (London: Oxford University Press, 1961); Kenelm Burridge, *Mambu* (New York: Harper and Row, 1960) and *New Heaven, New Earth* (New York: Schocken Books, 1969); Peter Lawrence, *Road Belong Cargo* (Manchester: Manchester University Press, 1964); and Michael Barkun, *Disaster and the Millennium* (New Haven, CT: Yale University Press, 1974).

Based on this panorama of religious activity, Cohn elicits five descriptive elements of the salvation which messianic movements seek: collective, terrestrial, imminent, total and miraculous.[19]

Cohn's understanding of the development of these medieval sects begins with the social situation in which they arose. In that period, the traditional life of the serf and small landowner had been characterized by poverty and oppressive dependence on the local nobility. The stressful condition was enhanced by the rapid social change brought about by the increasing shift from the traditional feudal economy and by the upheaval caused by repeated Crusades.

Traditional social and kinship bonds were gradually destroyed, and this destruction, coupled with chronic poverty and instability, resulted in disorientation among the lower classes. Deprived of emotional and material support due to the breakdown of feudalism,[20] this group of now landless rural poor and urban unemployed or casually employed was unprivileged, oppressed, unbalanced and confused. Overwhelming problems, such as the Black Plague and concomitant famine, and intolerable anxieties about the continuation and condition of life catapulted these people into the "mass delusion" of messianic belief.[21] They embraced the fantasy of messianism and the related religious anarchic and mystical beliefs and took up the practice of self-flagellation.

The menacing and hazardous lifestyle and the unstable social situation of the marginal groups in the lower class led to a "collective flight into the world of demonological phantasies." From their state of "chronic and inescapable insecurity," messianic movements offered emotional release in the form of the group practices, especially flagellation, which it encouraged.[22]

The messianic movements were led by pseudoprophets and pseudomessiahs, ambitious and inventive individuals who shaped eschatological fantasies to conform with the dreams and hopes of their followers. These followers, the unskilled workers, dispossessed farmholders and marginals, fairly tottered on the brink of mass psychosis; they were

---

19   Cohn, *Pursuit*, p. 13.
20   Ibid., p. 282.
21   Ibid., p. 87.
22   Ibid.

prone to messianic activity and might be provoked by any extraordinary or abnormal occurrence.[23]

Although Cohn offers considerable historical detail throughout the study, he fails to provide significant connections between the social circumstances and the psychological state of the people involved or between their psychological state and their choice of religious activity. Cohn asserts that the change from traditional society resulted in anxiety, self-delusion and near-psychosis, and these in turn resulted in the tremendous support for messianic movements. This analytical progress relies on two assumptions: first, a social-psychological assumption that poverty and social instability cause individual or collective emotional disturbance; and second, a psychoanalytical assumption that religion is based upon self-delusion and even psychosis.

The proffered explanation of messianic movements explains Cohn's own perspective before all else: it explains how Cohn believes people might act in a particular situation, based on current theories of psychological behavior, and how he views religion and, specifically, messianism. His uncritical suppositions of human reactions and motives, combined with the hybridized psychoanalytic generalizations, severely undercut the comparative base for his historical treatment of medieval messianic movements.

Kenelm Burridge deals with the problems of Cargo Cults in *Mambu*, discussing the New Guinean scene and people, and in *New Heaven, New Earth*, which is primarily a theoretical review.

The immediate explanation for Cargo Cults is the presence and activity of the Europeans in New Guinea and, particularly, the dominant economic and political position they assumed. Yet, while political unrest and economic disturbance play significant roles in this history, Burridge emphatically relates Cargo Cults to the native New Guineans' perception of and affective response to the turmoil around them. What Burridge characterizes as the ideological problem or the moral dilemma of the New Guinean situation may be better understood as their emotional response to the difficulties they endured.

Faced with the external pressures and changes brought about in the colonization of New Guinea and the resultant internal reorganization in social relations and status, the natives sought a new system for understanding their changing position in the world. They were caught

---

23   Ibid., p. 88.

between traditional mythology and the disruptive effect of the European presence and turned to produce a new cosmogonic myth, a sort of "community daydream," which would comprehensively reorganize their situation.[24] This Cargo myth then related the story of a primal error on the part of the black brother which enabled the white brother to flourish at his expense. The new myth-dream replaced older, challenged myths and incorporated the blacks' own guilt as inferiors, a new perspective of divine forgiveness and a new model for behavior — the moral European.[25] This last image, derived from the teachings of European missionaries, would allow access to cargo — material possessions and the power inherent in them — through a program of moral regeneration.

The New Guineans struggled to fit the Europeans into their newly formed cosmological and ethical systems. The New Guineans felt confusion and, particularly, resentment against the economically and politically superior European, that is, the immoral European, who blocked their progress in their quest for personal integrity and who refused to enter into an appropriate relationship with them.

The purpose of the Cargo Cult, for the perplexed New Guineans, was first to create a new man and then a new society which could incorporate the European material and intellectual imports. As new men, the New Guineans could get *cargo*, or at least access to it. Cargo, in these circumstances, was more than material goods; it was the symbol of manhood, of correct moral position and of power.

According to Burridge's explanation, Cargo Cults and Cargo myths were invented as part of the natives' emotional readjustment to colonization. They sought to change their self-image along with their world view. The primary difficulty with this approach is that Burridge accepts this confusion of irrational Cargo Cults as an appropriate response by the people, given what he views as their extremely limited understanding and confused psychological state.

The reader is barely able to recognize the non-European foundation of Cargo Cults. The ethical concepts such as primal guilt, conflict of morality and immorality and resultant moral dilemma are part of a Western Christian religious terminology imposed from without by Burridge and cannot be assumed to be integral to the Cargo Cults or myths.

---

24   Burridge, *Mambu*, p. 104.
25   Ibid., p. 207.

Burridge does construct tenuous connections between social circumstances and the affective response of resentment and confusion, and between the resentment and confusion felt and the reconstruction of mythology in the Cargo Cults. However, his explanation relies on an assumed pattern of behavior based rather loosely on Western psychological theories and on a contradictory understanding of New Guinean mentality as primitive, emotional and easily disturbed. This latter assumption is not uncommon in studies of Cargo Cult activities and finds echoes in the work of Peter Worsley, discussed above, and of Peter Lawrence, a discussion of which follows.

The approach chosen by Peter Lawrence combines a detailed account of the political history of New Guinea with a parallel study of what he calls the native epistemology or system of ideas. While the majority of the text of *Road Belong Cargo* presents a fairly straightforward narrative of the colonization process, Lawrence emphasizes that Cargo Cults were not the direct result of oppressive conditions or social disintegration but instead expressed the native resentment, confusion and misunderstanding.

Excepting the earliest arrivals, New Guineans found the Europeans to be untrustworthy, cruel, arbitrary and, significantly, incomprehensible. Strong feelings of hostility resulted from forced labor, seizure of property and the assumption of superior economic and political positions by the Europeans. Because of a lack of understanding of the Europeans, or, better, a lack of categories for understanding, New Guineans created Cargo myths and cults.

The traditional New Guinean society relied on the principles of reciprocity and redistribution of wealth in order to maintain economic stability. As their ideology (or mythology) held that material wealth was received from the deities, a cosmological stability was thereby maintained as well. The arrival of the Europeans and their refusal to adopt appropriate behavior, that is, to distribute manufactured goods and accept native products as equally valuable in exchange, disrupted native self-perception and forced the creation of new cosmogonic myths.

The New Guineans could not understand the historical process in which they found themselves. They reverted to irrational traditional belief structures or, as Lawrence expresses it, traditional epistemological structures. They returned then to their established structure of religious beliefs, altering its mythic content in order to account for the European presence. They further reorganized ritual activities in order to secure cargo, so that stability could once again be achieved. The

adoption by New Guineans of Christian beliefs was superficial, in
Lawrence's view, and only minimally affected the pattern of their
beliefs. The cultists in particular accepted Christian terms and rituals
as additional information in their pursuit of cargo. In general, Cargo
Cults were conservative: the participants retreated from the emotionally disturbing contact with the Europeans and relied on old ways in
radically new external circumstances.[26]

In the analysis of these Cargo Cults, Lawrence extensively discusses
native epistemological structures and their change in content. Beneath
his awkward choice of terminology, however, he is actually referring to
religious beliefs and ritual activity. The historical changes he describes
are continually connected with the emotional disruption felt by the
New Guineans.[27] The final conclusion is that the natives, confused and
irrational, retreated from the effects of colonization into their mythic
world and that this reaction was inherently inferior to Western rational
behavior.

While Lawrence continually demonstrates a comprehensive
knowledge of the New Guinea scene, his information is marred by the
attempts at analysis. As a result, the New Guineans have no religion,
only epistemology, and their Cargo Cults are seen as the products of
ignorance or dementia.

Michael Barkun explains the appearance of messianism in relation
to what he calls the "disaster syndrome" — an extreme psychological
reaction of individuals subjected to life-changing crises. Barkun briefly considers several millenarian-type movements, taking among his examples the Vailala group of New Guinea, the Ghost Dance movement
of North America and the Taborite sect of fifteenth-century
Bohemia.[28] Drawing parallels between these apparently peripheral
episodes in exotic locales and historically important revolutionary
movements, he emphasizes the innovative social structure and capacity
for change of the millenarian groups. He also includes separate treatment focusing on ecstatic behavior, one ritual aspect which recurs in a
number of these groups, and on the more modern or Western examples

26   Lawrence, *Road Belong Cargo*, p. 232.
27   Examples of this in *Road Belong Cargo* are: "Their low economic status
was...bitterly frustrating" (p. 59); "the...natives were sullen" (p. 71); "[the natives]
became increasingly surly" (p. 72); and so on.
28   Barkun, *Disaster and the Millennium*, pp. 11-18.

of millenarian activity. Barkun contends that with respect to the wide variety of millenarian movements, the similarity of the psychological reaction of the participants in various and differing historical situations allows for meaningful lateral comparison.[29]

All of the situations in which messianism or millennialism occur may be characterized as disasters. They involve destruction of "true society" for one particular group of people. "True society" is defined as that combination of elements—political, social and material—which a community holds to be essential and irreplaceable for life in their environment. The destruction may stem from successive natural disasters (earthquake, drought, and so on) or from stressful social change. Further examples of disastrous situations are the oppressive conditions of colonization, under which cultural and social traditions are disrupted; relative deprivation, that is, the negative discrepancy between a group's expectations and their actual condition, especially relative to a superior or dominant group, during a period of change; and decremental deprivation, that is, a progressive loss of actualizing capabilities in a group.

While a single disastrous situation may produce the "disaster syndrome" which leads to messianic activity, repeated disasters provide the optimal setting for the appearance of messianism. Following a disaster or series of disasters, the survivors are affected by the syndrome. Some individuals are only temporarily or superficially affected by the disaster. Many, however, are seriously emotionally disturbed for a prolonged period of time. These latter undergo two phases in the syndrome: first, at the time of the disaster, these victims suffer sensory over-stimulation which triggers both panic and psychological disorientation; and second, following the disaster they suffer sensory deprivation, which results in extreme feelings of desolation. Individuals afflicted with disaster syndrome are characteristically withdrawn, passive and easily swayed by a strong personality.[30]

During the stressful and destructive situation, and through the two phases of the reaction, the individuals do not respond rationally but instead feel themselves to be both vulnerable and incapable of direct response to the disaster. They believe that their traditional political and social structures are on the verge of collapse and are therefore

---

29   Ibid., pp. 129-165, 166-199.
30   Ibid., p. 53.

unreliable as means for rectifying their problems. It is at this point that messianism emerges.

The desolation and confusion of the survivors of a disaster impel them to turn to the utopian and salvific hopes of messianic beliefs. The communal structure affords them psychological support and the dominant leader provides orientation.

Barkun's work, although itself not commonly cited, is highly representative of the category of theories which base their explanations of messianism on the psychological reaction to extreme or extraordinary deprivation. The theory of the reaction, or in this case, syndrome, is based on individual psychological reaction to extreme stress and does not necessarily apply to group reactions or to non-Western cultures. Considerations on the psychological reactions of people in historical situations as remote as fourteenth-century Italy can rarely advance beyond speculation.

More important, however – and this is the recurrent criticism of these studies in messianic movements – is the fact that only the most tenuous connections are made between the emotional condition of a group and the messianic beliefs which it holds. It cannot be shown that a severely disturbed group which had never before held messianic beliefs adopts or invents extremes of such beliefs in direct response to the emotional upset. Barkun does not delineate the relationship operative here; the reader can only suppose the connections and the result.

This category of theories, those which rely on psychological analysis of the followers of messianic cults, runs into serious problems on two distinct levels: the first, that of the psychological assumptions themselves; and the second, that of conclusions with regard to religions. While these above-presented studies and many others inject psychological theory into the treatment of historical crises and the related religious developments, they generally neglect several problems which inevitably arise with regard to their psychological theoretical assumptions. On the one hand, an easy or accurate gauge of psychological reactions is difficult to obtain from a great geographic or temporal distance. Even when certain points may be granted, the psychological theories used generally derive from Western industrialized culture and are not necessarily suitable for studies of serfs in the thirteenth century or of nineteenth- and twentieth-century nonliterate groups. On the other hand, further misunderstandings may occur as psychoanalytical theories of individual behavior are uncritically applied to group behavior. The results of misapplication of psychological theories are confused and nonanalytic terminology, sweeping generalizations on human responses to stress, and unreliable conclusions.

The most problematic assumption, however, is that which relates emotional disorientation to the development of messianic movements in their diverse forms. Using this assumption, these theorists may portray messianism as crazy activity—irrational, absurd and dreamed up by psychotics. This perspective obviously distorts the understanding of religious activity and calls into question the reliability of these studies, from their initial data base to their controvertible conclusions.

Psychological Response of the Leader

Several authors proposing the psychological explanation have chosen to isolate the leader in describing the psychological response or characteristics which lead to messianic movements. This leader is then portrayed as a single extraordinary individual who manipulates his or her followers and their beliefs. He or she is shown to be aberrant in belief, liminal in relationship to normal social patterns and hypnotic in group interrelations.

This approach, with the slightly more sophisticated supportive theory of charismatic leadership, has seldom been taken up in the more recent theories of messianic movements. It may be found in its characteristic formulation in the work of the Brazilian author, Euclides da Cunha.[31]

Euclides da Cunha wrote *Os Sertões* as a thorough study and historical account of the messianic movement led by Antônio Conselheiro in the late 1890s near Canudos, Brazil. From the opening chapters of the book, it is apparent that da Cunha's motive was to make the occurrence and particular characteristics of the movement understandable to the reader (of the early 1900s) through an investigation of the conditions of the Northeast of Brazil where the movement developed and of the people of the backlands who joined the movement. The book then follows the cult from its background in the *sertão* (backlands) to the decimation of its followers by militia attacks in the Canudos Campaign of 1897.

---

31 *Os Sertões*, fifth ed. (Rio De Janeiro: Tecnoprint Gráfica Editora, 1967). It has been translated as *Rebellion in the Backlands*, trans. S. Putnam (Chicago: University of Chicago Press, Phoenix Books, 1944).

Da Cunha offers a graphic portrait of the desolate scrub-desert which constitutes the *sertão* of Northeastern Brazil and a harsh characterization — typical of late nineteenth-century Brazilian ethnographers and historians — of the retrograde backlanders who eked out their lives there. The backlanders or *sertanejos* were rough, crass types whose inheritance of racially mixed traits (from native Indian, few black African, and primarily Portuguese ancestors) inclined them toward physical weakness and mental instability. This mental deficiency particularly affected their choice of religious beliefs — the *sertanejos* were mystical, superstitious, and tended to fanaticism of all kinds. The religion that they clung to was "a religious phase of misunderstood monotheism contaminated by extravagant mysticism, within which the fetishism of the Indian and the African collided."[32]

The leader of the emergent messianic movement, Antônio Conselheiro, was immersed in the contradictions of this setting and, in a way, epitomized its extremes. He was born into one of the pair of great feuding families of the Northeast and lived an unsettled, even tumultuous life. When his wife ran away with a police officer, Antônio retreated to the backlands to live as a wandering religious penitent. Gradually adopting the fantastic appearance of a bedraggled hermit, Antônio was a "living example of atavism," and the religious beliefs he espoused were of a "remote phase of evolution," a "strange mysticism" of the backlanders.[33]

With the support of the *sertanejos*, this "monster" became a counselor, healer and preacher, and further, a prophet and emissary from God. He was called *Santo Antônio Aparecido*, Saint Anthony on earth. He hypnotized and perverted his followers, in da Cunha's view, with his bone-chilling sermons, and incredible legends grew about his life. His poverty became an enviable apostolic asceticism and his simple way of life an extraordinary discipline of penance.

The messianic beliefs that Antônio preached, drawn from Portuguese Sebastianism and the missionaries' apocalyptic sermons, gathered a band of credulous followers and the group settled in

32 Da Cunha, *Os Sertões*, p. 122; cf. *Rebellion*, p. 110.
33 *Os Sertões*, pp. 131, 133, 142; cf. *Rebellion*, pp. 117, 127.

Canudos, a run-down settlement of outlaws. In 1897 the messianic movement was destroyed by military attack.[34]

Da Cunha paints Antônio as a hero and a madman — and suggests that the readers only imagine "a buffoon enraptured with a vision of the Apocalypse" so as to envision him.[35] He then compares the messianic beliefs of the group in Brazil with those of second-century Montanism and shows Antônio to have deluded and manipulated his followers. Antônio was a madman and dreamer, a psychotic who was nonetheless the creative force of Canudos. A personification of all the retrogressive characteristics of the backlanders, he instituted the rituals, crystallized the beliefs, drew the people together and held them together under the fatal onslaught of the militia.

Da Cunha's explanation of the messianic movement at Canudos as the result of the machinations of the warped mind of Antônio Conselheiro is, of course, extreme. As was the case with Norman Cohn, this analysis serves primarily to illuminate the author's own prejudices and preconceptions. The claims and predictions Antônio made were not the ravings of a madman, but were integrally related to the beliefs of the backlands, the hopes of his followers and the social upheaval during the establishment of the Brazilian Republic.

The emphasis placed on the manipulative or seductive role of the leaders of messianic movements denies the independent volition of the followers and their own expectations and messianic beliefs in a critical situation. Mass hypnosis by a single psychotic individual cannot be a viable explanation for the occurrence of a messianic movement.

This second type of analysis, focusing on the psychological responses of followers and leaders which then lead to the founding of messianic movements, has produced various and uneven results. The unfortunate individuals trapped in crises and disasters lapse into neurotic or psychotic beliefs and behavior — of which messianism seems to be characteristic. Participants or leaders of messianic groups have been pictured as unstable and their religions as delusion or fantasy. Even the apparently sophisticated treatments which deal with morality and epistemology require, as a function of their conclusions, that the members of the messianic movement be confused, ignorant or mentally retrogressive.

---

34   For a different perspective on Canudos, see Chapter 8, below.
35   *Os Sertões*, p. 149; cf. *Rebellion*, p. 133.

These analyses develop and rely upon a thoroughly negative interpretation of group and leader behavior, of messianism and, inevitably,
of religion. The psychological explanation of messianic movements, exemplified by the above-considered theorists, is unacceptable: even
careful analysis is capable of leaping to extreme conclusions and the
understanding of messianism is not furthered.

As has been shown, past theories of messianic movements have invoked an interesting array of elements which could serve to explain or
at least shed light on the problematic occurrence and configuration of
these movements.

The first category considered has relied upon external crises in the
political, economic and social situations. These crises, variously construed, impel the members of the community to seek recourse in a messianic movement as a sort of solution for their problems. This
perspective offers only hypothetical connections between the historical situation, the people involved and the religious activity, tending
toward a mechanistic interpretation of human behavior and religions.
It relies upon the coincidence of historical events, that is, the coincidence of a social or political crisis with the occurrence of a messianic
movement, in order to prove actual causation where none clearly exists.
Further, this approach simply cannot incorporate the development of
religious beliefs and rituals as an appropriate response and instead
reduces religion to an ideological overlay on stunted social movements.

The second category of studies makes use of psychological interpretations; it explains messianic movements in terms of the psychological instability of individuals in stressful conditions. Drawing upon
ill-defined or questionable psychological and psychoanalytical assumptions, these interpretations conclude that the development of
messianic movements and, by extension, religions in general occurs as
a result of psychosis or, at least, misunderstanding. The leader of a messianic movement may be cast as a misguided mystic who hypnotizes his
followers or, conversely, the followers as suffering from mass delusion.

These two approaches, in their simplest forms, reduce messianism
to political unrest or hysteria and effectively eliminate it as an historical factor. The various models used at this level of analysis of messianism—as everything except religious activity—leave aside the
problem of the formation of these religious movements.

Aside from the various political, social and behavioral factors, it is
entirely possible to analyze messianic movements in the context of the
religious tradition from which they emerge. The other approaches

treated above, because of their methodological assumptions, have eliminated, skewed, and left unexamined the religious beliefs and rites of the specific messianic movements studied, as well as the religious history of the community involved. As a result, they cannot explain either the continuation of a movement after the *denouement* of the critical situation or account for the lack of similar movements in parallel situations.

In place of the focus centered on political structures or psychological patterns, the emphasis may instead be shifted to the *religious* situation, as it were, in order to understand messianic movements as religious activity and in terms of religion. In this way, in the place of the assumption of the static nature of religion in the absence of external crises, full consideration may be given to independent development and change in religious beliefs and rituals over time. For, while religious changes are often related to various crises, they are not contingent on them for initiation or significance.

Further, it may be seen that religions, in fact, affect political and social situations and that religious beliefs such as messianism are historical factors in their own right. Messianism is, for example, recurrently significant in sectarian or heterodox groups which constitute themselves in opposition to the ecclesiastical institutions.

The primary hypothesis operative in this perspective of messianic movements within the context of their respective religious histories is that these movements are present only where previously existed suitable religious belief and behavior patterns. That is to say, messianic movements develop in those groups in which the legitimacy of apocalyptic or messianic ideology as well as the acceptability of sectarian groups is established. This hypothesis and the concomitant model of religious tradition will be considered extensively in the following chapter.

Chapter 3

An Alternative Model for Study

The preceding chapter considered the two categories of studies, emphasizing sociopolitical circumstances or psychological distress on the part of the participants in the interpretation or explanation of the phenomenon of messianic movements. Common to the various theories under these categories is the tendency to reduce messianic movements and thus religion to something other than religion, such as the expression of political stances or psychological disturbance. In the study of religious phenomena, this reductionism is untenable; for, while political events, social relations and psychological conditions have an effect on religious movements, emphasis on these in theories such as the above results in the elimination of religion as an historical factor.

The classification and analysis of messianic movements and the related groups — such as Cargo Cults and millenarian sects — has not been an organized pursuit. There have been, however, several distinct trends or assumptions operative in many of the espoused theories which divert and bias the interpretations offered.

First, each historically pinpointed messianic movement has been considered an isolated, unique religious event comparable with but not related to other similar movements. That is to say, each group may be compared with other groups of similar or even radically different circumstances, primarily on the basis of beliefs apparently held in common, yet the parallel derivation of two groups from the same religious tradition is rarely investigated. Messianic movements of the same geographic area or religious background have been studied individually and each given a separate history dependent upon the distinct character of the founder or leader.

Second, the comparisons made between messianic and similar movements are constructed laterally. Groups of the same religious tradition are not related based upon their shared beliefs and rituals or on the pattern of the transmission and development of these in history.

Rather, broadly conceived comparisons are offered, such as between fourteenth-century European millenarian cults and twentieth-century African prophetic sects, in order to emphasize the ubiquitous nature of messianic-type beliefs. These lateral comparisons, however, result in predictably superficial conclusions on structural similarities.

Third, each single movement has been separated from its continuing messianic and nonmessianic religious tradition of beliefs and rituals. This separation occurs for two distinct reasons: first, these religious movements are construed as primarily political or social movements and may therefore only be related to political or social events; or, second, the religious tradition of the participants in the messianic movements is not recognized as a complicated and dynamic force which is capable not only of bearing diverse and intense eschatological beliefs through long periods of time, but also of accepting and even stimulating change and development in these and other beliefs. As a result of the separation of each movement from its religious background, each movement is cast as an epiphenomenal, one-dimensional event — an extraordinary occurrence — and as the exception to the religious rule.

Finally, in the study of messianic movements, external causation has been used to explain the appearance, growth and internal configuration of the movements. This external provocation may range from climatic crises to mass psychosis. This emphasis, however, again denies the possibility of change and development in religions and of crises related to religious history itself.

These assumptions and trends are the results of a singularly ethnocentric approach to the study of messianism, an approach discoverable in nearly all of the theories considered above. This approach relies primarily on the imposition of categories foreign to the study of religions and, particularly, to the specific movements under scrutiny. This has especially occurred in the study of messianic movements in the Third World. The interpreters employ typologies and terminology derived from Western Christian theories of theology, psychology and sociopolitical relations and apply them uncritically to radically different religious groups. As a consequence, data which may be relevant but which does not fit is deleted, unusual elements are restructured to fit the chosen categories and dissimilar groups assembled under the same, over-general rubric. From these investigative efforts, redundant and reductive conclusions are then drawn.

In the present study, an alternate model for the study of messianic movements will be proposed. From this new perspective, messianic movements will be considered in relation to and derivable from the continuing, accessible religious tradition of the participants. Emphasis will be shifted to comparison of movements of the same tradition in order to indicate the existence of change and development of religious beliefs and practices and to attempt to understand these in chronological sequence. Purely external causation theories will be abandoned and replaced to a certain degree with consideration of the ongoing religious events which influence or precipitate the actual occurrence of each messianic movement. The categories for interpretation used in this endeavor will be those which are integrally related to the movements under study for the purpose of understanding the specific religious context and structures.

The religious traditions from which messianic movements emerge are not easily defined or limited. This tradition consists of the total religious context, that is, the complex of beliefs and practices of a designated religion. It includes the literary tradition of the religious institution, the normative doctrine or theology of the hierarchy, the oral tradition of conservative and local religious beliefs, the so-called folk religious practices, and special healing and votive rituals, that is, the range of religiosity from complex doctrines to simple daily rituals.

Within this religious tradition from which messianic movements emerge, a smaller tradition may be described. It is the hypothesis of the present study that there exists prior to the occurrence of any single messianic movement a *messianic tradition* of messianic and related religious beliefs, as well as rituals and structures integral to the eventual appearance and formulation of the messianic movement. This messianic tradition serves as the foundation and connection for chronologically separate movements within the same religious tradition and contains the totality of elements—derived from the larger religious tradition—which dominate and determine each movement which occurs. In each messianic movement, certain separable categories or aspects may be designated as, specifically, those containing the core religious beliefs, religious rituals and the organizational or social structures present. The messianic tradition may therefore be said to comprise the contents of these three categories, including the complete complex of particular beliefs, practices and organizational principles and related and supportive elements which recur historically.

The significance of the hypothesis of the messianic tradition may be explained on two levels: first, the positing of the pre-existence of the messianic tradition with respect to a given messianic movement serves to ground that movement in established religious beliefs and practices rather than characterize it as a separate, freak occurrence; and, second, the resultant study of the messianic movements relates these to religious events and the religious continuum rather than to political movements and nonreligious phenomena.

The hypothesis of the existence and effect of the messianic tradition will be tested through a specific historical case study, that of the Brazilian messianic movements. In the nineteenth century in Brazil, three chronologically separate messianic movements occurred; this thesis will elicit, through historical investigation, the messianic tradition from which these movements emerged. The study will commence with the messianic and related beliefs and practices, together with contingent group structures, of a determinate beginning era and follow these in their development through history to the later messianic movements. In the past, these three messianic movements in Brazil, at Serra do Rodeador (1819-1820), Pedra Bonita (1838-1839) and Canudos (1882-1897), have been treated separately, as independent social or political events, related to one another only superficially. The present study will, instead, integrate the three movements into the messianic tradition of Brazil and of its parent country Portugal in an historically expanded investigation of the individual elements and structures present and transmitted in that tradition. As indicated in Chapter 1, the "Introduction," Portugal claimed and colonized the Brazilian territory in the sixteenth century; the eventual participants in the messianic movements of the nineteenth century were primarily of Portuguese descent and maintained religious beliefs and practices of Portuguese origin. For these reasons, Portugal was the source for the messianic tradition developed in Brazil and is the geographical starting point for this study. The temporal beginning will be the sixteenth century, the period of the claiming of the new Brazilian land by the Portuguese and thus the period of the first transmission of elements of the messianic tradition to the colony; it was a time of heightened messianic activity in Portugal as well. The religious tradition of Portugal and thus of Brazil was Roman Catholicism, with the special addition of Iberian and Portuguese folk beliefs and practices.

For the purposes of this study, the three basic aspects present in the Luso-Brazilian messianic tradition, that is, the religious beliefs, the religious practices and the organizational structures, will be investigated under the following categories: (1) messianic and related beliefs, including certain derivative rituals, (2) lay religious activities, and (3) penitential practices.

The first category of messianic and related beliefs and rituals includes the doctrinal eschatological teachings of the Roman Catholic Church in Portugal and Brazil, associated messianic-type beliefs of the cult of the saints, related motifs in legends of Portuguese and European hero-kings and heterodox religious beliefs. The rituals included are integral to the cult of the saints and expressive of this category of belief. Messianism itself, the eschatological belief in the coming or return of the Messiah—for Christianity, Jesus—is the root paradigm for the Luso-Brazilian messianic tradition, persisting through changes and development and necessarily present in the nineteenth-century movements in Brazil. These messianic and related beliefs provided the belief content and mythic structure for the continuing tradition and for each movement which occurred. Their originative presence in the Roman Catholic doctrine—the foundation for this tradition—supported their persistence through history to the later dissenting groups, for they were continually held to be appropriate religious beliefs.

The lay religious activities, at the individual and group levels, provided the required and approved relational patterns for the formation of the later messianic movements—which were themselves religious activities initiated by the laity—and for the role and function of the lay leaders of those groups. The group structure of the messianic movements and their separatist inclination as dissent groups, as well as the pattern of behavior for the leader, are thus part of the Luso-Brazilian messianic tradition. Included under this category for study are the religious groups of late medieval Portugal such as beghard and beguine groups and unofficial orders and lay religious associations such as devotional brotherhoods. These organizational models continued through the tradition and allowed for the expression of messianic and related beliefs, particularly through non- or anti-institutional groupings. The basic structure of these groups consists of a single leader with an immediately subordinate level of disciples or coadministrators of up to twelve in number, with the remaining numbers of participants, taken as a whole, under these.

The role of the messianic leader as a lay religious individual is intricately related to both ordained and lay religious behavior patterns;

included in this category are the models of ordained missionary, religious pilgrim, initiators of devotional shrines and lay holy men.

The penitential practices of the Portuguese and Brazilians form a complicated aspect of the messianic tradition. The practice of extraordinary penance, particularly fasts and self-flagellation, was in continual parallel with messianic beliefs, part of the rituals connected with those who believed in messianism, and recurred in the messianic movements. As a group practice, flagellant activity supported the same organizational principles as did other lay religious practices. Further, such extreme penitence was intimately related to belief in the imminence of the end of the world and preparations for the arrival of the messiah. These practices were thus the behavioral supports both for the messianic ideology and for the related group structures.

The practice of self-flagellation as a salvific technique in itself will not be introduced in this study. *Imitatio Christi* is an individually performed activity, expressive of the desire to achieve closer proximity to the Deity and one's own salvation; it is not part of the messianic tradition which emphasizes group salvation and redemption through supernatural agency rather than through individual merit.

The means for the persistence of these three elements of the Luso-Brazilian messianic tradition will be sought in determinate means of transmission, from Portugal to Brazil, over this extensive period of time. Primary among the possible means for communication were the official organs for transmission of appropriate beliefs, organizations and practices: the agents of the Roman Catholic Church in Portugal and Brazil. These agents included the Portuguese king, under his right of patronage, members of the ecclesiastical hierarchy, ordained parish priests and the numerous missionaries, in particular the Franciscans and Jesuits. Lay groups which were officially constituted, such as the Third Orders attached to religious communities and religious brotherhoods, also transmitted key religious beliefs and practices. Finally, the oral or folk communication preserved and passed on messianic and messianic-like beliefs and approval of appropriate rituals and groups through two means. The first involved strictly oral transmission from parent to child and from itinerant singers and storytellers; both of these are conventional means for transmission of traditional religious beliefs and practices. The second means involved the Luso-Brazilian poetry and prose found in *cordel*, or small pamphlets.

The literature of the *cordel* took as its beginning the romances and troubadour tales of the late Middle Ages in Portugal. In small manuscript notebooks bound by a cord, heroic and romantic legends, poetry and history were set down; these books were sold in local markets to literate elites and to those few of the rural peasants who read. The *cordel* pamphlets were imported to Brazil by individual colonists in the sixteenth and seventeenth centuries and produced there independently from the latter century on. As occurred in the related *corrida* of Hispano-American colonies, the *cordel* books in Brazil began to contain more recent history, popular poetry and legends and were read aloud by a literate family member or villager. In the nineteenth and twentieth centuries these pamphlets were printed on rather crude presses and illustrated by excellent examples of primitive woodcut and lithographic prints. The stories these contained were laid out in a standardized poetic form composed by famous local poets and storytellers.[1] These *cordel* books communicated, through their romances and legends, traditional mythological beliefs and thus contributed to the transmission of the messianic tradition.

These four sources, the institutional and adjunct means of communication, and the oral transmission and *cordel* literature, will be indicated and included as the historical study of the development of the Luso-Brazilian messianic tradition proceeds.

This study will investigate and discuss the existence, formation and continuation of the three aspects of messianic and related religious beliefs, lay religious activities and penitential practices which form the Luso-Brazilian messianic tradition, progressing historically from the sixteenth through the nineteenth century and moving from Portugal to Brazil. The first historical chapter will review the content and structure of the messianic tradition in Portugal, with related discussion on the development from similar forms of the late medieval period. The chapters following will discuss the elements of the messianic tradition as they recur in the Portuguese colony in Brazil in the sixteenth, seventeenth, eighteenth and nineteenth centuries. The discussion of the nineteenth century will include the appearance and formulation of the

---

1   Manuel Diégues, Júnior, *Literatura de cordel*, Cadernas de Folclore, no. 2 (Rio de Janeiro: Ministério da Educação e Cultura, 1975), pp. I-II; Renato Carneiro Campos, *Ideologia dos poetas populares do Nordeste*, second ed. (Recife, Brazil: Instituto Joaquim Nabuco de Pesquisas Sociais, Ministério da Educação e Cultura, 1977), pp. 9-10.

three messianic movements. Each chapter will begin with a brief look at the significant historical circumstances of the century which represents the temporal limits for that chapter; the elements of the Luso-Brazilian messianic tradition will subsequently be discussed, in separate sections. All of the diverse parts of the three aspects or threads of the messianic tradition will be included as they occurred in the Northeast of Brazil in the region including the states of Bahia, Pernambuco, Ceará, Alagoas, Piauí and the territory of Maranhão. The messianic movements of the nineteenth century were based in this region, which represents a separable, unified part of the vast territory of Brazil; only those religious elements determined to have undeniably appeared and persisted there may be considered integral or influential with regard to the messianic tradition under study.

As the historical discussion progresses, the purpose will be twofold: first, to elicit the structure of each separate aspect of the messianic tradition and its development through the centuries as a single trajectory; and, second, to uncover the interaction of these aspects as integrally related or simply superficially linked, from the sixteenth century in Portugal to the expression of the Luso-Brazilian messianic tradition in the three nineteenth-century Brazilian messianic movements. It is hoped that through this detailed historical investigation of the single case of the Luso-Brazilian messianic tradition and the resultant messianic movements a refined model for the further study of other such movements may be suggested. The strength of this model or approach, grounding messianic movements in a pre-existent messianic tradition, will be contingent upon the historical presentation of this thesis and will be discussed in the conclusion.

Chapter 4

Portugal in the Sixteenth Century: The Beginnings

Just as the political beginnings of the nascent Brazilian colony are to be found in its homeland of Portugal, so the beginnings of the Luso-Brazilian messianic tradition are to be discovered in the religious beliefs and activities of sixteenth-century Portugal. This first chapter on the messianic tradition will consider the wide range of influential religious elements which, from their Portuguese roots, were brought by colonists in the sixteenth and seventeenth centuries to Brazil. Religiosity and religious expression in that Christian nation certainly varied by region and from north to south; however, special attention will be focused in this chapter on those common beliefs and practices which would have readily been transplanted to the colony.

Following a brief discussion of the historical situation of imperial Portugal from the later Middle Ages through the end of the sixteenth century and its relationship with early colonial Brazil, the specific elements of the European and Portuguese messianic beliefs, lay religious activities and flagellant practices will, in turn, be explored.

Historical Circumstances

In the political history of Portugal in the sixteenth century, one uncertainty followed another and, by the end of this period, the Portuguese crown was in the hands of their closest rivals, the Spanish.[1] In

---

1   Information on the history of Portugal in the fifteenth and sixteenth centuries, its late medieval culture and its relations with its colonies may be found in H. V. Livermore, *A New History of Portugal* (Cambridge: Cambridge University Press, 1966); Charles Boxer, *The Portuguese Seaborne Empire: 1415-1825* (New York: A. A. Knopf, 1969); Eduardo Alvarez, *Memoria açerca da batalha de Alcacer-Quibir* (Lisbon: Imprensa Nacional, 1892); Fortunato de Almeida, *História de Portugal*, 4 vols. (Coimbra: Imprensa Acadêmica, 1910-1922); and A. H. de Oliveira Marques, *Daily Life in Portugal in the Late Middle Ages*, trans. S. S. Wyatt (Madison, WI: The University of Wisconsin Press, 1971).

1494 João II had died with no legitimate heir and was succeeded by his cousin and brother-in-law, Manuel I. Dom Manuel and his son, João III, sponsored the great exploratory voyages around the African cape which led to the incursions in the Asian spice trade and the discovery of Brazil.

When the only heir of João III, his grandson Sebastião I, was slain in an ill-starred battle in 1578 after a brief reign, Cardinal Henriques, brother of João III, ruled Portugal for two years as the last of his dynastic line, the House of Avis. Thus, in 1580, with no designated heir for the Portuguese throne, King Philip II of Spain (I of Portugal) annexed the crown by virtue of his relation to the House of Avis from the various intermarriages between the Spanish and Portuguese monarchs of the three preceding generations. Under Philip III (II of Portugal) and, in 1621, Philip IV, Iberia remained a united empire, although the Portuguese *Côrtes* (parliament) and ministries maintained their integrity and a certain degree of independence.

In spite of the dynastic problems, Portuguese trade had thrived and expanded. By the time of the beginning of this historical case study of messianic tradition, the midsixteenth century, Portugal was the metropolis of a successful and highly dependent trade empire. Its subject territory included commercial ports in India and the Eastern and Western coasts of Africa, colonized islands in the Atlantic Ocean, and *Vera Cruz* — that part of the southern continent of the New World later called Brazil.

It was the exploratory impulse, guided by Prince Henriques (Henry the Navigator), especially from 1418 to 1460, and continued by João II (1481-1495) that launched the history of Portugal's essentially maritime empire. Clearly undertaken to challenge other European and Muslim access to the spice trade of the East, the exploration and conquests of scattered but crucial seaports in Africa, India, and Japan established for Portugal the pattern of indifferent and unwavering hegemony over its colonies.

Portugal, as the mother country, was distinctly dominant in its relationship with Brazil from the opening of that colony and remained so through the colonial period, until 1821. Portugal's primacy rested on its imperial political government but extended through every phase of economic and cultural life, for the maintenance of Brazil as a colony and its exploitation for trade commodities were understood to be undertakings solely for the benefit and profit of Portugal and the Crown.

On the one hand, highly restrictive trade policies regulated Brazil's economic relations and development: Brazilian ports were closed to all but Portuguese ships until 1818, and enforcement of the monoculture of sugar and rice resulted in extreme dependence on Portugal for luxury foodstuffs, salt, manufactured goods, and metals, especially iron.[2]

On the other hand, the Portuguese king made effective use of his right of *padroado* to extend politico-religious authority over the Brazilian colonists, inevitably affecting religious and ecclesiastical development in the colony. The essence of the *padroado*, or patronage right, dates from the first king of Portugal, Afonso Henriques, who in 1143 swore his allegiance to the Holy See of Rome and traded the protection of St. Peter and the Papal Court at Rome for an annual tribute from himself and his royal descendants. Evolving later from the establishment of the Portuguese ruler as the Grand Master of the Order of Christ, which granted him ecclesiastical jurisdiction over newly conquered lands during the Crusades, the *padroado* itself represented a contract between the king and the Holy See. The king was conceded the power to collect and administer the tithes or *dízimos* for the economic support of the Roman Catholic Church within his regime, to nominate suitable candidates for vacant ecclesiastical offices, to build and maintain churches and chapels and to accept and communicate the edicts of the Holy See. He was, in return, charged with the promulgation of the faith in the Portuguese dominions. With respect to Brazil, this last task was offered as the primary reason for the Portuguese colonization effort. João III, in his order to the first royal governor of Brazil in 1548, insisted that his plan "to conserve and develop...the lands of Brazil" was in "the service of God" and for "the exaltation of our holy faith."[3] João added that "the principal thing that moved me to order populated the said lands of Brazil was that the people there be converted to our holy catholic faith."[4] Thus, the

---

2   Subsistence foods, such as maize, manioc, beans and rice as well as some beef, provided the main portion of the colonists' diet. Caio Prado, Júnior, *Formação do Brasil contemporâneo: colônia*, seventh ed. (São Paulo: Editora Brasiliense, 1963), pp. 227-228.

3   "Regimento de Tomé de Souza (17 de dezembro de 1548)," Carlos Manheiro Dias, gen. ed., *História da colonização no Brasil*, 3 vols. (Porto: Litografia Nacional, 1924), 3: "A Instituição do govêrno geral," by Pedro de Azevedo, p. 345.

4   Ibid., p. 347.

Brazilian colonization effort and the mission of Roman Catholic evangelization in that New World territory were, from the earliest moment, inextricably linked.

With further and more explicit bulls from Pope Julius III and later popes, the *padroado* privilege was extended to the Brazilian lands, particularly under the establishment of the bishoprics, first of Salvador (Bahia) and, much later, of Rio de Janeiro. The Portuguese throne had secured *de jure* and *de facto* control over the Roman Church in its domain and tightly retained that subordination of Church to State until the end of the era. Roman Catholicism was thereby the state religion, to the exclusion of all others, and its representatives, from cardinal to monk, were maintained under Portuguese royal discretionary powers.

As all ships bound for Brazil in these early years travelled from Portuguese ports, so all goods, books, and immigrants destined for that land were either of Portuguese origin, or approved by the proper Portuguese authorities. The various groups of Roman Catholic missionaries, comprising at this time Jesuits and a few Franciscans, Carmelites and Benedictines, were particularly scrutinized by officers of the government. These restrictive measures, such that no missionary appear in Brazil except under the auspices of the Portuguese government, resulted in the sending of rather small numbers of predominantly native-born Portuguese religious to the colony.[5] The few missionaries sent to Brazil from other European countries — their numbers increased later — were generally under the direct supervision of a religious superior in Portugal. The numbers of all the missionaries, however, were determined by the needs of the enterprise of the Portuguese conquest, rather than by the religious needs of the colonists or natives.

From this beginning, Portuguese hegemony over its Brazilian colony was so extensive that Brazil remained an imported culture for three centuries, and its colonial inhabitants looked unwaveringly to Portugal for food supplies, household goods and building materials, as well as for law, polity and religion. Those Roman Catholic prelates and missionaries who attended the religious needs of Brazil were from Por-

---

5   Eduardo Hoornaert, "Primeiro período: evangelização do Brasil durante a primeira época colonial," *História da Igreja no Brasil*, eds. Eduardo Hoornaert, et al., 2 vols. (Petrópolis: Editora Vozes Ltda., 1977-), 1: 35-37.

tugal, approved by Portuguese authorities, and taught Portuguese Christian beliefs and rites.

Messianic Beliefs in Europe and Portugal

Along with the material commodities which embarked from Portugal to the shores of the new colony, messianic ideas and legends were also borne across the Atlantic Ocean by the sea travellers.

It has been contended by a few scholars of native Brazilian religions that the aboriginal Brazilindian beliefs, such as the belief in a Land without Evil, provided a major impetus to the presence of continuation of messianism in that colony.[6] While it may be possible that the existence, however fleeting, of a parallel native legend would allow for easier acceptance of the messianic beliefs among certain of the later bi-racial Euro-Brazilians, it is inarguable that the specific elements, structures, and final elaborations of messianic belief in Brazil sprang solely from European sources. This will become apparent as our study continues.

In order to indicate the sources of the Portuguese messianic beliefs which later found their way to Brazil, the thematic patterns in (1) contemporary Judaic and Christian messianic and apocalyptic beliefs, (2) the native Portuguese legends of the Hidden King, João Prestes, and the return of King Sebastião, and (3) the cult of the saints in Portugal will be discussed in this section.

Jewish and Christian Messianic Beliefs

Messianism in Europe and on the Iberian peninsula included a wealth of legendary themes through the Middle Ages to the sixteenth century. A significant portion of those themes persisted and developed in Portugal through the importation and adaptation of legends which were not Portuguese in origin, as well as through the messianic mythology which developed in Portugal itself.

By far the most important themes were those contained in the parallel belief patterns of Judaic and of Christian origin. The long-

---

6   For such analyses, see Hélène Clastres, *Terra sem mal*, trans. Renato Janine Ribeiro (São Paulo: Editora Brasiliense, 1978), and the excellent summary of other studies by Queiroz, *O Messianismo*, pp. 164-210.

established doctrinal Judaic expectation of a Messiah was a vital force among Jews during the Middle Ages and found strong believers in Jews residing in Portugal. Undoubtedly affected by the beliefs of the Spanish Kabbalists, who were among the Spanish Jews immigrating to Portugal in 1492, small groups of Portuguese "New Christians"[7] supported messianic figures and developed an apocalyptic literature during the sixteenth century.

Around the turn of the century, Isaac Abranavel, a well-known Portuguese Jewish financier, announced that the year 1503 would see the arrival of the promised redeemer. In fulfillment of that prophecy, a man claiming to be the Messiah appeared in Istria in 1502 and collected a small following.[8] David Rubeni, who preached his message of his messianic kingdom around 1526, and Luís Dias of Setúbal, who prophesied the imminent arrival of the Messiah during the 1540s, affected the development of this aspect of Portuguese religious beliefs.[9] The popularity of these figures indicates the depth of the Jewish response to the messianic legend.

The parallel apocalyptic literature placed emphasis on the imminence of this-world salvation for devout believers in the Messiah and recalled the classical imagery of Jeremiah and Isaias in the description of the triumphant kingdom and the proper preparation for it. The *Trovas* of Bandarra, considered at length below, were the dynamic and startlingly popular expression of these ideas combined with uniquely Iberian legendary structures and related Christian beliefs.[10]

The Middle Ages, especially from the tenth century, also saw the dramatic elaboration of the Christian myth of the Second Coming of Jesus, based particularly on the canonical Apocalypse, or Revelation

---

7   *Novos cristãos/novas cristãs* were Jews forced to convert to Christianity under threat of death or of expulsion. In Spain these were named *Marranos*.

8   João Lúcio de Azevedo, *A Evolução do sebastianismo*, second ed. (Lisbon: Livraria Clássica Editora, 1947), p. 24.

9   Ibid., pp. 23-27. See also Theophilo Braga, *O Povo portuguêz nos seus costumes, crenças e tradições*, 2 vols. (Lisbon: Livraria Ferreira Editora, 1885), 2: 243-244.

10   [Gonçalo Annes Bandarra], *Trovas do Bandarra* (Porto: Imprensa Popular de J. L. de Sousa, 1866) is an expanded edition of this New Christian's opus. See below, pp. 52-54.

of John.[11] In spite of the early doctrinal shift within the Church towards an emphasis on individual salvation and symbolic interpretation of the imminence of the Kingdom of God, sectarian belief in Jesus as a returning messiah found tremendous support among the populace. Canonical imagery, illuminated in florid detail by medieval artists, combined with influential prophetical tracts such as the Sibyllines and the later writings of Joachim of Fiore to bring the messianism of the Roman Church to the extremes of expression.

The active messianic movements, such as those led by Tanchelm (fl. 1110) and by Vincent Ferrer in the fifteenth century, as well as the Crusades of the Poor and related movements in the twelfth through the fourteenth centuries,[12] offer only partial indication of the widespread acceptance of messianic eschatology during those periods. Christians in many different parts of Western Europe participated in this outbursting of vibrant apocalypticism, both in practice and through the development of oral and literary traditions.

Although the Church did not officially consider the popularly phrased beliefs which led to these movements as anything but heterodox, its regular and secular clergy continued to include the vivid and orthodox messianic themes of damnation, salvation, the Last Days and the coming of the Antichrist in their sermons and writings.

Portuguese Christians, although not as demonstrative as Christians in other parts of Europe, accepted the current eschatological beliefs and, of course, received comparable religious instruction. Thus their messianic beliefs did not vary substantially from those of other European Christians.

Portuguese Legends

Apart from these doctrinal beliefs, heroes of folklore, whether taken as political saviors or as religious redeemers, also played a significant role in the formation of the European, and thus Portuguese, conception of the messiah. Among these heroes were the long-dead but vividly remembered great kings or emperors whose reigns had seen fantastic advances and whose second coming promised a return to that golden age. The legends include figures such as Charlemagne, who was to have

---

11   These messianic beliefs and movements are most extensively treated in Cohn, *Pursuit*.

12   Cohn, *Pursuit*, pp. 46-50; 61-70; 89-90; 94-107.

returned for the First Crusade (1096) or at least to found a new Holy Roman Empire; England's King Arthur, waiting, according to the circulating prophecies attributed to Merlin, on the enchanted isle of Avalon; and Frederick I, Barbarossa, whose legend of promised return supported not only his own grandson, Frederick II, but also the claims of several impostors.[13] Carried into Iberia by troubadours and by manuscript folias of romance-tales, these myths wielded a tremendous influence on Portuguese folk beliefs.[14]

These beliefs occurred in four thematic groups: the legends of the *Encoberto* or Hidden King; the legend of the vision of Afonso Henriques; the legend of João Prestes or Prester John; and Sebastianism, taken in its widest sense.

Of particular importance and duration was the Iberian belief in *el Encubierto* (Spanish) or *o Encoberto*, the hidden king. Strongly affiliated with the Arthurian legend, this belief appeared in the prophecies attributed to Isidore of Sevilla, who lived in the seventh century, and in other manuscript prophecies which emerged around 1520 in Spain and Portugal.[15] The "Hidden One" was a hidden king, reported dead but actually alive on a misty isle somewhere west of Iberia, temporarily doing penance for an infraction of the chivalrous code or a more serious sin. He was destined to return in glory and victory to his elevated and idealized empire. This legend was apparently connected with Charles V of Spain and, later, with Sebastião I and João IV of Portugal.[16] This king's enchanted or hidden island (*ilha encantada* or *ilha encoberta*) was believed at various times to be Arthur's Avalon or one of the Canary Islands, the Azores or the West Indies.[17]

Several of the Portuguese myths which inform the messianic tradition developed as their focal point the emerging triumph of Imperial Portugal, paralleling the mythic history of the Holy Roman Empire.

---

13 Braga, *O Povo portuguêz*, 2: 239; and Cohn, *Pursuit*, pp. 72-74; 111-112.
14 Braga, *O Povo portuguêz*, 2: 238.
15 Azevedo, *Sebastianismo*, pp. 18-19.
16 See below, pp. 55-58 and p. 104.
17 Braga, *O Povo portuguêz*, 2: 239-240.

The first of these involved the prophetic dream attributed to Afonso Henriques, the first king of Portugal, who secured the independence of the County of Portugal from Castile and there reigned from 1139 to 1185. His legend came to light in the fifteenth century and was elaborated even in the seventeenth as an appeal to the Portuguese as chosen people.[18]

According to the more common version of the tale, Afonso Henriques, abroad in one of the more ambitious campaigns against the Moors in Iberia, fell asleep over a Bible on the eve of the great battle in Ourique. During the night, he was visited by a vision of Jesus himself, in the guise of an old man, promising that the king's Crusade would be victorious and that Portugal would become a great empire. In confirmation of the vision, Afonso was to look for an old wandering hermit the next day. In the morning, Afonso found the hermit asking to see him and recognized him as the figure of his dream. This legend was repeated and became increasingly popular during the period of Spanish control of the Portuguese throne (1580-1640).

A second cycle of legends in Portugal was centered on the mythical figure of João Prestes, also called Presbyter or Prester John.[19] João Prestes, according to a widely circulated — but forged — letter attributed to him, was the bishop and monarch of a vastly wealthy Christian nation beyond the Moorish realm. The kingdom was sought by Portuguese explorers in India, Persia and the coasts of Africa. Particularly obsessed with this legend and hopeful of aid against the Moors, both João II and Manuel I included this legend as reinforcement of their more mercenary quest for spice and gold in Africa and Asia. The kingdom of Abyssinia (Ethiopia) was eventually accepted in fulfillment of their search, but the extraordinary stories of João Prestes remained to become associated with the hidden king, the *Encoberto*.

The third and by far the most significant Portuguese legend is in the cycle of myths surrounding Sebastião I, king of Portugal from 1557 to 1578. This cycle, as a whole designated Sebastianism, actually antedated the birth and reign of Sebastião, having begun in the *Trovas* of

---

18 Hernani Cidade, *A Literatura autonomista sob os Filipes* (Lisbon: Editora Livraria Sá da Costa, n.d.), pp. 162-163; Sebastião de Rocha Pita, *História da América portuguesa* (Lisbon: n.p., 1730; reprint ed., São Paulo: Editora da Universidade de São Paulo, 1976), pp. 135, 137.

19 Boxer, *Seaborne Empire*, pp. 19-20, 33-35. See also Livermore, *A New History of Portugal*, pp. 127-129.

Bandarra (ca. 1530), and persisted through the reign of João IV, the first Portuguese monarch after the Spanish Captivity, until our own time.

In the cycle of Sebastianism, three phases may be distinguished: the first, of expectation of an unknown *Encoberto*, embellished in the poetry of Bandarra; the second, of hope in the return of King Sebastião specifically; and the third, of the short-lived belief that João IV was the expected redeemer-king. These phases were not chronologically consecutive: the second phase both appeared before and continued long after the brief period of the third phase.

Between 1525 and 1531 a shoemaker and New Christian in the Portuguese village of Trancoso wrote a lengthy manuscript of prophetic verses.[20] The poet, Gonçalo Annes (or Eanes), called *o Bandarra*, "the doodler," condemned the corrupt society of urban Portugal and foresaw the arrival of a great and just prince. Bandarra was known locally as a sort of Biblical scholar and had directed his poems to the common folk as well as to people of learning.[21] His reputation and work were divulged rapidly: by 1531, when he travelled to Lisbon from Trancoso, he was sought after for explanations of his cryptic prophecies.[22]

The extant versions of the *Trovas* show the poem to be a complicated, often witty, nearly always obscure apocalyptic vision of a glorified Portuguese empire. The imagery is drawn primarily from Iberian and Portuguese folklore and poetry and, to a lesser degree, from Jewish and Roman Catholic messianic themes. The earliest version (1603) contained 107 verses, while later editions (from 1644 on) inserted thirty-five additional lines in one segment of the poem and added verses to the end.

---

20   The earliest version is from D. Joam [João] de Castro, *Paraphrase et concordançia de alguas profeçias de Bandarra, çapateiro de Trancoso* ([Paris]: n.p., 1603; facsimile rep., Porto: Officina Typographica de A. F. Vasconcelos, 1901); additional verses from the edition of 1866, taken from [Gonçalo Annes Bandarra], *Trovas do Bandarra*.
21   Innocêncio Francisco da Silva, *Diccionário bibliográphico portuguêz*, 7 vols. (Lisbon: Imprensa Nacional, 1859), 3: 151.
22   Braga, *O Povo portuguêz*, 2: 244.

The *Trovas* begins with a lengthy prologue directed to Bandarra's sponsor which describes the author, his shoemaking and, especially, his writing ambition:

> I determined to write
> In my shoe store
> To have Your Excellency see
> What comes of my stitching.[23]

Bandarra assures the reader of the reliability of his prophecies: "My work is very secure" and "I do work that endures/ And not superficially."[24]

He turns then to criticize the dismal historical conditions around him: "I do not see justice done/ To all in general." In that imbalanced society, the maleducated receive academic degrees and judges cannot tell right from wrong. Further, he tells of money-grubbing lawyers and clerics, lords with falsified lineages and the fragile reputations of women. All around him is "such a jumble/ Without a chief to command." In this prologue, Bandarra offers no solution and calls the situation totally accursed.[25]

Following the prologue is the section of his prophetic dream. In these verses, Bandarra describes the coming of a great king who will overturn the reign of the wolves. This king will have a new name and will raise the shield of Portugal with the five wounds of the Savior Jesus as his crest. Already in Portugal great omens have been seen.[26]

The long middle section of the *Trovas* contains an extended dialogue between the Head Shepherd and several interlocutors about the restlessness of the herds and a dance in which all should join.[27] These passages may only be understood as allegory referring to Portugal, its dynastic houses and its allies and enemies.

The last section of the *Trovas* repeats the prophecies on the coming of the redeemer-king. This king, "a great Lion," will come to overthrow the African kingdoms and to destroy all enemies within and without

---

23   Castro, *Paraphrase*, folio 7v; my translation in this and all following quotations.
24   Ibid., folio 9v.
25   Ibid., folios 12-20v.
26   Ibid., folios 22-51.
27   Ibid., folios 55-73v.

the realm. The corrupt leaders will be evicted and the rich made to pay great taxes. This "good hidden King" will emerge in triumph, "make peace in the world" and guard the true law. In concluding, Bandarra instructs the reader to "note well the prophecies" from Jeremiah and Daniel.[28]

The exact date of the first manuscript of these verses is impossible to determine. However, it is known that in 1537 Heitor Lopes of Trancoso requested a new copy from Bandarra, since his own book was old and torn.[29] The manuscript copies were widely divulged in the sixteenth century, as attested by their popularity and their appearance on the list of banned books, the *Index Expurgatório*, of 1581. The *Trovas* were first printed in 1603 in a rather piecemeal fashion in the concordance written by Joam [João] de Castro. A more complete edition appeared in 1644 in Nantes, subsidized by the Conde de Vidigueira, then ambassador to France; later editions appeared in 1688, 1812, and 1886. It was banned for the second time in 1665.[30]

Gonçalo Annes Bandarra was not left untouched by the popularity of his work or by the controversy it then created. One of the circulating copies of his manuscript was delivered to the Mesa de Consciência, one of the controlling offices of the Portuguese Inquisition. As a result, in 1545 he was seized in Trancoso and taken to Lisbon, tried before the Holy Office of the Inquisition, and instructed to cease writing heretical commentaries on Sacred Scripture and to keep no biblical materials in his home, save the excerpt editions approved by the Church. As part of the fulfillment of his sentence, Bandarra publicly admitted his errors in an *auto da fé* in Lisbon and, according to the records of those proceedings, the Mesa da Consciência determined to suppress the *Trovas*.[31]

Although the believers of the prophetic visions of Bandarra were not the majority of the Portuguese populace at first, the work and the legend became familiar within a very short time. The theme of Bandarra's poetry caught and expanded the spirit of Portuguese nationalism in the sixteenth century to such a degree that when Sebastião I, heir to D. João III, was born in 1554, his name was im-

28   Ibid., folios 78-126.
29   Braga, *O Povo portuguêz*, 2: 244.
30   Azevedo, *Sebastianismo*, pp. 76, 88; Braga, *O Povo portuguêz*, 2: 245-246.
31   Azevedo, *Sebastianismo*, pp. 123-134.

mediately linked with the legend of the expected great Prince, the *Encoberto*. Even before his birth, João III's heir was called *o desejado*, "the desired one*.*" This child was hoped to be a male heir for the failing dynastic line so that the eventual Spanish succession to the Portuguese throne might be staved off for at least another generation, if not permanently.[32]

The reign of Sebastião I, despite the great expectations of his subjects, proved to be of dismal outcome. He succeeded to the throne in 1557 but only took power in 1569 when, at fourteen, he reached his majority. In a parliament-directed plan to offset any subversive influence from his still-surviving Spanish mother and grandmother, Sebastião was given a conspicuously Portuguese education, tutored by a Portuguese Jesuit. The emphasis of his schooling was on military and religious training. He emerged a deeply religious youth and was reportedly obsessed with the idea of launching a new Crusade against the infidels, the Moors, who held Morocco.

In late 1578, Sebastião undertook an expedition which was meagerly financed and poorly planned with about 16,500 troops to establish a Portuguese stronghold in Morocco to be administered by a local sharif, one of his Moorish allies. His army was vastly outnumbered and he met with disastrous defeat in the Battle of the Three Kings at Alcazar-Quibir (El-Ksar el-Kebir). Both Sebastião and his Moorish ally were slain and barely 100 Portuguese soldiers survived the day. Upon his death, his great-uncle Cardinal Henriques reigned for two years, and subsequently the Crown passed to Spain, in whose possession it remained for sixty years.

The Portuguese nation, and particularly those citizens who saw in Sebastião the great hope for the glory of their empire, were devastated by the sudden loss of the young king. Sebastião was not blamed but was instead exalted for that defeat. Owing to a coincidence of several events, the shock of many of the Portuguese subjects turned to disbelief, and from that began the core legend of Sebastianism: that Sebastião was not, in reality, dead but merely in hiding in Africa.

Two factors may be noted as precipitous of the founding of the legend. First, serious difficulties arose in the identification of the King's

---

32   J. M. de Queiroz Velloso, *D. Sebastião*, second ed. (Lisbon: Empresa Nacional de Publicidade, 1935), pp. 5-6.

body. Found the day following the battle, stripped of armor and insignia and severely disfigured, the corpse was never indubitably ascertained to be that of Sebastião. Since his close companions were also dead, there remained no witnesses to his supposed capture and death. The body was originally buried in Africa and was finally moved to Portugal in 1582 when only bones remained – past recognition.[33]

Second, an influential tale of Sebastião's survival of the rout sprang up the night of the battle. Late that night, a small group of Portuguese horsemen fleeing the battle appeared at the gates of the nearest fortified city, Arzila, seeking admission. The few guards, fearing attack by the Moors, denied them entry. In desperation, one of the horsemen called out that King Sebastião was with them. The gates immediately opened. In order to carry out the lie, as they entered the fort one of the horsemen disguised himself with his cloak and the others maintained a properly respectful distance. Although these later admitted the ruse, the rumor had already spread to the nearby Portuguese fleet and thence back to Portugal.[34]

These two incidents, when combined with the dismay felt in Portugal at the sudden death of the King and the continued effect of the popular *Trovas* of Bandarra, led to the inauguration of legends in the second phase of Sebastianism. These legends, which continue in popular belief through the twentieth century, foretell the imminent emergence of Sebastião, unscathed from the battle at Alcazar-Quibir, to reunite and glorify Portugal (and Brazil).

The earliest tale was that Sebastião was hidden with his fleet and was soon to enter the port of Lisbon to reclaim his crown from Cardinal

---

33 When finally sepulchred in 1682, Sebastião's body was marked by a stunningly ambiguous epitaph:

> In this tomb is kept, if the report is true, Sebastião
> Whom premature death took on the plains of Libya
> Do not say they are wrong who believe that the king lives,
> According to the law, for the dead man, death is like life.

The phrase *si vera est fama* ("if the report is true") supported beliefs of the Sebastianists for several decades. António Belard da Fonseca, *Dom Sebastião*, 2 vols. (Lisbon: n.p., 1978), particularly 1: 165-175, offers a scholarly, though repetitive, argument on the dating of the inscription. The sepulchre itself is shown in that volume, fig. 1, facing p. 20.

34 Velloso, *D. Sebastião*, pp. 403-404.

Henriques or, after 1580, from the Spanish. A rival tale suggested that Sebastião was being held in prison by the Moors but that his release was soon to be miraculously accomplished.[35]

During the period of the Spanish reign, the myth crystallized to tell of the penitent Sebastião, hidden in a misty island, atoning for his foolhardy venture. He was to return in a cloud, riding a white horse.[36] This popular version persisted beyond the limit of years of Sebastião's normal life-expectancy, for it rendered Sebastião a figure immune to natural laws and under the protection of mystical beings beyond this time and space.

Accordingly, four different men stepped forward during the years from 1584 to 1625, claiming to be the returned Sebastião. The false claimants of Penamacor (1584) and Ericeira (1585) were quickly dismissed by questioners. The "Sebastião" of Madrigal (1594) also had a brief though brilliant career acknowledged by several nobles. The false Sebastião of Venice (1598), under the tutelage of João de Castro and with the latter's clever rewriting and selective interpretation of Bandarra's *Trovas,* received considerable support by Sebastianists despite his apparently limited command of the Portuguese language.[37]

The legend of Sebastião, quickly romanticized, also became the subject of literary creations: a large number of poems and dramas of the century following his death used this tragic theme, including English Elizabethan plays and, notably, John Dryden's *Don Sebastian* (1689).

The third phase of Sebastianism began with the Restoration of the Portuguese throne by João, Duke of Bragança, in 1640.[38] In the coronation of João IV, the vision of the hidden king was recalled and Bandarra received posthumous acclamation as a national prophet.[39] João, however, failed to fulfill the weighty expectations of the prophecies and ended his reign in 1656 after several years of ill health. Despite the extraordinary and ambitious writings of the Jesuit António Vieira, who

---

35   Ibid., p. 404.

36   Braga, *O Povo portuguêz,* 2: 242.

37   Fonseca, *Dom Sebastião,* 2: 33-129. See also Castro, *Paraphrase,* folios 140-167. For a comprehensive treatment in English, see Mary Elizabeth Brooks, *A King for Portugal* (Madison: University of Wisconsin Press, 1964).

38   The political history of the Restoration and the works of António Vieira will be treated in Chapter 6, below.

39   Azevedo, *Sebastianismo,* pp. 67-95.

proposed that João would soon be resurrected to continue his career, the national hope for a redeemer-king reverted to Sebastião.

Thus Sebastianism, as belief in the *Encoberto*, in Sebastião and his hoped-for return, and the special significance attached to the restoration of Portugal by João IV, was the leitmotif of Portuguese nationalism for over a century. This cycle of myths thrived, part of Portuguese folklore through the present era, and saw several enthusiastic revivals in the late eighteenth and early nineteenth centuries. The beliefs of Sebastianism, combined with the other Iberian legends of the *Encoberto*, D. Afonso Henriques, and João Prestes, formed an integral, stable part of Portuguese folklore and of the belief structure of the messianic tradition. These were pervasive, popular myths, readily transmitted to Brazil by the Portuguese immigrants in literary and in oral accounts.

The Cult of the Saints

The cult of the saints has in various modes been part of Christianity from its earliest years. It involves, as its core practice, special reverence paid to the memory of a deceased martyr or holy figure represented in an image or relic remains. This figure was petitioned to intercede with God on behalf of the individual devotee or community of believers for specific aid. Although historically controlled by ecclesiastical authorities, devotion to the martyrs has characteristically been a localized, lay religious phenomenon, centered at shrines attended by local communities and supported by individuals. The cult of the saints maintained two distinct levels of influence in medieval Christianity: at one level, the local shrine gave power, monetary support and prestige to the parish vicar or bishop under whose auspices it flourished, and at a second, it formed a focal religious center for the lay or family cult of Christianity, that is, of the traditional Christian beliefs and practices learned in the family.[40]

In late antiquity, the local or private cult of the martyrs, originally under the patronage of wealthy families in Western Europe and centered at the tomb site, was appropriated and developed as public

---

40   Hippolyte Delahaye, *Sanctus: Essai sur le Culte de saints dans l'antiquité* (Brussels: Société des Bollandistes, 1927), p. 123.

practice by bishops and Church authorities.[41] Through the medieval period to the eleventh century, lay devotion focused on the relic remains, usually the bones or the skull, of the local figures so honored; these saints included early martyrs for Christianity, holy men or women, and particularly devout priests or powerful bishops. This local cult was spread only through the physical transference of a small portion of the relic to a new shrine. After the eleventh century, with the introduction of sacred images such as statues and paintings into common Christian usage, devotion to the saints was separable from the original establishments of relics in cathedrals or churches and independent shrine sites sprang up. At this time special shrine devotion to Mary, impossible earlier for lack of relics, was also begun; the new shrines focused on her images.[42]

In the Iberian states the cult of the saints was implanted in the early medieval period and flourished as an integral part of religious devotion both in local villages and at greater shrine sites. The saints of special devotion were local bishops and martyrs, the aspects of Mary and, later, aspects of the deity and international saints whose devotion was limited to appeals for specific assigned problems.

The practice of devotion to these figures was primarily of a private contractual nature: an individual or village as a unit pledged a special vow or practice in return for relief from a designated problem. The devotee would pledge to honor the saint yearly, perform a single extraordinary ritual, donate to the shrine, make a pilgrimage to a far shrine, or, rarely, keep a vow of lifelong chastity or join a religious order. The saint was petitioned in times of drought or epidemic or to relieve an individual's affliction or personal calamity. The vow or *promessa* made was solemn and the failure to complete it considered a mortal sin.[43]

In Portugal, the early cult of the saints centered on Iberian figures of Saints Vicente and Eulália, the Portuguese Epitácio, and bishops and devout elites of the nobility. The Portuguese shrines were maintained and directed by an appointed ordained chaplain or by the

41   Peter L. Brown, *The Cult of the Saints: Its Rise and Function in Latin Christianity* (Chicago: University of Chicago Press, 1981), pp. 23-49.
42   William A. Christian, Jr., *Local Religion in Sixteenth Century Spain* (Princeton, NJ: Princeton University Press, 1981), p. 21.
43   Ibid., pp. 21-31.

local parish priest. The shrine itself, whether a tiny chapel in the village or a greater building set in the countryside and dedicated to one of the more powerful saint figures, housed not only the relics of the saint and his or her painted or sculpted image, but also gifts from the devotees, such as commemorative plates or valuable objects, and *exvotos*, that is, representations of healed body parts (head, arms, legs, feet) or painted depictions of the physical ailment cured by the saint.[44] Three kinds of celebrations were familiar to such shrines by the sixteenth century: *vigílios*, vigils held in commemoration of the death of the saint, usually with large numbers of attending devotees; *festas*, yearly feasts of the saint, either with the common participation of Christians throughout Portugal or specifically inaugurated by a local vicar; and *octavas*, celebrations of eight consecutive days of religious devotions, reenacting the life story of the saint.[45] Other public demonstrations included songs and dances held near the shrine and processions and pilgrimages to the site; confraternities or *irmandades* were formed in the village, devoted to the local saint or to a more internationally acknowledged Christian figure.

Although the Papal See had reserved for itself the right to designate saints, local cults were founded and feasts celebrated for numerous noncanonized individuals in Portugal. The cult of the saints there was particularly concerned with proper localization of devotion to each of its own saints. A village or community might claim as its own a holy figure who was born or had lived or died nearby, or one who had favored their town, or another simply by virtue of its possession of the relics.[46]

The cult of the saints also comprised village and familial religious beliefs and practices as well as devotion to the saints. Within the family, Christian doctrine was continued and common prayers, such as the Pater Noster and Ave Maria, taught by parent to child. This conservative and traditional religiosity represented Christianity at the local level, appropriate to all and accepted by the local clergy, and contained the religious beliefs and practices known to most Portuguese. When the institution changed or fragmented, as in the transmission of official

---

44   Ibid., pp. 95-96.
45   Jorge Cardoso, *Agiologio lusitano dos sanctos*, 4 vols. (Lisbon: Officina Craesbeekiana, 1652), 1: 43.
46   Ibid., p. 37.

Church doctrine to the residents in the Brazilian colony, these fundamental Christian beliefs were perpetuated by the individual immigrants.

For the Portuguese laity, the figures of the cult of the saints, approached as elsewhere through vows, represented in concrete form the basic beliefs of Christianity. The relationship between the suffering sinful individual and the holy and powerful agent of God was recognizably parallel to the structure of contemporary messianic beliefs; in practice, the devotion to the saints often effectively replaced participation in the established rituals directed to God and Jesus. The saints, in roles similar to that designated for Jesus, were perceived as familiar yet intensely potent celestial figures who could intercede not only for specific disasters but also for remission of one's sins and for one's salvation. Jubilees held in honor of saints extended remission of all previous sins to the participants, and relief from Purgatorial penance was gained through lesser devotional acts.[47] Included in the legends and attributes of the more influential saints such as Mary, Santa Úrsula and other nonlocal figures were distinctly messianic elements derived from their own mythic association with Jesus or developed from parallel legend structures. In this way, the cult of the saints provided a strong continuing support for messianic beliefs, both contributing new elements and absorbing established motifs of the messianic tradition.

The messianic beliefs of the Luso-Brazilian messianic tradition at this beginning point in sixteenth-century Portugal comprised the myths of the Judeo-Christian messianic belief systems, the European messianic-like heroic legends, the Portuguese legends of the vision of Afonso Henriques, the *Encoberto*, João Prestes and Sebastião, and the body of beliefs expressed in the Portuguese cult of the saints. These interrelated beliefs form the foundation for the messianic tradition as a whole, grounded in Portugal and to be followed through later centuries of colonial and postcolonial Brazil, to their expression in the Brazilian messianic movements of the nineteenth century.

Lay Religious Activities

The European Christian Church of the sixteenth century held, as in the Middle Ages, significant control over more than the religious

---

47   Christian, *Local Religion in Spain*, p. 144.

ideological aspect of the lives of its followers. As a powerful institution and the embodiment of the religion of the European states, the Church expended considerable effort in maintenance of its hierarchical structure and of continued adherence to its specified religious creeds.

The Portuguese Church, while it preserved considerable political independence under the right of *padroado*, still at every level bowed to the terms of most papal decrees. Through the late medieval period, however, attempts against the institution of the Church had been made by Christian lay individuals and lay groups who began, as counterparts to the rigid monastic structures, parallel or alternative religious formations.

Certain of these, such as guilds, brotherhoods, Third Orders, and shrine devotion groups, were accepted or even encouraged by the ecclesiastics, provided that clear, chartered regulations were established. Other lay religious activities, such as poverty brotherhoods, the beghards and beguines, and eremetic individuals, were discouraged or considered disruptive or heretical by the Church. Initiated by the lay participants themselves, these latter lay religious activities were consciously begun in counterpart or actual opposition to the monastic orders seen as lax, luxurious or too restrictive. The religious brotherhoods and Third Orders, however, were usually instituted by ecclesiastics, originally as lay groups complementary to other religious activity; in practice, though, the distinction between these types was never clearly drawn nor observed.

In this section will be discussed the different forms of popular Christian lay religious activities in Portugal of the sixteenth century. These activities constitute an important part of the messianic tradition for two reasons. First, their acceptability either for the ecclesiastical institution or for the dissenting laity and their legitimacy as alternate religious activities in place of standard attendance of rituals or entrance in monastic orders encouraged the continuation of innovative lay religious behavior crucial to the later messianic cult groups. Second, their established structures as lay associations, with a leader or small group of principals and larger number of participants under a more or less designated religious purpose, persisted as the model for formation of the later similar groups in Brazil.

In Portugal, as elsewhere in Western Europe, Christian lay religious activities were formed on two levels: first, that of group or collective activities; and, second, that of individuals in solitary devotion. In these ways, the laity in Portugal who sought to lead a better, more devotional

or more moral life could augment their religious practices without join-
ing the monastic or clerical orders. These orders were, at various times,
considered either too removed from ordinary life or too corrupted by
their own wealth and vices to be a suitable choice.

In collective activities, the laity chose to participate in one of the
several religious associations. These were (1) brotherhoods or
irmandades, (2) Third Orders, and (3) more loosely structured groups,
such as beghard-like groups or those connected with a local or
pilgrimage shrine.

The *irmandades* (brotherhoods), alternately designated confraternities or sodalities, developed from the medieval guild, a craft and arti-
san association. The *irmandades* were, however, constituted for a
distinctly religious end, that is, of devotion to a particular saint such as
were popular in Portugal, to an aspect of the deity such as the Holy
Spirit, Corpus Christi, or, especially, to Mary. The *irmandades* were
made up of persons with similar livelihoods or from the same class.[48]
It was not uncommon for a small community to maintain a brotherhood
for community-wide participation in devotional practice.

The devotional activities varied, particularly with the wealth of the
group. Commonly, the group gathered for a prayer service before a
special *oratório* or portable shrine of the holy sponsor or in its own
room or chapel. A special mass might be held or, as with later brotherhoods of the Rosary, a special set of prayers be chanted. Each year, on
the saint's feast day or the day established by the group for celebration,
a religious procession would be staged in which the *oratório* figure or
a banner would be displayed while the brotherhood, accompanied by
clergy, walked together to or from the church services.

Along with these expressions of religious faith, a few brotherhoods,
particularly with wealthier participants, indulged in charitable work for
the Church, for schools, and for hospitals. The Irmandades de
Misericórdia were founded during the early sixteenth century specifically for charitable as well as devotional purposes. They were wealthy,
prestigious groups and supported hospitals and orphanages. The
brotherhoods of artisans, along with their devotional activities, also
provided assistance for ailing or aging members.

The brotherhoods were founded by submission of a *compromisso*, a
type of charter, to the local parish or see. The more formally

48   Almeida, *Igreja em Portugal*, 2: 490-492.

constituted groups, such as the Misericórdias, established a *Mesa* or board of directors and kept records of donations and expenditures.

The first European confraternity, a lay devotional association dedicated to Mary, appeared in the thirteenth century in Paris under the direction of Bishop Odo. The first Portuguese brotherhoods appeared in the same century; these were for blacksmiths and for merchants and, later, for devotion to the Holy Ghost and to Saint Francis. A fifteenth-century *irmandade* in Lisbon, Servants of the Bom Senhor Jesus Christo, gathered during the time of the plague to pray for relief.[49]

This form of lay religious association was important, for as a stable continuing part of religious life it allowed considerable lay religious practices without direct involvement of the clergy. The Church, in fact, encouraged the founding of *irmandades* as lay-initiated participation in Christian cultic activities. The *irmandades* also contributed donations to local churches or parishes, a factor significantly in favor of their continued toleration.

Participation in Third or Minor Orders was also available to the more religious among the Portuguese laity, though these groups were more rigidly regimented. *Ordens Terceiras*, or Third Orders, were lay religious associations connected with certain monastic orders, specifically the mendicant orders such as Franciscans and Carmelites.

The first Third Order was founded by Francis of Assisi and approved by papal authority in 1221. Francis' orders were exemplary of the monastic reform groups of that time which, unlike the older eremetical orders whose members withdrew from the secular world, instead chose to live and work in the secular world, following the apostolic example. Francis founded his first order of male mendicants; the second under his tutelage was of nuns led by Clare. The third group, then, was for lay participants.

The purpose of this and later Third Orders was for the laity to achieve a degree of the dedication and discipline of the monastic life without breaking with family and the secular life. These lay groups lived under the spiritual guidance of the particular religious order to which they were attached and always established their center in the vicinity

---

49   Manuel S. Cardozo, "The Lay Brotherhoods of Colonial Bahia," *Catholic Historical Review* 33 (April 1947): 18-20; Marques, *Daily Life*, pp. 220-225.

of a monastery or seminary. Third Orders maintained more stringent rules than the early *irmandades*: each member took "minor vows" and wore a scapular medal under his or her clothing as a sort of habit. In processions, special habits similar to those of the friars or nuns could be worn. Members of the Third Orders were under the control of the superior of the related monastery or of a specifically designated friar.[50]

The *Ordens Terceiras* in Portugal formed a lay parallel to monastic life, an intermediate level between the secular and religious communities. Their activities, however, showed many similarities to the *irmandades* and, after the sixteenth century, they were understood as interchangeable with these, despite their own formal connections.

Besides the *irmandades* and *Ordens Terceiras*, there also existed more loosely structured lay religious groups in Portugal. These included the independent monastic-type communities of the beghards and beguines and the shrine-associated groups. In the twelfth century in Europe, small lay groups of men and women created monastic religious communities similar to but independent of the established orders and in defiance of ecclesiastical restrictions. The undertaking of these beghards and beguines was to reaffirm the true or pure ideal of devotional, apostolic, or monastic existence which they believed had been broken by the luxurious and unchaste lives of the monks of that time. They therefore inaugurated their own orders, often with a much more rigorous interpretation of monasticism, which emphasized extremes of poverty and ritual practices.

The Church considered these late medieval groups to be heretical. Although their actual beliefs may have been simply a more extreme position of the currently accepted views, rather than truly heterodox, the ecclesiastical authorities regarded the general trend as dangerous and subversive. In 1317 the papal bull *Sancta Romana* sharply condemned these unchartered groups, including among the *profanae multidinis viri* associations of "little friars" and beguines.[51]

The first such group for men in Portugal was recorded in 1294 under the name *eremitas pobres* — the poor hermits. Women also organized

50   Mário Barata, *Igreja da Ordem Terceira da Penitência do Rio de Janeiro* (Rio de Janeiro: Livraria Agir Ed., 1975), p. 59.
51   José Sebastião da Silva Dias, *Correntes de sentimento religioso em Portugal, séculos XVI a XVII*, 2 vols. (Coimbra: Universidade de Coimbra, 1960), 1: 4.

independent religious houses, as elsewhere in Europe, and these continued in popularity for several centuries. In the 1480s the Portuguese *Côrtes* was called upon to consider the problem of convents for women outside the approved orders.[52]

As a widespread activity, these Portuguese groups — small in number at the height of their popularity — declined as time passed, though "houses of charity" for poor or unattached women became an established part of Portuguese communities. The activities of these groups directly imitated those of reclusive monks and, later, those of mendicant friars. They proposed, however, to start afresh without the corruptive influence of the institutionalized religious orders and the decadence they saw there. The beghard and beguine groups did not submit their rules for papal approval as was required but, at least initially, admitted a stricter regimen than that of the older orders.

As elsewhere in medieval and postmedieval Europe, Portugal was the site of several popular pilgrimage shrines. These played an important role in the lives of the lay Christians as focal points of worship. Not only were they usually specifically dedicated to the more powerful or popular figures of the cult of saints — such as Our Lady of Nazare, Our Lady of Cabo, St. Maria of Escada, St. Vicente, St. Turcato and St. Donato — but they were also ancient sacred sites in their own right. Visits to these freed the pilgrims of the burden of sins committed and earned them indulgences or perhaps the granting of a special request.[53]

Because of their religious significance and popularity, pilgrimage sites also became the gathering points for small devotional bands of lay pilgrims. These bands formed a loosely structured community, not always permanent in nature, in support of the shrine. Their primary activity was prayer and ritual veneration of the saint of the shrine, though less frequently they would also tend to the physical and spiritual needs of the more transient pilgrims. This latter function, however, was also ministered by a local confraternity.[54]

From the time of the late Middle Ages continuing through the sixteenth century, a number of acceptable options for religious group activities were available to the Portuguese laity. Those among the laity

---

52   Ibid., 1: 65.

53   Marques, *Daily Life*, pp. 212-215; Mário Martins, *Peregrinações e livros de milagres na nossa Idade Média* (Lisbon: Edições "Broteria," 1957), pp. 19-22.

54   Martins, *Peregrinações*, pp. 22, 31.

who chose to intensify their involvement in religious devotion to the Church or to one of its saints, rather than seeking admission to the formal monastic orders, could instead participate in brotherhoods, Third Orders, beguine communities or other less structured groups.

These collective religious activities provided an alternative and usually legitimate means to better one's religious or moral standing in the eyes of the Church or of the community, often without abandoning the common secular life. The institutional lay religious groups acknowledged and therefore regulated by the Christian Church, primarily the brotherhoods and Third Orders, affirmed the appropriateness of religious practices outside of or parallel to the orders of the institutional church, while the groups begun in substitution for or in opposition to these orders suggested the superiority of noninstitutional religious practice. In this way, that is, as specific and distinct models for religious activity, both of these types of groups significantly contributed to the development of the Portuguese messianic tradition.

Lay individuals of the sixteenth century might also opt for a solitary religious life of contemplation and penitence, atoning for their own sins and the sins of others. Those persons, predominantly men, who followed this way of life adopted the practices of the established cenobitic and mendicant orders or of the apostolic ideal. The solitary lay individuals who withdrew into a religious life settled in remote, less populated or more rugged areas or near a holy shrine or pilgrimage site. Known in Portugal as *ermitães*, these penitents were usually respected for the extremes of poverty, suffering and devotional practices which they endured in order to achieve a superior religious condition.

Other individuals continued a mendicant or wandering life, at times from shrine to shrine, in a lifelong pilgrimage of penitence. Or they assumed the habits of the Franciscans or Carmelites and walked from village to village praying and preaching.[55]

Those who undertook the solitary religious life, though they were, like the lay groups discussed above, outside of or in opposition to the ordained religious orders, still often secured positive reputations and were even seen as holy persons or saints themselves. This further option for lay religious activity offered a radical model for religious behavior and for religious authority. It was not unusual that these individuals were at times held in higher repute than the local clergy or monastics.

55   Ibid., pp. 11, 161.

Thus in the sixteenth century in Portugal there existed several types of Christian lay religious activities which served as acceptable complements to the expected practices of attendance at Mass services and receipt of the sacraments. Even the beghard groups and the temporary or unstructured associations which sought to substitute for the institution found acceptance among the laity in Portugal as appropriate alternative forms of intense religious experience.

The presence of these lay activities indicates that for many of the laity who sought increased involvement in the Christian cult the monastic or clerical orders were not a suitable option. The lay persons chose instead one of these three: (1) participation in a lay religious community without withdrawal from secular life, as in the brotherhoods or Third Orders; (2) participation in a lay religious community vivifying the apostolic or monastic ideal, including withdrawal from secular life and the practice of poverty, abstinence and penitence, as in the beghard groups; or (3) solitary religious devotion in an independently determined role, as a wandering pilgrim, hermit or *ermitão*. While these last two formulations have been understood as anticlerical or, in more extreme cases, as protests against the Church itself, the participants nonetheless undertook these as means toward achievement of a more perfect religious life or toward the goal of a reward expected after death.

All of these activities, although in themselves not always messianic, offer distinct parallels with contemporary and later messianic movements in Portugal and Brazil. This is especially evident in the analysis of the more spontaneous groups and of the exemplary lifestyles of the *ermitães*. These all contributed substantially to the Luso-Brazilian messianic tradition – and are thus a part of it – by providing the legitimate, acceptable ideological and social structures mirrored in the development of the pattern of the messianic groups.

Nearly all of the lay religious activities discussed above were transported to Brazil during the sixteenth century or reappeared there after a brief hiatus. The *irmandades* and Third Orders were deliberately continued in the colony from its earliest days. The solitary religious *ermitão* as well as the loosely structured religious associations also occurred.

Penitential Practices

An integral part of the late medieval Christian cult, emphasizing as it did strict adherence to canonical and ecclesiastical laws, was harsh penance and penitence for moral wrongdoing. Physical deprivation in the form of special fasts, extremely long prayer services and self-flagellation was characteristically practiced as the most fitting penitence for sins.

The Portuguese penitential books of the late Middle Ages, drawing upon the rigorous recommendations of the early Church fathers and of the earlier medieval penitenciaries, ordained severe punishment, particularly fasting, for all manner of serious sins. Extended fasting was then practiced by abstaining from all animal meats and products except small fish and from wine and beer; on three days of each week the penitent was restricted to a diet of bread and water only. Most of the mortal or grievous sins — such as homicide or adultery — demanded a seven-year fasting period for atonement. Fornication by a priest, incest or robbing a church required fifteen years; lesser sins would be remitted after twenty to thirty days of a strict bread-and-water fast. All of these penances were set and their completion ascertained by the local rector or parish priest. Some penances were so harsh that in order to achieve full remittance the sinner might simply enter a monastery.[56]

Each of these penances could be interchanged with a fixed, corresponding amount of extended prayers or lashes with a whip. For example, the recitation of forty Psalms while kneeling in church was equal to one day of bread-and-water fasting. "Twenty blows with the hand or twenty strokes with a whip" had the same value.[57]

Consideration of penitential practices, specifically self-flagellation, is included in this study of the Luso-Brazilian messianic tradition because the practices historically parallel not only messianic belief and messianic movements but also lay religious activities, constituting a significant aspect of the latter's rituals.

Flagellation — viewed as the perfect penance — occurred as an important and even popular part of Christian life and custom from the time of the Middle Ages, though it was barely acknowledged in

56   Mário Martins, "O Penitencial de Martim Perez, em mediêvo-português," *Lusitania Sacra* 2 (1957): 59-102.

57   Ibid., p. 103.

contemporary or more modern literature. Many penitential practices, particularly self-flagellation, were specifically incorporated into the messianic movements from the twelfth century in Europe to the nineteenth century in Brazil. Flagellation also served as the *raison d'être* of many small lay religious associations which gathered temporarily during the Lenten season or sporadically over several years.

In this section will be discussed flagellant practices with other remarkable forms of penance in Europe and Portugal in the later Middle Ages through the sixteenth century. The attention of this study will first be turned to those penitential practices among the religious orders as these comprised exemplary and regulated behavior; discussion of the penitential practices and penitential groups among the laity will follow.

The monastic orders originally adopted the use of flagellation as penal corrections for transgressions by their own members against the regulatory codes of the order or for noted or confessed sins. Fasting and simplicity of lifestyle are already inherently part of these orders as they adhered to the apostolic ideal. For this reason punishment for disobedience or for grievous sins seemed to necessitate a more extreme measure, such as flagellation of the guilty individual.

Self-flagellation as a regular or common penitential mode was not encouraged by the Church or by the orders until well into the medieval period. However, before that time, saintly individuals practiced self-flagellation among their other more severe corporal mortifications in their quest for spiritual ascendancy and purity. The legends of Peter the Hermit, for example, and of William, Duke of Aquitaine, and Dominic Loricatus as well as the hagiographies of many of the medieval and later saints and fathers of the Christian Church emphasized the harshness of their continual use of flagellation.[58]

Damian of Ostia around the middle of the eleventh century recommended this self-inflicted penance and has been credited for the surge

---

58   James G. Bertram [William M. Cooper], *Flagellation and the Flagellants*, new ed., rev. and cor. (London: W. Reeves, [1904]), pp. 48-49. As stated above, the practice conformed to the description of the Passion of Jesus, specifically as described in Mark 21, scourging by the Roman soldiers. This *imitatio Christi*, or imitation of Christ, represented not hubris for the flagellant, but rather self-humiliation and mortification of the body in an imperfect recreation of the original perfect act of penance by Jesus.

in its popularity among both ordained and lay Christians alike. Self-flagellation, that is, the whipping of one's front or back with cords or leather thongs, some with iron tips, was to be undertaken to subdue the corporal and thus elevate the spiritual aspects of humanity.[59]

Voluntary flagellation was called "discipline," which term referred as well to the whip and to each stroke. The rules of many monastic orders, especially those established or reformed in the late medieval period, included as customary activity regular discipline for all monks and friars.

Discipline, in Portuguese *a disciplina*, was performed in Portugal primarily among the Jesuits and the Franciscans, although the documentation of the latter's activities remains scanty. The writings of the Jesuits, on the other hand, who were by far the more powerful group in Portugal in the late sixteenth and seventeenth centuries, provide ample records of their penitential practices, among which self-flagellation frequently figured.[60]

Ignácio de Loyola, before his founding of the Society of Jesus in 1534 (papal recognition came in 1540), had led an exemplary life of extreme penitence and deprivation. He performed discipline to the point of bodily disfigurement and illness, as well as other modes of penance, so as to rigidly subjugate his body to the control of his spiritual will. These activities were later moderated, partially owing to impaired health, and the recommendations he offered to the members of his new community in the treatise of *Spiritual Exercises* reflect that change.[61]

In that work Ignácio still recommends flagellation as self-inflicted punishment for sins, since "exterior penance is the fruit" of interior penance. Along with reductions in eating and sleeping, he advises

> chastising the flesh, thereby causing sensible pain. This is done by hairshirts, cords or iron chains on the body, or by scourging or wounding oneself...What seems to be the most suitable and safest thing in doing penance is for the pain to be felt in the flesh, without penetration to the bones, thus causing pain but not illness. Therefore it seems more fitting to scourge oneself with light cords, which cause exterior pain, than in another way that might cause internal infirmity.[62]

---

59   Ibid., pp. 49-50.
60   Ibid., p. 96.
61   Ignácio de Loyola, *Spiritual Exercises*, trans. Anthony Mottola (New York: Doubleday and Co., Inc., Image Books, 1964).
62   Ibid., pp. 61-62.

The Society of Jesus in Portugal had as its founder Simão Rodrigues, one of Loyola's earliest companions. Disregarding his superior's moderating advice, Rodrigues introduced severe bodily mortification in Portugal and found many willing participants. In 1542 Rodrigues inaugurated the Jesuit College of Coimbra whose students attended classes at the nearby University of Coimbra while completing their novitiate in the order. Rodrigues demanded extraordinary mortifications of his younger Jesuits. One novice carried a skull with him to his class in order to suffer repugnance and humiliation. Another, fifteen years old, tied himself to a post in a public square for a day. A group of novices — among them Manuel de Nóbrega, later a Brazilian missionary — were instructed to run through the city streets at night, yelling, "Hell for all those who are in mortal sin." Other special penitences were also arranged.[63]

In order that his followers might deny worldly vanity, Rodrigues had them wear torn, mended or short tunics and suffer the laughter and derision of their noble classmates. They were also sent out to beg for their daily food. Discipline, that is, self-flagellation, became a customary part of their religious observance, even in public, through the streets of the city.[64]

The continued influence of the instructions of Rodrigues may be clearly seen in the later practices of Manuel da Nóbrega and of other Brazilian missionaries who studied at Coimbra. Rodrigues himself was later reprimanded and then removed from the College, partly because of these excessive practices.[65]

Flagellant practices were also adopted by the laity in Portugal. These, part of the historical trend of lay flagellant groups in Europe, initiated flagellant processions and brotherhoods, cooperating with and following the lead of the Portuguese Jesuits.

As self-flagellation became a common practice among the members of the various European monastic orders, so it also spread through the Church as a whole, gaining popularity as a special form of penance among the laity in general. Flagellant groups appeared in Italy and

---

63   Francisco Rodrigues, *História da Companhia de Jesus na Assistência de Portugal*, 4 vols. (Porto: "Apostolado da Imprensa" Empresa Editora, 1931-1950), 2, Pt. 1 (1938): 365-367.
64   Ibid., 1, Pt. 1 (1931): 364-365.
65   Ibid., 1, Pt. 2 (1931): 41-55.

Germany in the thirteenth century and, despite the ban by Pope Clement VI in 1349, continued for several centuries. The highly organized processions of lay men lasted a specific symbolic period and included chants and prayers with their flagellation.

The ideology of many of these groups was evidently messianic: their penance was performed to save humanity from eternal punishment in the impending Judgement of the Last Days. A small number of flagellant sects can be considered messianic movements; these generally practiced their rituals in secret. Even when the eschatological aspect became muted, flagellant processions were held for yearly remission of sins, at least for the participants. Flagellant groups of the fourteenth century organized against the threat of the advancing plague to stave off with their own self-inflicted penance that punishment sent by God.[66]

In Portugal, these lay practices began later and continued longer than in other European countries. The Portuguese considered fasts and prayers private penance and flagellation in groups or processions acceptable public penance.[67]

Flagellant processions repeatedly occurred in Lisbon, even long after the ban of Clement VI. The so-called Procession of the Naked was held, with a brief hiatus, through the late eighteenth century. Partially clad and barefoot, men joined this yearly procession in fulfillment of a vow to God or a saint or to earn remission of sins. They walked between monasteries near the city of Coimbra, flagellating one another. The activity was halted temporarily in 1641 and finally in the eighteenth century, because it had become exaggerated and engendered considerable mockery.[68]

The *Procissões dos penitentes* ("processions of the penitents") became a Portuguese custom in the late Middle Ages and involved both lay men and women in a short Lenten demonstration of penitence. Self-flagellation was often part of this ritual as well.[69]

---

66   Cohn, *Pursuit*, pp. 127-147; see also Bertram, *Flagellation*, pp. 100-102.

67   Getúlio Cesar, *Crendices do Nordeste* (Rio de Janeiro: Irmãos Pongetti Editores, 1941), p. 131, n. 1.

68   Marques, *Daily Life*, p. 220; Martins, *Peregrinacões*, pp. 36-37.

69   Jaime Lopes Dias, *Etnografia da Beira*, 9 vols. (Lisbon: Livraria Feira, Ltda., 1926-1963), 9 (1963): 122-124.

Flagellation, along with walking barefoot or on one's knees, the wearing of unseasonably light clothing, and the carrying of heavy stones also added to the penitential value of long pilgrimages.[70]

While the Portuguese laity had themselves created a number of independent flagellant practices, they also participated in penitential services led by the religious orders, particularly those organized by the Society of Jesus. Attendance at such services began as devout practice, although some later achieved a certain social prestige among the nobility. In Lisbon, for example, a confraternity of men dedicated to extraordinary penance and frequent attendance at religious services inaugurated a group meeting in the Jesuit House on Friday nights under the guidance of those priests to hear the sermons of the Jesuits and to practice the "discipline" together. By 1548 this popular penitential confraternity numbered over two hundred men and was still growing; in 1550 even the Queen and the Prince of Portugal requested special admission to one of the services.[71]

The Jesuits held significant influence over the members of the royal court and introduced not a few of them into penitential practices. The large meetings of the penitential services were held again in the early seventeenth and late eighteenth centuries, each time with undiminished enthusiasm and noble participants.[72]

The seventeenth century also saw the founding of the Congregation of *Boa Morte*, or "the Good Death," again by the Jesuit Order. On Fridays, at night, the members of the Congregation assembled to contemplate the Passion and death of Jesus and to prepare for their own deaths. The service ended with a sermon on penitence and flagellation during the chanting of Psalms.[73]

In these ways, during the period of the late Middle Ages and of the Counter Reformation in Portugal expression of penance in extreme modes, particularly self-flagellation, became part of religious expression. Participants in these penances included members of religious orders as well as Portuguese lay individuals. As described above, among the religious orders discipline was held to be meritorious and saintly practice and found advocates particularly in the Jesuit Order in

---

70   Martins, *Peregrinações*, p. 37.
71   Rodrigues, *História da Companhia* 1, Pt. 1 (1931): 618-619.
72   Ibid., 2, Pt. 1 (1938): 427; Bertram, *Flagellation*, p. 97.
73   Rodrigues, *História da Companhia* 3, Pt. 1 (1944): 294-295.

Coimbra and Lisbon. This institutionalized practice by the religious orders kept the example of such special penitence constantly before the laity and induced the latter's involvement.

The Christian laity of Europe took part in the surge of popularity of flagellation by organizing flagellant processions and messianic-flagellant sects. Portugal also felt the effect of this trend: Portuguese lay men held flagellant processions, joined penitential groups led by the Jesuit fathers and added self-flagellation to the pilgrim's penances.

Two aspects of these flagellant activities are important in the historical development of the Luso-Brazilian messianic tradition. First, the use of flagellation was related to the historical occurrence of European messianic movements and often actually served as part of the core rituals of these movements. Second, flagellant practices provided a clear format and purpose for the organization of independent lay religious associations and, as organizing principles, affected the later formation of Brazilian flagellant groups and messianic movements.

In this first chapter on the historical elements of the Luso-Brazilian messianic tradition, the component parts of the beginning, the Portuguese messianic tradition, were presented.

First considered was the corpus of messianic mythology whose accumulated beliefs were disseminated in the sixteenth century in Portugal. The specific myths were of the Judeo-Christian creeds, that is, belief in a superhuman messiah whose arrival would cause or signal the end of this world, and of other legend cycles, that is, concerning the Hidden King, Portuguese King Afonso Henriques, the elusive João Prestes, and finally Sebastião, the redeemer-king.

This body of legends uniquely determined the messianic ideology in Portugal, affecting the structure of beliefs received from other European sources in two ways: first, by adding substantially new mythological content and thus making the ideology unmistakably Portuguese; and, second, by reaffirming the value of the continuance of these beliefs. The country-wide involvement after the death of Sebastião gives a clear indication of the extent to which messianism had become part of popular religious beliefs.

Next considered were the religious activities in various types of devotional associations available to the Christian laity in Portugal. Rather than seeking admission to inappropriate or corrupted institutional orders, certain lay individuals joined temporary or more permanent lay religious communities or brotherhoods. Others pursued a more perfect religious life alone as hermits. These several options opened up a different aspect of participation in intensified religious activity, that is, participation apart from the officially constituted and approved organizations within the Roman Catholic Church. Consideration of these types of activities as acceptable and even superior persisted among the Portuguese and Brazilian laity, and these activities provided the social structural framework for more radical and dissenting groups. As such they are an important organizational part of the Luso-Brazilian messianic tradition.

Finally, the Christian penitential practices and flagellant groups in Europe and Portugal were discussed. Religious and lay alike became involved in private penitence and public displays of self-flagellation. The practices themselves were focal ritual activity for a few messianic movements; the flagellant associations, as other lay religious associations, structured the lay Christians in intensive alternative forms of religious practice.

These three segments, comprising quite diverse elements, thus form the beginning of the Luso-Brazilian messianic tradition under study in this thesis. As Portuguese men and women colonized Brazil, elements from these three recur there, as will be seen in the following chapter.

Chapter 5

Brazil: 1549-1599

It is clear from the historical evidence gathered in the preceding chapter that the critical religious elements and structures of beliefs — those which will later be seen in the development of the nineteenth-century Brazilian messianic movements — were abundantly present in sixteenth-century Portugal. These beliefs in messianic salvation, in the redeemer-king, and in the power of the saints, together with the related lay religious social behavior patterns, made the transition to colonial Northeastern Brazil with the Portuguese colonists.

This next period under study for the traces of the messianic tradition, that is, the period in the history of colonial Brazil from 1549 to the end of the sixteenth century, represents the first direct effort by the Portuguese crown to establish political and religious hegemony over its colony in the New World. In the Northeast of Brazil during this era — that particular geographic section which later served as the site for the three messianic movements — the first capital city, Salvador, in the state of Bahia, began to flourish on the Bay of All Saints, and the sugar and related cattle industry were extending the colonial frontiers inland. The Portuguese Christians — ordained religious and lay alike — who disembarked at Salvador brought with them, as part of their religious heritage and in the books of doctrinal instructions for the colonists and natives, the elements of belief which constituted the messianic tradition.

This first chapter on the Brazilian aspects of the messianic and related beliefs, lay religious activities and penitential practices will consider the continuation of the various ingredients of the Luso-Brazilian messianic tradition from Portugal with their further development or change, if any, as part of Brazilian religiosity. Emphasis will be placed on following those specific beliefs and practices noted in the preceding chapter.

Because the people who inhabited the Northeast in the nineteenth century and took part in the messianic movements there were primarily of Portuguese ancestry, in this chapter and all following chapters on the religious beliefs and practices in Brazil only the material verifiably related to the Portuguese colonists and their descendants will be included. For this reason, information such as on the theory and effect of the catechizing of the Brazilindians will be absent.

The specific messianic beliefs, lay religious activities and penitential practices in the Northeast of Brazil of this period will be presented, preceded by a brief historical view of the colony in the sixteenth century.

Historical Circumstances

The governing of Brazilian colony, from the claiming of the territory for the Portuguese crown by the explorer Pedro Alvarez Cabral in 1500 until the establishment of the royal capital at Salvador, Bahia, in 1549, was a failed attempt at delegation of political authority in the colonization enterprise.[1]

After the securing of Portugal's claim to that portion of the New World by proclamation of possession, King João II chose not to govern the colony directly from the metropolis, but rather to implement the system that had succeeded in Madeira and the Azores, that of the *capitânias*, or captaincies. Thus, in 1534, João divided the coast of Brazil into fifteen segments of approximately fifty leagues from north to south, with the inland extension unlimited, and awarded them as inheritable lands to favored nobles in his court. The *donatórios*, the lords in possession of these parcels of Brazilian land, and their descendants could then exploit the land as they saw fit, with a significant portion of their trade or agricultural profit earmarked for the coffers of the royal treasury.[2]

Under the plan of the *capitânias*, very little colonizing actually took place. The majority of the *donatórios* simply lacked the means to launch an expedition to a piece of unknown property half a world away, let

1   Excellent works on the history of Brazil include these in English: C. R. Boxer, *The Dutch in Brazil: 1624-1654* (Hamden, CT: Archon Books, 1973), and E. Bradford Burns, *A History of Brazil* (New York: Columbia University Press, 1970). The best work on Catholicism and the Catholic Church in Brazil is Hoornaert, et al., eds., *História da Igreja no Brasil*. See also Serafim Leite, *História da Companhia de Jesus no Brasil*, 10 vols. (Lisbon: Livraria Portugalia, 1938-1950), which contains significant accounts of Brazilian religion from the perspective of the work of the Jesuits there.

2   Boxer, *Dutch in Brazil*, p. 17; Burns, *History of Brazil*, pp. 24-25.

alone establish an operating commercial center and defend it against aboriginal, French or Dutch encroachments.[3] Limited exportation of brasil-wood, along with other dye materials and rosewood or jacaranda, was undertaken. When sugar cane was introduced, however, *engenhos de açucar* or sugar plantations sprang up and flourished, especially in the rich agricultural areas in the Recôncavo of Bahia and in Pernambuco, both in the Northeast. These finally served as anchoring points for the Portuguese enterprise of the colonization of Brazil.

As a whole, however, the reality of the *capitânias* failed to achieve the potential envisioned by João II. In 1549, João III inaugurated a new era for the young colony: he commissioned the first Governor-general, Tomé de Sousa, to install Portuguese royal authority in the new capital of Salvador, Bahia, the port city of the sugar cane industry and *metrópole* of the Northeast. Tomé de Sousa and his second successor, Mem de Sá, were able executives and, through the rigid Portuguese governing structure, oversaw the collection of taxes and maintenance of military defense. The Governors-general of Brazil functioned as representatives of the King, though distance and reasonable leeway in interpretation of laws allowed their governments a degree of independence.

Under the royal *padroado*, the colonial governors were also responsible for certain aspects of the administration and organization of the colonial Church and of the local missions of Franciscans and Jesuits. Their functions overlapped those of the bishopric and order superiors to such an extent that conflicts were unavoidable. The missionaries, for their own part, on occasion disregarded both governor and bishop.

With Tomé de Sousa came the first six Jesuit missionaries under the guidance of Manuel da Nóbrega, constituting not only the first Jesuits in the New World, but also the first religious order to settle in Brazil. The Jesuits, through their influence at every social level and the prosperity of their industries, remained the most powerful single group in Brazil through most of the colonial epoch.[4] They also maintained a vast overseas correspondence with Portugal and Rome of letters, reports, financial statements, printed sermons and other written works, substantially increasing their information and authority.

---

3   Boxer, *Dutch in Brazil*, p. 17.
4   Luiz Beltrão, *Comunicação e folclore* (São Paulo: Edições Melhoramentos, 1971), p. 27.

The duration of the Spanish control of the Portuguese throne, from 1580 to 1640, did not irrevocably affect the growth and status of the colony: it remained a Portuguese possession ruled primarily by Portuguese.

Messianic Beliefs

The messianic mythology developed in Portugal was imported during this period by the incoming colonists, allowing for the continuance of an unbroken chain of belief to the later messianic movements. These beliefs, in the imminence of the Messiah and the historical circumstances preceding his appearance, in the savior-king and in the messianic role of the saints, set the pattern at this early point for a belief structure which continued essentially unchanged for three centuries in the Northeast of Brazil.

The messianic legends of Portugal arrived in the colony by means of two apparently distinct vehicles. First, the Jesuit missionaries, who dominated the evangelistic work during this period, expressed the supportive attitudes of sixteenth-century Christianity toward messianic expectations. Because of their own perception of their task in Brazil, the theme of salvation—by Jesus, or by his saints or emissaries—and the means to salvation through *bons costumes* (good habits) repeatedly appeared in their letters and writings.

Second, the Portuguese immigrants, including nobles, merchants, artisans and *degredados* (exiled criminals) naturally continued the Portuguese religious folk culture with which they had been raised. This included the legends of their favorite or village saints and of Sebastião, the *Encoberto*.

These two groups, the religious missionaries and the lay colonists, will be treated separately in this and later sections on Brazilian religious development, primarily because of the consciously separate status of the members of the religious orders. Their role as official disseminators of Catholicism extended a sort of legitimacy and the presumed approval by the Roman Church over all of their teachings, and the popularity of their writings made several of the members such as Anchieta and, later, Vieira singularly influential figures.

However, the beliefs and practices of the friars overlapped those of the laity somewhat beyond the expected priestly example. On the one hand, the Portuguese Jesuits were also participants in Portuguese folk culture, and they believed and repeated legends such as that of

Sebastião which were not considered to be strictly orthodox teaching by Rome. On the other hand, because of the scarcity of clergy in the sixteenth and later centuries in the Northeast, lay individuals took up the role of the missionaries, led prayers and preached as they did and were at times acknowledged as feasible substitutes by their hearers. This limited acceptance allowed them, again, to continue messianic legends which otherwise spread more slowly from parent to child, by village storytellers, or through circulating *cordel* pamphlets.

In this section on the messianic beliefs in the sixteenth century in Brazil, the teachings of the individual Jesuits will be considered, that is, the letters of Manuel da Nóbrega, the writings and prophecies of José de Anchieta, and the Jesuit catechism by Marcos Jorge, followed by the first noted appearance of Bandarra's *Trovas* in the colony and the continuance of the cult of the saints.

The two most important religious leaders in sixteenth-century Brazil were Portuguese Jesuit missionaries: Manuel da Nóbrega (1517-1570), the first Provincial of the new mission area, and José de Anchieta (1534-1597), called the Apostle of Brazil. Both received their instruction at the Jesuit College at Coimbra, Portugal, as did the majority of the early Jesuit missionaries in Brazil and other Portuguese possessions.

Manuel da Nóbrega first arrived in Brazil in 1549 and immediately launched the ambitious and aggressive campaign of the Jesuits to redeem the heathens and reclaim the sinful Portuguese. He was chosen to head the nascent Brazilian Jesuit community and his task to "expand the frontiers of the faith and of the empire" had begun with preaching among his shipmates during the long sea voyage from Portugal. Once in Salvador, Nóbrega could not lose sight of the fact that he must first bring the Portuguese residents back to the Church before turning completely to the enterprise of catechizing the Brazilindians.[5]

Thus, the first literary creation in the colony, written by Nóbrega alone or with the collaboration from José de Anchieta, was a religious drama, "Pregação Universal," a "universal preaching" directed to

_____

5   José Carlos Sebe Bom Meihy, "A Presença do Brasil na Companhia de Jesus: 1549-1649," (Unpublished Ph.D. dissertation, Universidade de São Paulo, 1975), p. 84; and Riolando Azzi, "As Romarias no Brasil," *Revista de Cultura Vozes* 73 (1979): 39.

immigrants and natives together in Portuguese and Tupí. Most of the
text has been lost, but its few extant verses and contemporary sources
indicate that its bilingual theme was the salvation of two sinners
through the mercy of Mary, mother of Jesus.[6]

The two themes of repentance and salvation dominate each writing
that Nóbrega intended for the colonists, even at the expense of the
canonical message designated for a particular religious feast-day. In
1552, in Bahia, he sent a missive to "the inhabitants of Pernambuco,"
enjoining them to take to heart the example of the suffering and
glorified Christ and to repent now for their later glory. He assures them
that "in the eternal life all will be one with God." He warns them,
though, of the limitations of God's mercy in those "last times":

> For, so much grace is given [to repentant sinners] and in such abundance,
> many times I am concerned, and it is for me a sign that the world will last
> only a short time.[7]

Nóbrega's preachings contain only muted motifs of messianic
beliefs; in this, he is representative of the normative doctrinal stance
which the Jesuit order adopted in Brazil. However, his writings, combined with the efforts of many others, offered ecclesiastical support for
belief in more radical eschatology.

The more influential and prolific figure of this period was Nóbrega's
disciple, José de Anchieta. He became legendary during his own
lifetime: tales of miracles, cures and all manner of visions were collected by his Jesuit companions as proof of his holiness.

Anchieta composed epic poetry, religious dramas and dramatic sermons in his role as apostolic missionary to the young colony. The letters which he wrote to his superiors and friends in Portugal echoed the
religious sentiments that his literary works portray: that life, particularly in Brazil, was a continual struggle against the Devil and the

---

6   Simão de Vasconcellos, *Vida do veneravel Padre José de Anchieta*, 2 vols.
(Lisbon: Oficina de João da Costa, 1672; reprint ed., Rio de Janeiro: Imprensa
Nacional, 1943), 1: 55-58; Richard Preto-Rodas, "Anchieta and Vieira: Drama as
Sermon, Sermon as Drama," *Luso-Brazilian Review* 7 (1970): 97.

7   Manuel da Nóbrega, *Cartas do Brasil e mais escritos*, ed. Serafim Leite
(Coimbra: Universidade de Coimbra, 1955), pp. 106-108 (my translation in this and
all following quotations).

temptation of evil and that only the true soldiers of the Christian Church could triumph.[8]

Anchieta reiterated the emphasis on the significance of salvation found in Nóbrega's writings. In his sermon preached on the day commemorating the conversion of Paul, for example, Anchieta instructs his audience that the Church is the means to salvation, through a common metaphor: "to no one does Jesus teach the way of his salvation, nor can one be saved, unless he first enter the city of the holy Church." The concept of the path to salvation appears repeatedly in Anchieta's other sermons and letters as well.[9]

In the 1580s, Anchieta wrote a trilogy of religious plays known together as *Na vila da Vitória*, that is, "In the village of Vitória."[10] The plays were intended to substitute for the more secular entertainment of that time, as well as the religious plays of poorer quality or lesser moral content. Because of the quality of writing and the inspirational and effective religious themes, these plays enjoyed great popularity in the late sixteenth century in Brazil.

The plays as a unit gave dramatic presence to Anchieta's version of the messianic paradigm: the world of colonial Brazil was corrupt, ruled by the Devil himself and on the brink of the Last Days—yet the conquering salvific force of God, in the persons of two popular saints, Santa Úrsula and São Maurício, would soon overthrow the evil and begin a New Age.

In the first act of the first play, also called *Na vila de Vitória*, Lucifer and his loyal servant Satanáz plan the temptation of São Maurício. Satanáz reminds Lucifer that he has already had one major reversal in the temptation of "he whom they called the Messiah." Maurício, when later confronted, argues that he has chosen the path to salvation.[11]

The second act finds the village of Vitória herself speaking: she recounts the stories of the first sin and of the son of God sent to redeem humanity. With "Government" and "Ingratitude," she complains of the

---

8   Preto-Rodas, "Anchieta and Vieira," p. 96.

9   José de Anchieta, "Sermão do Padre Jozé d'Anchieta: In die convertionis S. Pauli, 1568, Piratininga," *Revista do Instituto Histórico e Geográfico Brasileiro* 65 (1891): 120; Vasconcellos, *Vida de Anchieta* 2: 104-105.

10   José de Anchieta, *Na vila de Vitória e Na visitação de Santa Isabel*, ed. M. L. de Paula Martins, Documentação Linguística, no. 3 (São Paulo: Museu Paulista, 1950). The plays, for the immigrant audiences, are in both Castilian and Portuguese; the devils speak Castilian.

11   Anchieta, *Na vila de Vitória*, Act 1, lines 28-32, 333-335.

rampant sins of Brazil — pride, wrath, guile, lewdness, and greed — and asserts that all souls are lost. Further on, "Fear of God" and "Love of God" advise the audience on sin and repentance.[12]

The second play of the trilogy is *De São Maurício* ("Of São Maurício") and comprises a one-hundred-line poem praising his martyrdom.

The third play, *Quando, no Éspirito Santo, se recebeu uma relíquia das onze mil virgens* ("When, in Éspirito Santo, a relic of the eleven thousand virgins was received"), returns to the battle over the village of Vitória.

O Diabo, the Devil, challenges an approaching angel and calls Santa Úrsula and her accompanying troop of eleven thousand virgins to battle:

> We have objections, damsel,
> to your being in this place.
> You would not wish me to make worse,
> that, with sword and wheel,
> I must make you go back.
>
> If there in that sea battle,
> you trampled me,
> when you joined the eleven thousand,
> whom you made believe in God,
> it need not be so now.
> If then you triumphed over me,
> today I must conquer you.

The devil laughs at the angel, threatens her with a musket, and gloats:

> I have no opposition
> in the whole Capitânia.
> It earlier, without contention,
> under my hand
> Surrendered itself happily.[13]

The angel and devil exchange invectives through the first act, but the devil flees before the approaching Úrsula.

The village of Vitória speaks again in Act 2, praising the triumphant martyrdom of Santa Úrsula, who will be the patron of the village. Finally, in the third act the martyr Maurício arrives with his Theban troops.

---

12   Ibid., Act 2, lines 575-580, 769-771, 1442-1654.
13   Ibid., *Quando, no Éspirito Santo, se recebeu uma relíquia das onze mil virgens*, Act 1, lines 1-12, 13-17.

He reminds the audience that "human forces are not enough" to save the village, but that they can "reach salvation" with the aid of God's graces. Yet he praises those mortals who are "in perpetual war" against the "mortal vices" which have a stranglehold on the colony.[14]

Úrsula is soon welcomed into the village church where a special enthroning niche has been reserved. Before assuming her victorious stance, Úrsula comments that increased devotion to her cult would bring not only spiritual but also political benefit:

> If our Portuguese
> would always honor us,
> they would suffer few reverses
> and from the English and French could be secure.[15]

Through these three plays, Anchieta dramatized a recognizable apocalyptic situation. The Brazilian world had become evil to the extent that the Christian *persona* of evil, the Devil, was its sovereign. Recovery of this world was only to be effected by a savior; in this case, however, the messianic role was assumed by Santa Úrsula. Although this substitution demonstrates the popular preference for a familiar figure from the ranks of the saints as well as the perception of the increasing remoteness of Jesus himself, the paradigmatic structure of the messianic belief is not lost. This may be expressed in the following manner: First, salvation may be undertaken at the communal rather than the individual level. In this case, the entire population in Brazil was to have been redeemed and protected from foreign invasion. Second, when this world has become grossly sinful, salvation is only possible upon the descent of a messiah. It is these crucial points which were communicated to the audiences and which, reinforced by parallel messianic beliefs, were integrated into the beliefs of the tradition.

José de Anchieta reached and influenced many in the Portuguese colony through such excellent vehicles for the communication of ideas as these dramas and through sermons and letters. He also gave substantial support to the growth of Sebastianism in Brazil, according to the various legends of sixteenth- and seventeenth-century chroniclers.

The first version of these legends simply recounts that Anchieta announced the arrival of Sebastião in Africa on the very day it occurred, which date was substantiated later through ship-borne news.[16] Or,

---

14   Ibid., Act 3, lines 151-161, 185-186.
15   Ibid., lines 228-232.
16   Vasconcellos, *Vida de Anchieta* 2: 156.

Anchieta had a vision of the death of Sebastião on the battlefield on the very day that the young king died. One legend tells that Anchieta stopped in the middle of a prayer and called out to everyone in the monastery that the battle had been lost. Later, when the official notice had been received, the time of Anchieta's vision was determined to be the same hour as that of the death of Sebastião.[17]

In a second more elaborated legend, Anchieta had spent a sad day in Bertioga without speaking to his colleagues. When they then asked the cause, Anchieta replied only, "On this day great things are occurring in the world." The prudent among his companions noted the day, and when news later reached them of the fall of Sebastião, they verified the coincidence of the date. Later, Anchieta told his friend, Captain Miguel de Azevedo, how the defeat of Sebastião had been revealed to him. The captain questioned him whether Sebastião had actually died in the battle, and Anchieta replied that no, he had not. The captain then asked if Sebastião still lived, but Anchieta only responded, "These are the secrets that the Lord keeps to himself." A further version adds that Anchieta assured his listener that Sebastião would reign again.[18]

It is impossible to determine at this considerably distant date the historicity of these incidents; they may have been actual events in the life of Anchieta or imaginative additions by his admirers. However, his presence as a respected religious teacher and leader in these tales greatly increased their credibility and popularity. Their recounting also supported the legitimacy of belief in Sebastianism, for they suggested that even among the spiritual elite, the Jesuit Provincials, the death of Sebastião was not accepted and that his return to power was expected. Therefore, the circulation of these stories, even if untrue, in the time following Sebastião's death undoubtedly reinforced the Sebastianist beliefs among the laity.

In their method of teaching and in the subject matter, the Jesuits were given considerable latitude by their remote superiors in Portugal and Rome. Their method in Brazil was "not to have a method" and their subjects were limited simply by their general purpose of working to honor God by their efforts and to bring others to salvation.[19]

---

17   Pita, *História da América portuguesa*, p. 94.
18   Vasconcellos, *Vida de Anchieta* 2: 55-56; Azevedo, *Sebastianismo*, p. 64.
19   R. P. Americo de Novaes, "Methodo de ensino e de catechese dos Índios usados pelos Jesuítas e por Anchieta," *Terceiro Centenário do veneravel Joseph de Anchieta* (Lisbon: Aillaurd & Cia., 1900), p. 147.

However, several texts were created in the Society of Jesus in order to assist the newer missionaries and, in general, to make the teachings of the Jesuits somewhat more uniform. The earliest and most important of these in Brazil was the catechism called the *Doutrina Christã*. This catechism, written by Jesuit Marcos Jorge and redacted by his contemporary Inácio Martins, was ordered for Brazilian use in 1564, soon after its first appearance in publication. The *Doutrina Christã*, also known as the "Cartilha de Mestre Inácio" ("Little book of Master Inácio"), was used extensively and appeared in many editions, including translations into Tupí and the language of the Congo.[20]

Its contents reflect, again, the simplified Catholic doctrine which the missionaries offered to Portuguese colonists and Brazilindians alike, with specific emphasis on salvation, redemption and Jesus the Messiah. In the dialogue format, the student is taught that one is Christian not by one's own merit but through the redemption by Jesus, the King over all kings. A non-Christian is the "son of a curse, slave of the devil, and disinherited of heaven."[21] Christ crucified, who saved all from captivity, will come again at the end of the world in Judgement. According to the Church, the future holds death, judgement, hell or perhaps paradise.[22]

This summary of the authorized doctrinal teachings, which goes on to include ritual prescriptions in reference to sacraments and prayers and Church laws, repeats the simplified schema of Christian credences taught by Nóbrega and Anchieta. The catechism as a whole offers a clear image of salvation: that the Christian was to be saved and Jesus was the Savior. Given its weight as an official document, the *Doutrina Christã* in this important point reinforced the messianic teachings available from other sources.

This repeated motif, of salvation by Jesus, received increased stress through the Jesuits' favored methods of teaching: the popular missions and the baroque sermon.

Because of the limited number of Jesuit missionaries in Brazil, the Jesuits came to rely on a plan already known in Portugal, that of sporadic visits to outlying villages. The Portuguese settlers there

20   Valdomiro Pires Martins, ed. *Catecismo Romano: versão fiel da edição autêntica de 1566* (Petrópolis: Editora Vozes Ltda., 1962), p. 22; Rodrigues, *História da Companhia* 2, Pt. 1 (1938): 459.

21   Marcos Jorge, *Doutrina Christã*, rev. by Inácio Martins (Lisbon: Geraldo da Vinha, 1624), folios 2-2v.

22   Ibid., folios 4v-5, 32.

gathered for a short *santa missão*, a holy mission of intense "rechris-
tianization" through prayers, sermons and sacraments. As in more
familiar evangelical meetings, these missionaries evoked a vivid image
of threatening damnation and made a passionate plea for return to the
Church of the Messiah before the coming of the Last Days. The star-
tling number of sudden confessions recorded in their own accounts at-
tests to the efficacy of their rhetoric. Further, this heightened image of
Jesus and the imminence of the Last Days remained with the listeners,
as the core of the Catholicism brought through these popular missions.[23]

The Jesuits preached lengthy — up to four hours — and evocative sermons to their urban followers as well, particularly on these same
themes of damnation and salvation, and with the same dramatic results.

Messianic and Sebastianist beliefs were not found solely among the
religious orders working and traveling in Brazil during this period; the
lay immigrants then coming to the colony also bore witness to these
beliefs. For example, the presence of a follower of Bandarra in Bahia
is noted in the Inquisition Records of the Denunciations of 1591 in Salvador.[24] In the entry "Contra Gregório Nunes" of August 13, 1591, an
immigrant from Lisbon named João Bautista denounced Gregório
Nunes, or Gregório Nidrophi, for various heretical acts. Bautista informed the Inquisitors that four years earlier he had traveled with
Nunes and that the latter had several times referred to the "*trovas* of
the shoemaker of Trancoso whom they call Bandarra" and had also
recited these verses:

eagles and lions
reach the fortress,
and climb up to such heights,
that they tame the dragons
and all rebels in the fight
turn in their confusions

---

23   Hoornaert, "Primeira período," *História da Igreja no Brasil* 1: 132; Mello
Moraes, Filho, *Festas e tradições populares do Brasil* (São Paulo: n.p., 1846; reprint
ed., São Paulo: Editora da Universidade de São Paulo, 1979), p. 139; Leite, *História
da Companhia* 2: 303.

24   Heitor Furtado de Mendoça, *Primeiro visitação do Santo Ofício às partes
do Brasil: denunciações da Bahia, 1591-1593* (São Paulo: Editora Paulo Prado, 1925),
pp. 316-318.

the free lions climb
with one of the blood of David.[25]

From this the denouncer understood that Gregório Nunes was expecting the Messiah. Bautista then accused Nunes of trying to lead him astray with this and other "Jewish" notions.[26]

It is remarkable that such records remain on this specific incident which thus clearly demonstrate the presence of the *Trovas* of Bandarra in Brazil in 1587. This further indicates the natural transmission to Brazil during this early period of the Portuguese messianic belief in their savior-king, particularly expressed in the widespread belief in Sebastianism. Undoubtedly, there were more similar instances of the importation of Bandarra's work, together with other popular stories of Sebastião and legends of King Arthur and the favorite saints. The *cordel* literature[27] was present and popular already in Brazil during this period, having been brought from the publishing sources in Portugal by the colonists and by the ships transversing the Atlantic route to the new land. These pamphlets preserved Sebastianist and prophetic teachings as well as the abundant legends of traditional histories or romances known in Iberia.

The Portuguese laity also brought with them to the Brazilian colony, with undiminished enthusiasm, their village saints and patrons. From this beginning the cult of the saints grew tremendously in its New World territory. It eventually formed the core of the Brazilian Catholic religion and the most consistent element for many of its northeastern practitioners.[28]

The baroque culture of Portugal had placed a unique emphasis on the exteriorization of the cult, connected with the increase of practices of novenas, processions, and so on, and on an idealization of life relating to the vision of the royal court. This latter found expression in the continuation of legends of João Prestes and Sebastião.[29]

In Brazil, the imported statues and paintings of the saints found a place of prominence in the religious devotion of individuals and of

25   Ibid., p. 317. This verse, in a mixture of Portuguese and Castilian, does not occur in early editions of the *Trovas* but was part of one of the many circulating alternate versions.

26   Ibid., p. 318.

27   See discussion above, pp. 40-41.

28   Eduardo Galvão, *Santos e visagens*, second ed. (São Paulo: Companhia Editora Nacional, 1955), p. 29.

29   Sônia Siqueira, *A Inquisição portuguesa e a sociedade colonial* (São Paulo: Editora Ática, 1978), p. 18.

collectives such as in the festivals of entire villages and in brotherhoods, as will be seen below. God the Father and Jesus received reverence as part of official worship but were considered remote figures; the saints, on the other hand, were more approachable personalities. Thus, to the extent to which one of the saints replaced God in cultic practice, so that saint or a similar figure replaced Jesus in the role of Messiah.

While the Portuguese colonists were bound to fulfill the official religious obligations and attend the rites of the Church, they also opted to express their religious beliefs in the cult of the saints. In this, Luso-Brazilian Catholicism exhibited a tolerance and malleability unknown to its Spanish counterpart: it was adaptable by popular initiative to the expansive practices of that cult.[30]

The nature of the cult in Brazil changed somewhat; it did not conform exactly with the Church calendar or liturgy and in fact could have been considered heretical in its tendency to make each saint a deity. The popular figures, the Virgin Mary, Santo Antônio, Santa Úrsula, São Bento, were believed to be present in their images— not in heaven or invisible— and aware of the needs of each family or village. Their devotees believed their direct personal intervention to be irreplaceable in the struggle to deal with the inconstancies of life and environ.

These believers interacted with the saints by means of a straightforward reciprocity— by a *promessa* or compact. The individual vowed to light a candle, say a prayer, or complete a more arduous task so that the saint would provide a good crop, a husband, proof against hexes or the cure of disease. These promises rarely included increased attendance at Mass services or moral rehabilitation.[31]

The favored saints in Bahia were the *Onze mil virgens*, that is, the eleven thousand virgins who accompanied Santa Úrsula. The arrival of a relic skull and other related objects in that city in 1583 caused great excitement and celebration, as well as the inspiration for several dramas, including that written by Anchieta.[32]

The deep-seated popularity of the cult of the saints, now in Brazil, indicates several important features of the nascent form of Brazilian religious beliefs which have a direct connection with the messianic

30   Thales Azevedo, *O Catholicismo no Brasil* (Rio de Janeiro: Ministério da Educação e Cultura, 1955), pp. 26-28.

31   Ibid., p. 28; and Emilio Willems, *Followers of the New Faith* (Nashville, TN: Vanderbilt University Press, 1967), p. 36.

32   Fernão Cardim, *Tratados da terra e gente do Brasil*, second ed. (São Paulo: Companhia Editora Nacional, 1939), pp. 254-297.

tradition. First, the believers continually showed a preference for present supernatural figures who could act in crucial life events and be acted upon in a significant way. Second, through their own initiative, the laity placed emphasis on immediacy in the religious cult: they reduced more esoteric or removed religious concepts to the here-and-now. This outstanding feature finds similar expression in messianic beliefs. Third, the believers expected direct and concrete intervention and constant supernatural assistance in their difficulties, allowing a near-messianic role for all of their saints.

In this section on messianic beliefs in sixteenth-century Brazil, a complex set of elements has been included. In the teachings of the Jesuits have been found the recurrent themes of salvation and the Last Days, as in the sermons and letters of Nóbrega and Anchieta, and in the *Doutrina Christã*, the messianic ideal in Anchieta's plays and his own Sebastianist beliefs. The lay community continued propagation of Bandarra's *Trovas* and of the increasingly important cult of the saints.

By means of the religious sermons, plays and missions to the colonists, the Jesuits communicated the key Christian belief in salvation, that is, a sort of guaranteed admittance to Paradise through the aid of Jesus. This is certainly not radical messianism; however, it contributes three significant points to the belief structure supporting the messianic tradition: (1) human force is not sufficient to achieve Paradise, whether here or in another world; (2) a supernatural agent is required; and (3) the community is to be saved as a group.

The confluence of these contributing factors gave substantial support to the imported messianic beliefs, for the continued usage of the *Trovas* and the parallel beliefs adjunct to the cult of the saints further these points. Thus, those who believed in Sebastião saw the image of their redeemer mirrored in the salvific aspect of Jesus and the saints and their entire belief verified by Anchieta himself.

The official position of the Catholic Church is especially unclear, even contradictory, through all of this. While acknowledged sources taught salvation by Jesus, salvation through the saints had also become an acceptable belief. The Sebastianist beliefs enigmatically voiced by Anchieta were considered miraculous visions, while use of the *Trovas* of Bandarra was a matter for denunciation to the Inquisition. The complicated interweaving and amplification of these varying beliefs nevertheless constitutes the historically recorded appearance of the messianic beliefs in this period.

Lay Religious Activities

The significance of the first lay religious activities lies in their continuation of a thriving social action system from Portugal, which system
would later serve in the formation of the nineteenth-century messianic
movements. The lay groups, such as *irmandades*, penitential groups
and associations for devotion to a saint, provided a vehicle for communal participation in religious practices separate from the more permanent or institutionalized orders constituted within the Roman
Church. As was the case in Portugal, so it was in Brazil, that activity in
these groups, or in solitary eremetical devotion, was an appropriate
outlet for religious expression.

The lay religious activities in the sixteenth century in Brazil included
the collective activities of brotherhoods (*irmandades*), confraternities
(*confrarias*) and the solitary devotions of the *eremitão*.

The Portuguese immigrants to Brazil naturally imported the
socioreligious structures known to them in their native towns and villages. The *irmandades* were not instruments or organizations of the
elite of the colonial government—whose stay in the colony was often
only temporary—but were rather vital expressions of religious involvement for the common people.[33]

From the perspective of the Roman Catholic Church, these lay
groups constituted a suitable means for pious devotion and, more important, for material support of the Church through charitable work
and donations. Generally the brotherhoods organized for devotion to
a special saint or aspect of God and provided for the maintenance of
their own church or chapel.[34]

From the perspective of the lay participants, the brotherhoods expressed their desire to form distinct religious communities, however
impermanent, separate from the interference of the greater colonial
institutions. In reality, the brotherhoods served in effect to balance the
conflicts of the developing colonial society. In the history of *irmandades*
in Brazil can be noted a "complex dialectical action between the
genuine popular expression and the attempts at cooptation" by the

---

33   R. Joviano Amarel, *Os Prêtos do Rosário de São Paulo: subsídios históricos*
(São Paulo: Edições Alvárico, 1953), p. 27; A. J. R. Russell-Wood, *Fidalgos and
Philanthropists: The Santa Casa da Misericórdia of Bahia, 1550-1755* (London:
Macmillan, 1968), pp. x-xi. Brotherhoods only rarely admitted women.
34   Cardozo, "Lay Brotherhoods," pp. 20-23.

government or the Church. In the history of the Brazilian Catholic Church the brotherhood was "a structure which sought to escape" the rigidity of colonial institutions.[35]

Certain of the brotherhoods, or better, confraternities, were devotional associations established by and under the guidance of the Jesuits for the purpose of maintaining pious communities. Their special tasks were devotion to the particular saint chosen, decoration of the niche or altar in the chapel or church, visits to the sick, aid in the burial of the dead, and processions on the feast-days. The *confrarias* under the Jesuits included the Confraria dos Meninos de Jesus (Confraternity of Santa Úrsula and [her] martyr companions) of 1579 in Salvador, also for students, and the Congregações Marianas, confraternities devoted to Mary.[36]

The majority of these lay associations were constituted independently. Their stated religious purpose was to encourage special religious devotion; their social purpose was to aid and support the members when sick or in difficulties and to provide Christian burial. Specialized *irmandades* of the wealthier classes built and maintained their own churches or only performed charitable works for the care of the sick. The Irmandade da Misericórdia in Bahia, already functioning in 1549, the brotherhood of the Rosary, and the Confraria of São Marcos of Pernambuco (1596) were the earliest official brotherhoods in the Northeast.

As the pattern and purpose of the Brazilian brotherhoods in this period partially replicated those of the Portuguese, so the appearance of lay hermits in Brazil also recalled the parallel phenomenon in the homeland. As in Portugal, these lay individuals choosing the eremetic life were called *eremitão* (hermit), *irmão* (brother), or *monge* (monk), and were dedicated to an austere ascetic existence in devotion to a particular saint or to Jesus. In most instances they resided far from urban centers and built or stayed near a chapel-like *ermida*, or hermitage.[37]

---

35   Hoornaert, "Terceiro período: a cristandade durante a primeira época colônial," *História da Igreja no Brasil*, 1: 305.

36   Leite, *História da Companhia* 2: 323-324, 329.

37   Riolando Azzi, "Eremitas e irmãos: uma forma da vida religiosa no Brasil antigo," *Convergência* 94 (July 1976): 371. In this era, only men undertook these roles.

In the early period of the colony only a few *ermidas* or shrines were noted, such as the "hermida" of São Braz near Vila Velha and the Jesuit *ermida* of Nossa Senhora da Escada north of Salvador.[38] The primitive *ermida* in Brazil was not a full church, but rather a devotional chapel or smaller structure.

During this period, however, it was primarily the religious missionaries who, during their long excursions through the Brazilian backlands, kept up the role model of the Portuguese *ermitão*. These practiced a truly ascetic life in solitude, poverty, and continual prayer. The Jesuit missionaries, scarce as these were, necessarily took lay men, orphans or boys along as companions and aides and in this way perpetuated this form of lay religious devotion.

The first renowned "hermit" in Brazil was an immigrant named Pedro Palácios, apparently connected with the Franciscans and probably a member of their Third Order. After a brief spell studying with the Jesuits in Bahia and accompanying them on local tours, Palácios left the city for a cave on a *penha*, a hill or mount, in Espírito Santo near Vila Velha and Vila Nova.[39] With a painting of Mary and a cross, both brought from Portugal, he established his chapel and kept to a life of prayer and intermittent preaching, catechizing and begging in the nearby communities until his death in 1570.

While the historical sources on lay religious activities are less than generous during this period, the framework of the Portuguese pattern is recognizable in the nascent forms in Brazil. The structure and purpose of the lay *irmandades* and *confrarias* were readily reestablished in the colonial towns as the laity sought to continue their supportive socioreligious groups. The beginnings of the development of the eremetical movement has also been noted, particularly in the role model of the peregrinating missionary.

These examples of the collective and individual lay religious activities in the late sixteenth century in Brazil are significant in two aspects as they form part of the continuum. First, the *irmandades*, confrarias and *ermitães* were imported Portuguese formulations and constituted a direct development from those earlier and contemporary

38   Gabriel Soares de Sousa, *Tratado descriptivo do Brasil em 1587*, third ed. (Rio de Janeiro: Companhia Editora Nacional, 1938), p. 152; Edgard de Cerqueira Falcão, *Encantos tradicionais da Bahia* (São Paulo: Livraria Martins, 1943), text of plate XVIII.

39   Hoornaert, "Primeiro período," *História da Igreja no Brasil* 1: 105. In Brazil, as in Europe, this type of hill was an auspicious site for a chapel or shrine.

Portuguese phenomena discussed above. Second, they established and made available to the Brazilian laity these popular and highly adaptable structures for lay religious expression and devotional activity. These will be seen to flourish in the late seventeenth and early eighteenth centuries.

Thus, at the levels of the collective and of the individual, the acceptable social pattern had been introduced into Brazil already during this early period. As noted earlier, the later development of the social groups was closely related to the formation of messianic movements, while the role of the *ermitão* was paralleled by the person of the messianic leader.

Penitential Practices

While it is comparatively difficult to locate historical accounts of messianic beliefs and lay religious activities during this early period, contemporary histories, particularly the voluminous reports of the Jesuits, preserve for our study a large number of accounts of the penitential practices of the late sixteenth century, with especial emphasis on self-flagellation.

Clerical and lay penitential activities, in individual and group practice, parallel both in structure and in function other lay religious activities. That is to say, they provide the focal purpose for the assembling of a temporary association, with a dominant leader or instructor or model, and serve as an alternate means of intense religious expression.

Because of the association of the practice of self-flagellation with monastic orders and especially individual favored saints, this particular practice was acknowledged as not only appropriate but also exemplary religious behavior and was in this aspect adopted by the laity. Thus, individual flagellants with the religious orders, such as Nóbrega or Anchieta, established a concrete motif for devotional activity understood to entail extraordinary or saintly status. The lay individuals who followed these examples imitated one strong aspect of the developing role model of the lay holy man, paralleling the *ermitão* as well.

In this section on the penitential practices in late sixteenth-century Brazil will be included exposition of the flagellant practices by the Jesuits, particularly the special examples of Nóbrega and Anchieta, followed by consideration of the lay flagellant practices established under the Jesuits and of the independently initiated lay penitential processions and groups.

Following the teachings and examples of their founder and superiors in Portugal, the Jesuit missionaries in Brazil regularly practiced self-flagellation, deeming it at once an act of humility and an indication of superior virtue. Extreme castigation was necessary to "break the passions" of body.[40] The refectory of the Jesuit House in Salvador, Bahia, saw more acts of penitence than meals: there, novices prostrated themselves and struggled under the weight of a cross or, on their knees, flagellated themselves and recited their sins publicly in atonement for their evils. The practice of self-flagellation was common and of two distinct kinds: "dry" discipline with a rod or cords and discipline "of the blood" with crueler instruments which caused the penitent to bleed.[41]

The Jesuits undertook extraordinary penances as part of their own quest for religious perfection and to set a striking example for the less morally diligent among the Portuguese colonists. João de Aspicuelta Navarro, in order to call the attention of the Governor in Bahia, Tomé de Sousa, flagellated himself in a public square near the Governor's mansion. This same Jesuit notes in a letter to Coimbra from Bahia in 1550 that after spending Monday through Thursday visiting native reductions, the Jesuits regularly returned to the city on Friday for a special penitential service featuring self-flagellation.[42]

Manuel da Nóbrega, a protégé of Jesuit teacher Simão Rodrigues while at the Jesuit College of Coimbra in Portugal, was an advanced proponent of "the discipline." He practiced self-flagellation privately within the monastery walls, together with other members or while traveling on extended mission tours between colonial towns or to native settlements.

Nóbrega believed that the spirit of the Jesuit missionaries in Brazil should be reduced to two simple points of behavior, penitence and obedience, to which all would adhere. In his own penances, his "mortifications" of the flesh, he continued to follow the example of the Portuguese Rodrigues in what some have called the "excesses of

---

40   António Franco, *Imagem da virtude em o noviciado da Companhia de Jesu no real collégio de Coimbra* (Évora: Officina da Universidade, 1717), p. 51.

41   Simão de Vasconcellos, *Chrônica da Companhia de Jesu do estado do Brasil*, 2 vols., second ed. (Lisbon: A. J. Fernandes Lopes, 1865), 2: 82; Leite, *História da Companhia* 2: 337.

42   Leite, *História da Companhia* 2: 336; and Serafim Leite, ed., *Cartas dos primeiros Jesuítos no Brasil*, 3 vols. (São Paulo: Commissão do IV Centenário da Cidade de São Paulo, 1954), "Documento 14. Baia 28 de Março de 1550 do Padre João de Aspicuelta aos Padres e Irmãos de Coimbra," 1: 183.

Coimbra." Shortly after his arrival in the Brazilian mission in Bahia he reported to Simão Rodrigues, his Superior in the Order, that

> now we live such that we have the discipline on Fridays... It is for those who are in mortal sin and for the conversion of the heathens, and for the souls in purgatory; and the same thing through the streets accompanied by a bell on Mondays and Wednesdays.

Nóbrega advocated the practice of such extreme penitence to all Christians; he preached to them that with the example before them of the loving, suffering Jesus, all should feel compelled to "do penitence for sins, with much blood running down" during whipping.[43]

For himself, Nóbrega made self-flagellation part of his regular religious observance in order to curb all physical desire or passion: in 1563, during a mission tour, he turned down the offers of native women, showing to all the whip that he carried with him in his robes and announcing that the disciplines "assured continence and defended against lascivious impulses and undesirable urges of the flesh."[44]

José de Anchieta was no less enthusiastic in the flagellant practice and also carried the instrument with him on his travels. Flagellation was normally included in his daily devotional prayers and he was reputed to have said that on the day that he ceased mortifying his body in this way, he would cease to be a missionary. This practice, accompanied by extended fasts, arduous journeys and the wearing of a rough cord (*cilício*) under his clothing, was noted by his contemporaries as a further mark of his saintliness.[45]

According to the regularity and abundance of the accounts of the practice of extreme penances among the Jesuits, it may be understood that flagellation was a truly common activity or, conversely, believed by the writers to be of such value that every virtuous Jesuit must necessarily have been a flagellant.

These extraordinary examples by the Jesuit clergy during this period in Brazilian history, that of the late sixteenth century, reinforced among the colonial religious values the efficacy of flagellation as a penance for sins and its importance as a sign of holiness. More important, however, was the active example of flagellant activity which was set by these

---

43   Leite, *Cartas*, "Documento 7. Baia 9 de Agosto de 1549 do P. Manuel da Nóbrega ao P. Simão Rodrigues, Lisboa," 1: 131; ibid., "Documento 45. Baia 5 de Junho de 1552 do P. Manuel da Nóbrega aos Moradores do Pernambuco" 1: 331.

44   Vasconcellos, *Vida de Anchieta* 1: 91.

45   Ibid., 2: 216.

religious outside their own monastery walls. The Jesuits enthusiastically enlisted their seminary students and other residents of Salvador in their penitential services.

Manuel da Nóbrega personally encouraged participation of the lay in the ongoing Friday night services which he had inaugurated. In 1552 in a report to his superior in Portugal, he noted the participation of many lay men in most of the Friday flagellant sessions, "especially [during] Lent, Advent and after [the feast of] Corpus Christi until [the feast of] the Assumption of our Lady." He remarked that while it caused "much devotion among the people," the Bishop of Bahia, who had already been alienated by the ultramontane Jesuits, disapproved of such public display.[46]

During the epidemic of 1554 the Jesuit Anchieta led nine solemn processions of lay men and women begging for God's mercy. These carried candles in their hands and some bore heavy crosses, while many whipped themselves until their backs ran with blood.[47]

With the examples of the Jesuits before them and their further solicitation in these services and processions, the laity also chose to undertake voluntary flagellant processions and other services independently for the salvation of sinners, for the souls in Purgatory, for the success of local battles or faraway European wars and in commemoration of Jesus' suffering on Good Friday. In 1559, a special penitential procession was held to pray for the termination of a drought in the Northeast, in 1560 for the success of an expedition by Mem de Sá against the French holding Rio de Janeiro, and in 1592, again for peace with the French.[48]

Along with these particular penitential events, the laity in the Northeast of Brazil also inaugurated and redeveloped the ritual known as *encommendação das almas* (literally, commendation of the souls), commonly called *a penitência* (the penitence) or simply *Procissões de Penitência* (Penitential Processions). The ritual of *encommendação das almas* had been known in Portugal: there, on the Fridays in Lent, small groups of village women or men would climb the steps of the

46   Leite, *Cartas*, "Documento 51. Baia de Julho de 1552 do P. Manuel da Nóbrega ao P. Simão Rodrigues, Lisboa," 1: 371.
47   Vasconcellos, *Vida de Anchieta* 1: 38-39.
48   Leite, *História da Companhia* 2: 317-318.

church or to the highest place near the village, ringing a bell and praying and singing for the easing of the suffering of the souls in Purgatory.[49]

In Brazil, however, the *encommendação* came to incorporate the practice of self-flagellation, inevitably becoming a more rigorous and structured ritual. It continued to be dedicated to the aid of the souls in Purgatory, though, and closely correlated with the services — accompanied by a bell — held in Bahia by Nóbrega with the Jesuits and laity there.[50]

The processions of the Brazilian *encommendação* were composed of men only, dressed in white and usually naked above the waist. These announced their progress and warned women and children away with a wooden noise-maker, the *matraca*, rather than with a bell. The rituals took place on the Fridays of Lent at midnight and proceeded from the church or chapel through the village or town to the cemetery. Several of the penitents would wear crowns of thorn, but the favored act of penitence was self-flagellation with an iron-tipped whip until blood ran. The men sang or chanted litanies and special hymns composed for this procession. Women were strictly prohibited from accompanying or watching the ritual.[51]

In the penitential practices of the Jesuits, of the Jesuits and lay colonists together, and of the colonists independently are found repeated the penitential modes of Portugal. In Brazil a distinct shift to the more violent practice of self-flagellation can be discerned, particularly among the laity. For example, the ritual of *encommendação das almas* in Brazil became a flagellant procession, quite dissimilar from the simpler Portuguese version.

In the study of these practices in general, it is important to note the consistent trend toward lay formulations, in groups, and by individuals. While not all of the lay groups which in this period adopted the flagellant practices formed independent cult groups, the temporary activities were repeated and established a social behavior pattern among the laity. This pattern of associative and individual activity maintained and further developed the independent or alternative lay religious activity, whose later culmination was achieved in the nineteenth-century messianic movements.

---

49   Dias, *Etnografia da Beira* 1 (1926): 135-136; 5 (1938): 169-170; 6 (1942): 87-90.

50   Leite, *Cartas* 1:131.

51   Moraes, Filho, *Festas*, p. 158; Manuel Querino, *A Bahia de outr'ora*, second ed. (Bahia: Livraria Econômica, 1922), pp. 79-80.

In this first Brazilian time frame, from 1549 to 1599, the complete
pattern of the credal and ritual components of the messianic tradition
may be elicited. Although not all elements were present and the forms
of the elements occurring were not static but were rather in various
stages of development, the pattern that existed nonetheless clearly
demonstrates the ongoing transition of Portuguese religious beliefs
and practices to colonial Brazil.

The core belief in messianism, that is, the belief that salvation is only
possible in the community and by means of an external agent—the
Messiah—was supported in the catechistic and sermonic doctrines of
the institutional Roman Church. Manuel da Nóbrega and other Jesuit
missionaries instructed the Portuguese colonists accordingly, emphasizing the path to salvation in their letters, while José de Anchieta
dramatized the salvific powers of Santa Úrsula and, tangentially, São
Maurício, in his cycle of religious plays. The catechistic texts used by
the Jesuit missionaries in Brazil also underscored these themes.

At the same time, popular literature and oral tradition imported and
reinforced the enduring legends of Sebastianism, as indicated by the
Inquisition records concerning Gregório Nunes, together with the
beliefs present in the cult of the saints.

The early lay religious activities, the brotherhoods, the confraternities and the less formal groups, while in this time lacking the support
of a large colonial population, still continued the structural model for
group function separate from the normative modes of the institutional
Church.

Parallel to these last, the flagellant penitential practices in the late
sixteenth century in Brazil, performed by the Jesuits and imitated in
the lay services led by the Jesuits and in the *encommendações das
almas*, also served to perpetuate the framework for alternate modes
for intensive religious activity which was formulated in Portugal.

These three aspects, noted in this period in Brazil in developing
forms, thus reestablished the messianic tradition in this Portuguese
colony.

Chapter 6

Brazil: The Middle Colonial Period, 1600-1699

With the seventeenth century, Brazil entered its second century of colonization. For most of the first half of that century, Brazil was controlled by the remote rule of the Spanish; not until 1640 did Portugal regain its Crown.

The population of the colony grew continually, both from the influx of immigrants from Portugal and from the descendants of the Portuguese who had settled there in the preceding era. Cattle ranchers pushed further inland along the banks of the São Francisco River, spreading the population into the *sertão*, the scrub-desert backlands.

The continued immigration maintained the importation of Portuguese religious beliefs and practices from the homeland and, thus, the importation of those special religious elements which constituted the Luso-Brazilian messianic tradition. These, joined with the elements of the messianic tradition already established in Brazil during the sixteenth century— discussed in the above chapter — determined the unique character of the Luso-Brazilian messianic tradition of the seventeenth century.

This chapter will consider the formulation of the Luso-Brazilian messianic tradition in the Northeast of Brazil during this period, noting particularly the influence of the increased numbers and variety of colonists as well as that of the surge of Portuguese nationalism in connection with the political events in Brazil and in the homeland. Following a brief outline of the history of this century in Portugal and its colony, the messianic beliefs, lay religious activities and penitential practices of the colonists will be presented.

Historical Circumstances

During the first four decades of the seventeenth century, Portugal, and thus Brazil, remained under the control of the monarchs of Spain. While Portuguese administrators were usually appointed to handle

101

affairs in Portugal and its colonies under the three Philips of Spain, Portugal was also inevitably entangled in Spain's foreign conflicts, particularly with Holland.

During the reigns of Philip III (II of Portugal) from 1598 to 1621 and Philip IV (III) from 1621 to 1640, the incremental intervention of Spanish administrative officials in the treasury and Council of Portugal had incurred the growing resentment of the Portuguese people. In 1640, Portugal regained its throne through a quick and well-planned coup, and João Duke of Bragança became João IV of Portugal. His claim to the throne was established through his mother, Catarina, niece of João III. However, the success of the Restoration was chiefly due to the machinations of Portuguese elites, including the Duchess of Bragança Luisa Gusmão, and the covert support of allies in France. The coup was accomplished during the time of a rebellion in Catalonia which diverted the attention and troops of the Spanish king; the Spanish garrisons left in Portugal surrendered quickly.

The Restoration of the Portuguese throne was greeted by an outburst of nationalistic sentiment in Portugal and its colonies and was acclaimed as the redemption of the glorious Empire. The prophecies of Bandarra, which had found increasing support during the "Spanish captivity," were now reinterpreted and rewritten to signify the coming of João IV as the *Encoberto*. Bandarra was a national hero: his remains were moved to a magnificent tomb in Trancoso that honored him as the visionary who had foreseen Portugal's miraculous recovery.

João IV had assumed the throne in a difficult era: his authority lacked funds, allies and an army. Most of his diplomatic efforts were expended in unsuccessful negotiations with European rulers and the Papacy for recognition and alliance. João made considerable use of one of his counselors, the Jesuit António Vieira, in diplomatic missions in the early years of his reign. In spite of his different attempts, Spain did not recognize the autonomy of Portugal under the House of Bragança until 1669, and the Papal See of Rome, under Spain's considerable influence, also remained uncooperative until that time. João managed in 1641 to conclude a truce with Holland, still at war with Spain without, however, resolving the issue of the Dutch encroachments in Brazil.

In 1656 João IV died and Portugal was governed by the Regent Queen Luisa. The heir, Afonso VI, assumed the throne in 1662. While not illiterate as some sources have claimed, Afonso was poorly educated and extremely vulnerable to the manipulations of a series of court favorites. In 1668 he agreed to his own deposition and retired to the estate of Bragança; his brother Pedro II[1] then ruled as Prince Regent from 1668 to 1683 and as King until 1703.

During the "Spanish captivity" Brazil had been administered by various Portuguese members of the circulating corps of governors and viceroys. The vulnerability of Brazilian enterprises increased under the more remote Spanish rule, however, and left the colony open to the eager attack from Holland during the Dutch rebellion from Spain. Dutch expeditionary forces held Bahia only briefly in 1624-1625 but were more successful in Pernambuco: they invaded in 1630 and secured control of lands and the sugar trade there until the inhabitants rebelled in 1645. The Spanish kings had made no attempt to oust these invaders, and João IV only sent military aid after the rebellion had achieved its goal. The Dutch had conquered but not colonized that portion of Northeastern Brazil; the rebels were nationalistic Portuguese immigrants revolting against the rulers whom they saw as foreign heretical interlopers.[2]

Although the Luso-Brazilian economy nearly foundered in the first few years after the Restoration, by the end of the seventeenth century the customs duties and transport charges on the Brazilian sugar and tobacco crops had once again stabilized the empire's income. Brazil was raised to the status of a principality in 1646, perhaps in recognition of its financial importance; from that year, the heir to the Portuguese throne held the title, Prince or Princess of Brazil.

In 1693, a band of colonists raiding the backlands for Brazilindian slaves discovered alluvial gold in the area later named Minas Gerais ("General Mines"). This discovery led to a rush of immigration to the colony, as well as to vast demographic changes within Brazil, and inaugurated a golden age for Portugal and Brazil in the eighteenth century.

Even before the discovery of such mineral wealth, the population of the colony was substantially augmented by the immigration of the poor, unemployed and landless from Portugal and the Azores. Because of its reputation for a healthful climate, Brazil also lured aging or ill

---

1   This was Pedro of Portugal, not to be confused with the Emperor Pedro of Brazil (1841-1886), Brazil's last monarch. The latter Pedro was an enlightened despot whose popularity during his reign became glorification afterwards.

2   The Pernambucanos did not even learn the language of the invaders, and it is now reported that only two Dutch words survive in the Brazilian Portuguese of that area. Boxer, *Seaborne Empire*, pp. 120, 125.

Portuguese in search of longevity. Nearly 2,000 Portuguese men arrived in Brazil each year and, because of the relatively short and safe sea passage, a large number of Portuguese women also chose to immigrate during this period.

Messianic Beliefs

In the seventeenth century in Northeastern Brazil, a diversity of elements were comprised in the messianic belief structure, including Sebastianist beliefs, legends brought from Iberia, and Catholic sermonic themes. This section will consider, first, the messianic beliefs expressed in the sermons and writings of Jesuit and other religious preachers in Brazil, particularly António Vieira and Eusébio de Mattos, and, second, the body of related beliefs in *cordel* literature and popular religious and folk tales of the Northeast.

During the Spanish control of the Portuguese empire and in the wave of nationalism which followed the Restoration, Luso-Brazilian messianic beliefs at times signified or paralleled political doctrines. At this time, there was an understandable expansion in the Sebastianist and prophetic writings published or circulated in Portugal; as a group, these works mourned the loss of Sebastião and the throne and looked to the swift demise of all things Spanish. Many of the Jesuit fathers in Lisbon and Évora were known to be supporters of Sebastianism, and several of these wrote poems or essays on their beliefs. Of the numerous pamphlets circulating in Portugal, two were popular enough to have been brought to Brazil: the *Life of Simão Gomes* and the *Anacephaleosis da monarquia lusitana*.

In 1625 the Jesuit Manuel da Veiga, a recognized adversary of Castile, wrote and published *The Life of Simão Gomes*, on the prophet known as the Shoemaker of São Roque. Gomes had been a contemporary of King Sebastião and temporarily an astrological advisor to the King in Évora. He had predicted even then the loss of the kingdom of Portugal and its later restoration. *The Life of Simão Gomes* raised this shoemaker to a status equivalent to that of Bandarra.[3]

The Portuguese mathematician and astronomer, Manuel Bocarro, wrote in 1624 a four-part poem entitled, *Anacephaleosis da monarquia lusitana* ("Summary History of the Portuguese Monarchy"), dedicated to Philip IV (III), in which he recounted the glories of Portugal. The fourth section of the poem suggests that Sebastianists look to others of

---

3   Azevedo, *Sebastianismo*, pp. 63-64.

the same noble line; for the *Encoberto* Bocarro specifically indicates Teodosio Duke of Bragança (coincidentally father to João) as a likely candidate. Bocarro was later seized and imprisoned for his treasonous writings and activities, but he escaped to Italy to republish his work.[4]

The most widely known messianic writings and sermons of seventeenth-century Brazil were those of the Jesuit António Vieira. His actions and beliefs were considered controversial and even heretical during his own lifetime, but he wielded significant political and religious influence, both in Portugal and in its colony. His writings have remained popular through the present era.

António Vieira was born in Portugal but raised and educated in Brazil, attending classes at the Jesuit College in Salvador. In 1623 he entered the Jesuit novitiate and was ordained in 1634. Two years later he was appointed Professor of Theology and had already secured a reputation as the finest religious orator in Brazil.

Vieira was a member of the Brazilian ambassadorial party to the Lisbon court following the Restoration and, owing to his eloquence and boldness, immediately became a favorite of João IV. Vieira exercised tremendous influence in Portuguese political affairs for over a decade, consulting with João on all matters of state and serving as messenger to The Hague, Paris and Rome. João IV called Vieira "the greatest man of the world."[5]

The Jesuit's skill as a preacher won him numerous followers during this time and throughout his career, but his contentious support of free Brazilindians and the "New Christians" together with his novel interpretation of Sebastianism encountered powerful enemies in Lisbon and Brazil.

In 1652 he returned to Brazil and continued extensive missionary work in Maranhão. He remained there until 1661, when the local plantation owners, faced with increasing shortages of Indian slaves because of the humanitarian intervention of the Jesuits, expelled, with the consent of the government, all members of that order from the region. Returning to Lisbon, Vieira was brought before the Inquisition for his heretical messianic statements. From there, following a seven-year exile in Rome, Vieira returned to Brazil.

---

4   Ibid., pp. 54-59; José Pereira de Sampaio, *O Encoberto* (Porto: Livraria Moreira Editora, 1904), pp. 276-278.

5   Thomas R. Graham, *The Jesuit António Vieira and his Plans for the Economic Rehabilitation of Seventeenth-Century Portugal*, Coleção Monografias, no. 1 (São Paulo: Secretaria da Cultura, Ciência e Technologia, 1978), p. 26.

Many of Vieira's sermons and writings dealt with the controversial subjects of messianism, Sebastianism, the role of João IV as the *Encoberto*, and that of Portugal as the ultimate World Empire. Vieira was totally opposed to Sebastianism in its usual form, holding that Sebastião, long dead, would not return and could not be the prophesied *Encoberto*, or Hidden King.

In one of his first sermons preached in 1634 on the day of Saint Sebastian, Vieira satirized the belief in the return of King Sebastião which was evidently held by many Bahians. He acknowledges that Sebastião was the *Encoberto* only

> because the reality of life had hidden him under the illusion of death....What a miracle! What marvelous divine providence! In the opinion of all Sebastião was dead, but in truth and in reality Sebastião was living; wounded, yes, and wounded badly, but cured of his wounds; left, yes, for dead on the day of the campaign, but at night stolen away from it, with voices, yes, of the tomb and of the entombed, but alive, sound, valiant and as strong as he was before.[6]

Others of his sermons also assumed familiarity with and belief in the prophecies of Bandarra. In 1641, for example, before the news of the Restoration had reached Brazil, Vieira instructed his audience in Salvador to support the "unconquerable King Philip," for the special date of "forty years," that is, 1640, had passed without fulfillment of Bandarra's vision. Sebastião could only help the Portuguese empire — which "his too-great valor had lost for us" — by prayers in heaven.[7] He carried his own messianic theme further by comparing the city of Salvador, rescued from the hands of the Dutch, to a new Jerusalem.

In his first sermon in the Capela Real in Lisbon in 1642, Vieira's dramatically revised vision of Sebastianism was first revealed: João IV, the living king, was the true *Encoberto* promised by Bandarra and other seers, while Sebastião was only a tragic and dead king. This sermon, the "Sermão dos Bons-Anos" or New Year's Sermon, begins with an oblique statement from Vieira:

---

6   António Vieira, *Sermões* (Lisbon: J. M. C. Seabra and T. Q. Antunes, 1854-1856), Vol. 9, pp. 220ff., quoted in João Lúcio de Azevedo, *História de António Vieira*, 2 vols., second ed. (Lisbon: Livraria Clássica Editora de A. M. Texeira and Ca., 1931), 1:40 (my translation in this and all following quotations).
7   Vieira, "Sermão do Dia de Reis (1641)" in *Por Brasil e Portugal*, ed. Pedro Calmon (São Paulo: Companhia Editora Nacional, 1930), pp. 167, 204.

> I do not wish to refer to the prophecies of the good which we now enjoy, be-
> cause I suppose they have been often preached in this place and [are] well-
> known by all; I would like to alter and deepen their intent.[8]

Digressing from the stated textual theme for that day, on the Cir-
cumcision of Jesus, Vieira continues by explicitly correlating passages
from the Old and New Testaments to the events surrounding João IV
and the Restoration. For example, the new king of Portugal was like
Sarah's unexpected child, come after an inordinately long and sterile
wait. Or, as Peter had escaped Herod, so Portugal had escaped the
clutches of Spain after "sixty years, under a captivity so hard and so unjust!"[9]

In this sermon, Vieira cites Frei Gil, a Dominican and a renowned
visionary of Sebastianism in Portugal, as the source of his incontrover-
tible proof that João, not Sebastião, was the promised redeemer-king.
Frei Gil had said that "Portugal will be redeemed unexpectedly by an
unexpected king." Sebastião was the expected savior and therefore did
not qualify; João was the figure predicted. João was, indeed, like Christ
unrecognized by Mary Magdalene on the day of the Resurrection, an
unrecognized, unexpected ruler. In conclusion, Vieira adds the as-
surance that many of the prophecies were yet unfulfilled, and Portugal
could look forward to a glorious future under João.[10]

Through his close association with the King, Vieira seemed to become obsessed with his belief in João IV as the messiah of Portugal —
and the world. In 1644, Vieira informed another audience in the Capela
Real that João IV, then King of Portugal, would shortly become the
King of the Universe.[11] João, however, did not live up to the extensive
prophecies concerning the redeemer-king and fell ill around the time
that Vieira returned to Salvador in Brazil. There, during a service for
the monarch's health, Vieira asserted that João would surely not suc-
cumb to his illness, for the prophecies — especially those concerning
the rout of the Moors and the conquest of Africa — had not all been accomplished.[12]

When João IV died in 1656, Vieira continued to cling to his neo-
Sebastianist beliefs and altered them only slightly. Still assuming the

8   Vieira, *Obras escolhidas*, ed. António Sergio and Hernani Cidade, 12 vols.
(Lisbon: Livraria Sá da Costa Editora, 1951-1954), 10 (1954): 158.

9   Ibid., pp. 160, 164.

10   Ibid., pp. 165-168, 182-183.

11   Azevedo, *História de Vieira* 1: 97.

12   Azevedo, *Sebastianismo*, p. 81.

validity of the prophecies of Bandarra, Frei Gil, and other visionaries and the applicability of canonical prophecies to Portuguese history, Vieira began to write to members of his order and to other noble and religious elites that João IV would soon come back to life to fulfill the remaining prophecies. Vieira first expressed this belief in his sermon for the memorial services held following the death of the monarch in Maranhão, the far northern section of the colony. Such, too, were the conclusions of his several works written in Brazil, including *Esperança de Portugal, Quinto Império do Mundo* (Hope of Portugal, the Fifth World Empire) in 1659, *História do Futuro* (History of the Future) completed in 1664, and *Clavis Prophetarum* in 1677.

The document entitled *Esperança de Portugal* was originally written as a letter to the Bishop of Japan, Jesuit André Fernandes, who expected the return of Sebastião.[13] Vieira wrote to Fernandes in order to persuade him of the upcoming resurrection of João IV and of the suitability of Bandarra's prophecies with relation to João. He begins:

> Your Excellency tells me of the prophecies of the world, and hopes of happiness for Portugal, and Your Excellency says that all of these refer to the return of the King Dom Sebastião concerning whose coming and life I have already told Your Excellency of my feelings. Finally Your Excellency orders me that I send you some greater clarification of that which I have many times repeated to Your Excellency on the future resurrection of our well-loved lord D. João IV.[14]

Vieira had constructed a syllogism which he outlines and explains to Bishop Fernandes by way of proof of his own beliefs:

> In summing all, then, in a fundamental syllogism, I state thus: *Bandarra is a true prophet; Bandarra prophesied that King D. João IV was to perform many things that he has not yet performed, nor would he perform [these] unless [he were] resurrected: soon King D. João IV must return to life.*[15]

Vieira demonstrates each statement of the syllogism through complicated arguments which are based on a vast array of assumptions concerning the validity of prophecy, of tales of revived men and of his own insights.

Bandarra is first shown to be a true prophet. A "true prophet," according to Vieira's cited Church rulings, is one who foresees detailed

---

13   Vieira, *Cartas do Padre António Vieira*, second ed., edited by João Lúcio de Azevedo (Lisbon: Imprensa Nacional, 1970), pp. 468-525.

14   Ibid., p. 468.

15   Ibid., p. 469. Emphasis in original.

and specific events which later come to pass. Through careful creative analysis of many passages from the *Trovas* and some significant textual alterations, Vieira concludes this proof positively. The prophecy of the reign of João is established here through the change of a single letter: the line which read "His name is D. Foão" is amended to become "His name is D. João."[16]

In order to demonstrate the second statement of the syllogism that there are points of the prophecy yet unfulfilled, Vieira again combs the text of the *Trovas* and offers his interpretations.[17] Finally, while admitting that João had actually died and was buried, Vieira insists that the king must be resurrected. He cites cases of other men revived through the ages, five by the grace of the Jesuit Francis Xavier himself, and uses passages from the work of Bandarra in support of his claims. Vieira concludes with a lengthy argument against Sebastianism and with an intricate numerological calculation of the possible date of João's resurrection.[18]

Esperança de Portugal, sent to Bishop Fernandes in Lisbon and subsequently circulated there, led to the censuring of Vieira by the Inquisition. In 1663 the proceedings began, and in 1667 the *Santo Ofício* in Coimbra, having consulted with Rome, deprived António Vieira of the right to preach and the option to live outside an official Jesuit House. In this verdict was reflected the official disapproval not only of his work, but also of Vieira's considerable effort to prevent the enslaving of the Brazilindians and to ameliorate the position of Jews (or converted Jews) in Christian Europe. Vieira, by way of defense, asserted that the document had been intended as consolation for the King's widow.

In the meantime, Vieira had written additions to a related work which he had begun in Brazil in 1649 but later abandoned before completion: the *História do Futuro*.

The plan of this work was considerably more ambitious than that of *Esperança de Portugal*, for its purpose was to demonstrate that Portugal was the Fifth Empire of the World, the ultimate Christian Empire, successor to the four ancient empires described in the biblical

16   Ibid., pp. 469-472, 473. This alteration was the cornerstone for belief in D. João IV as the Hidden King described in the poem by Bandarra and was further supported by an earlier reference to a King João.

17   Ibid., pp. 483-506.

18   Ibid., pp. 506-525. 1666 was the favored date for the resurrection of João because of the significance of the number 666 in the canonical book of *Revelation*.

book of Daniel.[19] After confirming through logical argumentation that the Kingdom of Christ was to be on earth and temporal and established by Portugal, this *História* ends abruptly. Vieira had, however, already circulated a plan for this work which indicates that the remainder of the book was to have focused on Iberia, Portugal, the House of Bragança and finally João IV.[20]

Clavis Prophetarum, which Vieira conceived as his ultimate work, was finished during his stay in Rome around the year 1677 and circulated in Bahia after 1682. This writing concerns the Kingdom of Jesus as the fulfillment of the Old Testament prophets and as witnessed in the New Testament. Vieira also discusses aspects of the future Kingdom and who will be saved in it.[21]

The period during which Vieira lived and wrote witnessed an upsurge of Portuguese messianism and of Sebastianism in Brazil as well as in Portugal. The messianic beliefs which Vieira espoused, specifically, that King João IV was the *Encoberto* heralded by Bandarra and that João would be revived years after his death, became increasingly marginal with respect to contemporary beliefs after João's death. Vieira was, however, greatly respected as a religious orator and theologian, and his sermons and later publications were extremely popular. His obsession with João IV did not detract from his popularity outside the elite circles of Lisbon; although he was satirized by several writers,[22] Vieira continued to receive the admiration and support of the Portuguese colonists in Brazil.

His writings and sermons form, therefore, the primary source for the messianic tradition in Brazil in the seventeenth century. On the one

19   Vieira, *Obras escolhidas* 9: 1-160.
20   Ibid., pp. 161-170.
21   *Clavis Prophetarum* has not yet been published, but a Latin summary of it (from 1715) and later Portuguese translation is contained in *Obras escolhidas* 9: 173-267.
22   Gregório de Mattos, a satirical writer of seventeenth-century Brazil, wrote of Vieira:

> The Sebastianists listen
> To the prophet of Bahia
> The highest astrology
> Of all the gymnosophist sages
> ....
> As I create clarity
> I say in the literal sense
> That the king promised by God
> Is: who? His Majesty.

Taken from *Obras de Gregório de Mattos*, cited in Vieira, *Por Brasil e Portugal*, p. 132.

hand, he gives ample record of the widespread Brazilian belief in
Sebastianism, particularly in his sermon on the day of Saint Sebastian,
preached in Salvador in 1534. On the other hand, his own beliefs, expressed in the published and orated sermons and circulated writings,
contributed substantially to the content and continuation of the messianic beliefs in Brazil. In his *Esperança de Portugal*, for example, he
not only expounded his own interpretation at length, but he also cited
numerous verses of the *Trovas* so that the readers might consider the
prophetical text for themselves. However, his peculiar belief in the
resurrection of João was barely accepted even in Brazil: those who had
acclaimed João IV as the foreseen *Encoberto* in 1641 generally
returned to belief in Sebastião after 1656, the year of João's death.

Vieira's writings and the numerous sermons which he gave in Bahia
on messianic themes — which include many not discussed here — gave
what may be considered the decisive impetus to the continuation of
messianism and Sebastianism in Brazil for the next two centuries.

António Vieira was not alone in his consistent and dramatic use of
messianic themes in his sermons during this period. One of his disciples
and contemporaries, Eusébio de Mattos (1629-1692), emulated him in
this regard. Mattos entered the Society of Jesus in 1644, studied under
Vieira and eventually replaced him in the pulpit in Salvador; later, after
some unspecified difficulties, he left the Jesuit Order to join the Carmelites. Mattos continued as a noted preacher, however, and his sermons were well attended and, in published form, recommended
reading for their moral content.

In his sermons, which are characterized by their vehement or enthusiastic style as well as by their length, Mattos gave precedence to
the motifs of the Passion of Jesus and its import for the Brazilian
colonists. In his famous sermon on *Ecce Homo* of 1677, Mattos explains:

> You the faithful have understood that we are touching on the point of
> greatest importance that can be brought to the pulpits, because here it
> touches on the entire subject of our salvation, that there is no salvation
> without divine help.[23]

Nearly every one of the numerous sermons which Mattos preached
and circulated in printed form in Brazil included extensive exegesis on

---

23   Eusébio de Mattos, *Ecce Homo: Práticas prégadas no Collégio da Bahia às
sestas feiras à noite, mostrando se em todas o Ecce Homo* (Lisbon: Ioam de Costa,
1677), p. 8.

passages from the canonical Apocalypse of John. He interpreted these texts, as did Vieira in similar instances, in terms of contemporary history, particularly in Brazil:

> The Evangelist [John] says, that a new Heaven and a new earth will come... Constantly is America called the new earth, and new world.[24]

The themes which Mattos repeatedly employed spoke of salvation — of the means to secure it, of the significance of the sufferings in the life of Jesus, of the glorious Second Coming of the Messiah and of the imminence of the Last Days. While these motifs may appear to lack the drama of those of the Jesuit Vieira, Mattos' passionate style of preaching insured consistently large audiences for his sermons in Bahia. In this way Mattos reinforced, in perhaps a more orthodox manner than his mentor, the messianic beliefs of the colonists in the Northeast.

Mattos, together with Vieira and other evangelists of the seventeenth century, continued the various elements of the messianic tradition through their application of ancient and contemporary religious prophecies and texts to the contemporary historical situation. The canonical and noncanonical writings to which they referred were used to explain the political and social events in Portugal and Brazil. They sought, on the one hand, to reveal the significance of local events in connection with universal history or Christian history and, on the other hand, to determine the course of the future. This concept, that biblical and other accepted prophecies (such as the Sibyllines and those of Isidore of Sevilla) may be understood to be applicable to local history, figures preeminently in the development of messianic beliefs and is, in fact, supportive of the entire messianic belief structure. This concept is at the core of Luso-Brazilian messianism, for the believers accept that a universal prophecy — of the Second Coming, of the Last Days, of the return of Sebastião — may be realized in their own particular historical time and locale; they are capable of visualizing Portugal or Brazil as the promised Kingdom of God on earth and of welcoming the return of the Messiah in their own lifetime.

The means which the preachers employed in their expressions of the message of messianism were particularly appropriate to these topics; the baroque sermon, still widely utilized, was a complex and involuted format for Brazilian Catholicism. The baroque style of literature, in prose, sermons and poetry, had developed in Portugal following the

---

24   Eusébio de Mattos, *Sermoens do Pe. Mestre Fr. Eusébio de Mattos* (Lisbon: Miguel Deslandes, 1694), p. 41.

decline of the classic ideal of the Renaissance under the influence of Spanish gongorism, the style of poet Luis de Gongora. Known in Portugal as *culturismo* and "the Jesuit style" (*barroco* is a more recent term), the baroque style was an extraordinary and somewhat affected rhetorical device, employing neologisms, *doubles entendres*, revivals of ancient poetic forms and inserted Latin and Spanish terms in dramatic albeit stylistic expression of complex and discursive topics. Unconventional words and word order were combined with complicated grammatical structures in the works of Portuguese and Brazilian authors of the fifteenth through the seventeenth centuries. This style particularly flourished in Brazil between 1650 and 1750. It had been adopted for religious expression during the Counter Reformation, drawing obscure classical and mythological references and non-Portuguese themes to the expression of the Catholic spiritual reaction against rationalism and humanism.[25]

In sermons, baroque "conceptism" frequently relied upon the use of antitheses and paradoxes to dramatize the religious content. While the proposed topic of each sermon was generally of exegesis of a selected biblical text, this rhetorical form characteristically emphasized a strict dichotomy between heaven and hell and illuminated the means to salvation in an elaborate and vehement vocabulary which the listeners retained — in brief phrases or poetic amalgams — long after the main sermonic themes were forgotten. Rarely touching on mundane problems, these sermons also served to express, couched in elaborate metaphors, the views of religious factions and "communicated a magical and mysterious vision of Christianity."[26] This type of sermon was a highly appropriate vehicle for the communication of such volatile topics as António Vieira propounded, as well as for the dramatic messianic themes which were often the favored subjects for Brazilian preachers.

During the early years of the seventeenth century, Franciscan missionaries, specifically Capuchins, arrived in greater numbers from Portugal and initiated their contributive work in the development of Christianity in Brazil. While never as numerous or as ambitious in their task of evangelization as the Jesuits, the Franciscans in the Northeast traveled extensively in the interior and influenced the formation of the

---

25   Afrânio Coutinho, *An Introduction to Literature in Brazil*, trans. Gregory Rabassa (New York: Columbia University Press, 1969), pp. 75-110.

26   Azevedo, *Sebastianismo*, p. 75; Hoornaert, "Terceiro período," *História da Igreja no Brasil* 1: 332.

messianic tradition among the colonists there, particularly in the late seventeenth and eighteenth centuries.

During the period under consideration in this chapter, the Capuchins recorded their doctrine for catechizing the wayward colonists which, like that of the Jesuits, consisted of simplified and repetitive statements on the life of Jesus, salvation and the dreaded result of a sinful life. The Franciscans who held their missions in Bahia and further north focused their teachings on the Passion of Jesus, emphasizing his death for the salvation of humankind and his imminent Second Coming. These also added the more theological details of the mortality and immortality of Jesus in order to further illustrate the significance of his act of redemption of all souls.[27]

The plays of José de Anchieta, discussed in the preceding chapter, also remained popular through the first half of the seventeenth century. Published versions were read and used, chiefly by other members of the Society of Jesus, thus keeping his messianic beliefs in circulation and in support of other parallel contemporary beliefs. After Anchieta's death in 1638, his popularity diminished somewhat and the impact of his works decreased.

António Vieira, Eusébio de Mattos and others of their orders, together with the Capuchins, persisted in the communication of the doctrine of salvation and thus of messianism to the colonists. At the same time, the legends and romances which supported parallel beliefs, brought from Europe by the Portuguese settlers, were becoming an integral part of the Brazilian folk culture. Tales of the special heroes and heroines of Iberian folklore, such as Princess Magalona, Roberto do Diabo, Charlemagne and the Twelve Peers of France and, of course, King Sebastião, formed, from the seventeenth century on, the core of popular folktales in the Northeast.[28] *Cordel* pamphlets, in Castilian as well as Portuguese, were read to the family or villagers by the few literate colonists and the tales were repeated by storytellers. Professional singers, late troubadours, also perpetuated versions of these legends.

Similar to the tales of Sebastião, the legend of Charlemagne and his twelve French knights was well known in the Northeast. The first *History of Charlemagne*, in Castilian, had come to Lisbon in 1530 and

---

27 Claude d'Abbeville, *História da missão dos padres capuchinhos na Ilha do Maranhão e terras circumvizinhas* (Paris: n.p., 1614; reprint edition, São Paulo: Editora da Universidade de São Paulo, 1975), pp. 88-89.
28 Queiroz, "Três sobrevivências," p. 186.

thence also to Brazil, becoming in the seventeenth century one of the few literary works found in the sugar-cane plantations of this area. The structure of this legend, which recounts the mythically enhanced adventures of the early medieval Emperor with his twelve noble companions, reinforced the mythic image of the savior-king in the beliefs of the colonists there. *The History of Charlemagne* was not recognized as the legendary history of a foreign king, but was believed to be inseparable from the historical reality of Brazil and Portugal; eventually Charlemagne was incorporated into the Portuguese dynastic line, as one of the rulers "in the old days."[29]

The cult of the saints of this period assumed the position of a sort of domestic cult for the Brazilian colonists. That is to say, the practice of devotion and prayer to the special saints of the family or local community, together with ritual services, remained on a small scale — except for the yearly feast-day — and was kept within the home or chapel, separate from the official cultic activities sponsored by the Church. This resulted in the consolidation of these religious beliefs and practices and the integration of the elements of the messianic tradition as well, thus forming the foundation for so-called popular Catholicism in the Northeast region of Brazil.

In the seventeenth century in Northeastern Brazil, the messianic beliefs of the Luso-Brazilian messianic tradition were, in these ways, perpetuated and augmented through the religious and legendary expressions of the colonists. Eusébio de Mattos and other contemporary religious orators and missionaries drew the attention of the Portuguese settlers and their descendants to the messianic and salvific themes derived from Christianity by their emphasis and repetition. The Jesuit António Vieira went beyond this by offering a different version of the Sebastianist beliefs in connection with King João IV. Through these ordained and thus official purveyors of Christian beliefs, messianism continued and gained renewed support.

Parallel to these, the legendary tales of Sebastião and Charlemagne, together with the popular religious expression of the cult of the saints, also gave support to the form and content of messianic beliefs. In the view of the participants, the cult of the saints had begun to assume a slightly separate role in their religious life, apart from the official Roman Catholic cult, and messianic beliefs shared in this developing distinction.

---

29   Ibid., p. 190.

Lay Religious Activities

The lay religious groups, seen in nascent form in the sixteenth century in Brazil, continued and increased in number during this period. The presence of these groups in the colony, together with the role of the solitary hermit or *ermitão*, indicates the viability of these alternate forms of religious associations and accompanying religious activities within the scope of the Brazilian religious situation.

This section on the pattern of lay religious activities in the seventeenth century among the colonists in the Northeast will include discussion of the continuing brotherhoods or *irmandades*, penitential groups, special processions and pilgrimages, as well as of the significant increase in the lay individuals who chose the solitary eremetical life.

The lay religious groups in seventeenth-century Brazil provided the general structural example for independent, noninstitutional religious devotion, as did groups of the earlier periods. These further offered the model for more spontaneous group activities for the later messianic movements.

The lay brotherhoods and confraternities stabilized in form and membership during this period. These voluntary associations, for the most part originally constituted for religious or pious ends, also took up major charitable work. In the larger towns, brotherhoods organized from a specific class or race and excluded all who did not qualify. The Irmandades da Misericórdia, for example, were for European white males of the upper class and their pure-blood descendants, while the brotherhood of Nossa Senhora do Rosário dos Homens Pretos, as the name indicates, was for black slaves.[30]

While these brotherhoods continued powerful and numerous and offered the primary model for small socioreligious organizations in Brazil, their closed ranks and identification with the institutional Church effectively removed them as options for those seeking independent religious devotional groups. Membership in certain of the elite brotherhoods was sought solely for social prestige and personal gain, rather than for intense religious expression. Further, the licensing regulations for brotherhoods in Brazil were stricter than those for their

---

30   Julita Scarano, *Devoção e escravidão* (São Paulo: Companhia Editora Nacional, 1975), pp. 25-28. While the membership of the brotherhood of Our Lady of the Rosary of Black Men was composed solely of male slaves, the administrative board was white; this structure was standard for slave brotherhoods and continued even later among brotherhoods for freed slaves.

parent or parallel organizations in Portugal so that the ecclesiastical authorities might maintain tighter control over them.[31]

The Third Orders, *Ordens Terceiras*, were founded in Salvador in the early seventeenth century. These lay associations, closely linked with the religious orders, maintained their distinctly devotional purpose during this period.

Shrine sites, called *santuários* (sanctuaries), increased in number in the seventeenth century. The shrine consisted of a small independent constructed chapel or naturally formed grotto with a focal image of the patron saint. It established a physical and spiritual location for the devotion to that saint. Shrines were founded by the local village community, by a single ordained missionary, or by a lay religious on hills or spires or in caves deemed religiously auspicious. These shrines, often modeled after the *ermidas* erected by Jesuits or Franciscans for their own private use, became pilgrimage centers, drawing increasing numbers of visitors, and also often collected a spontaneous resident association. The lay *capelão* or chaplain of the shrine was a regular, often official adjunct: this was the conservator of the special legends, rites, prayers and hymns of the saint. While this role might be filled by an ordained friar delegated from the city for this purpose, often it was simply the religious *ermitão* who had originally established the shrine or another lay man who had chosen to devote his life to the patron saint.[32]

In connection with the local shrines and related to the resident association, penitential groups also organized and held processions for feast-days or anniversaries of the shrine. These processions usually began at the local church or chapel after brief services; the members then walked to the shrine, carrying crosses or images.[33]

While none of these pilgrimage centers were constructed on a large scale or supported by great numbers of devotees, they nevertheless increased in importance to the degree that they constituted a challenge to the officially designated local church and cult. In the late seventeenth century, the ecclesiastical authorities systematically began to draw these centers into their sphere of influence and, in the next century, established regulations.

In general, however, the lay religious groups which were not rigorously regulated, that is, the lesser confraternities and devotional

31   Ibid., p. 19.
32   Queiroz, "O Catolicismo rústico no Brasil," *O Campesinato brasileiro*, pp. 87-89.
33   Ibid., p. 88.

groups, gathered increasing numbers of lay participants and thus a significant position of influence in this era in the Brazilian Northeast.

Parallel to this trend is the sharp growth in the seventeenth century in the numbers of lay religious *ermitães*, a development which has been characterized as the single most significant factor in Brazilian Catholicism.[34] These lay individuals who chose the solitary or wandering life of religious devotion had as their predecessors the religious hermits of Europe and Portugal and the lay individuals associated with the Portuguese shrine sites. In Brazil, a further role and function model was present, that of the peregrinating Jesuit or Franciscan missionaries who traveled the Northeastern *sertão* or backlands. The long routes of these missionaries and their plan of sporadic visits to the small towns evoked the model for behavior for their lay followers and imitators. All of the missionaries carried with them a breviary and a staff which remained as symbols of their religious task and solitary life.

The lay men in the seventeenth century who opted for the solitary penitential life turned their backs on the customary ways of towns and cities to wander through the sparsely populated regions of the backlands or to settle near or erect their own *ermida* or shrine. Because of the endemic shortage of ordained priests in the backlands, these lay *ermitães* substituted for the priest or missionaries and were actually treated by the *sertanejos* (backlanders) as representatives of the Church. They were asked to solve religious questions, correct half-forgotten prayers, lead litanies, pray over the sick and dying, and hold funeral services.

These *ermitães* generally resembled the missionaries: they adopted as the symbols of their penitential or devotional life a heavy dark robe with a rope knotted at the waist and they walked barefoot or wearing leather sandals. Over their long hair and long beards they wore a broad crude hat and carried the pilgrim's walking staff. The *ermitães* bore a small reliquary box, worn on a string around the neck, which contained a tiny image of the saint to whom they were devoted, together with other relics, medals and scapulars. If they could read, they also kept a prayer book. The *ermitães* spent their hours in continual prayer, whether

---

34   Riolando Azzi, "Segundo período: a instituição ecclesiástica durante a primeira época colonial," *História da Igreja no Brasil*, 1: 241.

walking or in the chapel. They lived on alms collected from local inhabitants in return for a special prayer or counsel.[35]

This form of religious life was in its ideal form respected by the ecclesiastical authorities. Conflicts developed, however, when individuals became particularly influential and remained beyond the direct control of the Catholic Church. These figures progressively displaced the less admired parish priest and the scarce missionary as religious leaders for the backlands communities. Symbolically, the presence of the *ermitão* substituted for that of the priest, his holy reliquary for the sacred objects of the Mass, and the little chapel for the parish church. A local saying of the Northeast reflects that situation: "Much prayer, few masses/ much saint, few priests."[36]

The first *ermitão* of this type was Antônio Caminho; he established his chapel not in the Northeast but in Rio de Janeiro in the second half of the seventeenth century. Adopting the robe of the Franciscans and carrying his hand-carved statue of Our Lady of Glory, he founded his *ermida* in 1671 on a hill which is at present a few blocks from downtown Rio. At his *ermida* a number of devotees gathered, and an *irmandade* was later chartered with a donation stipulating a permanent shrine on that site and a sepulchre for the donor.[37]

A second *ermitão*, Francisco Mendonça Mar, called Francisco da Soledade ("of Solitude"), was more widely known and gathered a large following during his career, which extended from the end of the seventeenth to the beginning of the eighteenth century.

Francisco Mendonça Mar appeared in Salvador in 1688, working as a painter or muralist. After an apparently unjust imprisonment, Francisco was reportedly converted by a sermon preached by António Vieira; he abandoned the city and began his solitary religious life in the *sertão* near the São Francisco River.[38] Francisco carried with him a large crucifix and a painted image of the Virgin Mary and wore a

---

35   José Ferreira Carrato, *As Minas Gerais e os primórdios do Caraçá* (São Paulo: Companhia Editora Nacional, 1963), pp. 184-188; Hoornaert, "Terceiro período," *História da Igreja no Brasil*, 1: 399.

36   Hoornaert, "Terceiro período," *História da Igreja no Brasil*, 1: 398-399. This saying, here literally translated, is not grammatically correct but is expressive of *sertanejo* beliefs nonetheless: "Muito reza, pouco missa/ muito santo, pouco padre."

37   Riolando Azzi, "Eremitas e irmãos," pp. 375-376.

38   Hoornaert, "Primeiro período," *História da Igreja no Brasil*, 1: 106; Azzi, "Eremitas e irmãos," p. 377.

version of the habit of the *ermitão*: a coarse dark robe belted with a rope and wooden-soled sandals. He let his hair and beard grow long, avoided large towns and performed continual, rigorous penitences and fasts, such as eating only herbs and roots. His wandering near the river brought him to an unusual rock grotto whose interior was fashioned like that of a traditional church, with a main cave or "altar" and two side "altars." The crucifix and image he carried from Salvador fit perfectly into the appropriate niches, and Francisco thus established the shrine of Bom Jesus da Lapa e da Maria da Soledade ("Good Jesus of the Grotto and Mary of Solitude").[39]

Francisco then lived at the cave and traveled through the neighboring countryside, to ranches and communities, to hold prayer services, give religious instruction to the settlers and beg alms for his own sustenance. His sacred shrine gained renown throughout the area in a very short time, and large numbers of the laity made long pilgrimages to see and visit the site and to pray with Francisco and receive his blessing.

During this period of growth, Francisco himself wrote to King João V, the religious head of the Portuguese empire, asking for funds. The news of the popularity of the new shrine thus reached the ecclesiastical authorities in Salvador, and the Bishop of the diocese directed missionaries to investigate Francisco and the growing community at the shrine. Francisco was later integrated into the institutional Church, ordained as a brother of the Order of St. Peter, and the grotto or chapel was recognized as part of the official Catholic cult. Francisco, now "da Soledade," and the grotto of Bom Jesus da Lapa lost no popularity in this cooptation by the institution, but rather continued as the focal religious shrine in the *capitânia* and state of Bahia through the twentieth century.[40]

Legends of miracles and sudden cures at the hands of Francisco or in connection with the shrine increased with the number of pilgrims to the site, and a permanent lay religious community formed a settlement next to the grotto in the early eighteenth century.

Those lay individuals who chose a life of religious devotion — more numerous than in the earlier period — generally modeled their behavior in group and in solitude after the early Portuguese examples. During the seventeenth century, the numbers of participants in lay religious

---

39   Turíbio Vilanova Seguro, *Bom Jesus da Lapa*, third ed. (São Paulo: Gráfica São José, 1948), pp. 93-97.

40   Hoornaert, "Primerio período," *História da Igreja no Brasil*, 1: 106; Azzi, "Eremitas e irmãos," p. 378.

groups increased, both in the more institutional *irmandades* and in the more spontaneous or temporary associations of penitents or devotional groups at pilgrimage centers. A variety of *irmandades* were founded in Salvador and the Northeast during the early years of this century, but as a whole these brotherhoods demonstrated a tendency toward rigidity of structure, exclusivity of membership, and an emphasis on charitable or secular activities and thus no longer offered an alternative form for religious expression for the laity. *Confrarias*, *Ordens Terceiras* and unregulated lay religious groups replaced this latter function and thus perpetuated the religious social action structure in this area.

Parallel to this lay trend in group formation was the eremetical movement of the second half of the seventeenth century. Modeling themselves on the earlier examples of lay religious hermits and missionaries in Brazil, lay religious individuals called *ermitães* radically altered their own religious lives by undertaking a solitary penitential program of devotion to a special saint or aspect of God. These *ermitães*, whether settled at a shrine or chapel or wandering as preachers and counselors among the small towns of the interior, replaced many of the functions of the scarcer ordained clergy and deeply affected the development of religious beliefs and activity apart from the institutional Roman Church. Further, as religious leaders, some of these began separate communities or simply gathered followings, thus initiating the group formation pattern later found in the messianic movements.

Penitential Practices

Brazil in the seventeenth century witnessed the continuation and intensification of penitential practices, particularly self-flagellation. The exemplary penitential activity of the missionaries and priests combined with the advocating of universal penitential practice from the pulpit to renew lay interest in extreme modes of penance. As illustrations of these developments, in this section the penitential themes of seventeenth-century Brazilian preachers, specifically Eusébio de Mattos and António de Sá, and the continuing flagellant practices by members of the religious orders will be discussed, followed by consideration of lay enactment of the penitential ideal, in processions, penitential groups and in the practice of *encommendação das almas*.

Eusébio de Mattos, whose sermons have been seen to emphasize apocalyptic and messianic beliefs, also devoted sermonic passages to the theory and practice of extreme penitence and self-flagellation.

In his sermon *Ecce Homo* of 1677, Mattos develops the argument for extreme modes of penance based on sin and guilt and expectations for forgiveness by God. He warns his listeners and later readers of the challenge that Jesus will offer on Judgement Day:

> Christ wounded will appear on Judgement day, and advising us, will repeat the ancient complaint..."Here are the wounds that I suffered, and what did you suffer for your sins? what penances did you perform? what mortification did you suffer? what hairshirts? what disciplines? what tears? for satisfaction of your sins; then am I alone bloodied? [While] I was suffering wounds, in atonement for the sins of others, you did no penitences for your own sins, so beaten the innocent, and the guilty so little mortified!"[41]

Mattos tells his audience that if one believes in the judgement and commits sins with no atonement or penitence before the Last Day, one should fear the coming of Jesus. He reflects that the greatest saints on earth who had few marks on their purity performed penitences that left them "rational monsters, or living cadavers," while the true sinners neglect to atone or perform penances.[42]

Mattos admonishes these sinners and, in an unparalleled exegesis of a passage from the New Testament, suggests that the world will come to an end and Judgement Day arrive during the time when men "walk dry," that is, commit sins without tears of atonement.[43] He concludes his warnings with his own perspective that eternal damnation is inevitable if the sinner neglects penances.[44]

Mattos also wrote a dramatic series of sermons on the Passion of Jesus, each unit devoted to one iconographical detail of the Stations of the Cross, in which the themes of penitence and flagellation figure predominantly. In the sermon "Of the suffering of Christ at the Column," Mattos vividly depicts the flagellated and bleeding image of

---

41   Eusébio de Mattos, *Ecce Homo*, p. 55.

42   Ibid.

43   Ibid., p. 56. The passage to which he refers is from Luke 21:26; the usual translation is "men fainting with fear and foreboding." Mattos rendered the phrase *arescentibus hominibus* as "men walking dry." Similar unusual readings, or novel interpretations, occur in others of his sermons; these apparently derive from the standard Latin translation of that time.

44   Ibid., p. 57.

Jesus after five thousand strokes of the whip, thus presenting the model for penitent sinners.[45]

One contemporary of the preacher Eusébio de Mattos, the Jesuit António de Sá, was also a renowned religious orator of this period. Like Mattos and Vieira before him, Sá used the vehicle of his evocative sermons to remind the Catholic Brazilian audiences of the struggle for salvation and the possibility of the sudden end of the world. His sermon of "the day of ashes" (Ash Wednesday) echoes the sentiment expressed by Mattos, for Sá also warns the Brazilians that sins, which lead to damnation, must be atoned:

> If we have faith, and we believe that there is no pardon of sins without the repentance of the sinner, we must necessarily repent one day, then if it must be one day, why not today?

Sá suggests immediate penitence for sins committed, because human life comes to a sudden end: "how many have seen the sun rise, who did not [live to] see it set?"[46]

Another contemporary of these preachers, the Jesuit Affonso do Valé, recommended the practice of self-flagellation to his compatriots, delineating his own intent:

> What moves me to perform great disciplines... is the desire for two things. The first thing, to imitate Jesus Christ our Lord in some manner, and also to suffer something for his love, seeing that for love of me... he suffered five thousand strokes of the whip... The second thing... is to want to do penance in this life for my sins.... For this I want to discipline myself until blood runs, so that by that blood that I draw out, I might pay for my sins.[47]

During this period, as in earlier times, the members of the religious orders, through their sermons and by personal example, exalted the ideal of self-flagellation and penitence in general for the atonement of sins committed. Even the long and often difficult journeys of the missionaries were considered penitential acts. The repetition of these themes was, again, not lost on the laity, for these latter also performed the extreme penitences of fasting and the discipline.

Special penitential processions were organized under the auspices of the Jesuits during the times of droughts or outbreaks of yellow fever in the seventeenth century. In 1614, when many cattle died because of

---

45   Mattos, *Sermoens*, pp. 253-255.

46   António de Sá, *Sermam do Dia de Cinza que pregou o P. António de Saa da Companhia de Jesu* (Coimbra: Rodrigo de Carvalho Coutinho, 1673), p. 19.

47   Franco, *Imagem da virtude*, pp. 694-695.

drought, particularly rigorous and frequent penitential services were held in order to end the evil and assuage the Divine Wrath: the laity used prayers, celebration of Masses, and flagellant processions to bring the rains. On Fridays, the men of Bahia participated in the two types of flagellation, the first which drew blood and the second, milder, which did not, during the chanting of the *Miserere*, a rhythmic litany.[48]

In 1649 the Procissão de Cinza, or the Procession of Ashes, was inaugurated by brotherhoods of the laity in the city of Salvador. This event, held on the first day of the penitential period of Lent, was like the comparable processions on Friday and Saturdays of Holy Week. It gathered large groups of men and women, not only from the city but also from the surrounding area, usually dressed in long white robes, who sang and prayed in unison as they walked through the streets of that Northeastern city. Small bands of flagellants characteristically participated in these solemn processions, which were held for atonement of sins committed during the previous year. Similar processions were also organized further north, in the province of Pernambuco, although these latter services were forced to cease before the end of the seventeenth century.[49]

The practice of *encommendação das almas*, the Lenten penitence dedicated to the souls in Purgatory, continued, though usually under the simpler name "penitence." This practice, involving a small group of men in flagellant procession on late Friday or Saturday nights in Lent or throughout the year, was not unlike the larger-scale Processions of Salvador and Pernambuco. However, although the men returned to village life after each ritual, they considered themselves a formal group — often called an *irmandade* of penitents — and usually continued the weekly penitence for a specific number of years to complete their vows. The men adopted white robes or skirts for these meetings and sang or chanted as they walked and struck their backs with whips. The devotion of each penitent was sacred and not to be halted until the period, typically of seven years, ended. Completion guaranteed eternal salvation; willful interruption could result in sickness or death.[50]

48   Leite, *História da Companhia* 2: 319-320.
49   Marieta Alves, *História da veneravel Ordem Terceira da Penitência do Seráfico Padre São Francisco da congregação da Bahia* (Bahia: n.p., 1948), p. 193; Francisco A. Pereira da Costa, "Folk-lore pernambucano," *Revista do Instituto Histórico e Geográfico Brasileiro* 70, Pt. 2 (1907): 199.
50   Queiroz, "Os Penitentes," *O Campesinato brasileiro*, pp. 171-173; Fernando Altenfelder Silva, "As Lamentações e os grupos de flagelantes do São Francisco," *Sociologia* 24 (March 1962): 22.

During the seventeenth century, the *ermitão* himself also exemplified the penitential ideal; he practiced self-flagellation and encouraged other lay religious individuals to adopt the practice as well.

Near the end of the century small lay flagellant bands of a temporary nature also appeared, gathering for the sole purpose of extreme penitence through fasting and the discipline. These groups joined the organized processions or the lay associations of the shrine centers but dispersed after a brief period – of months or years – together.

Together with the other elements of the messianic tradition, the extraordinary penitential practices transported from Portugal by the early missionaries and settlers persisted during this time. Members of the religious orders themselves continued to practice flagellation and to exhort the Brazilian laity to emulate them. Through lay processions, "penitences" and independent penitential activity of the *ermitães* and temporary flagellant bands, this extreme form of penitence was accepted as part of religious devotional activity in the Northeast. As such, this special penitential practice would later serve as the purpose for organization of more permanent lay religious groups and as part of the religious rituals of the messianic movements of the nineteenth century.

During the period from 1600 to 1699 in Northeastern Brazil, the component elements of the Luso-Brazilian messianic tradition continued as strong, integral parts of the religious beliefs and practices of the colonists. The messianic beliefs and Sebastianism of António Vieira communicated through his sermons and tracts gave significant impetus to the spread and acceptance of such beliefs in Brazil as well as in Portugal. Other preachers, such as Eusébio de Mattos, also emphasized messianic imagery in their sermons and published works and thus drew the attention of the colonists to their support of these beliefs.

The lay religious activities developed as a major factor in the religious expression of the settlers in this region. The beginning of the eremetical movement and the progressive increase in lay groups indicate the strength and acceptability among the laity of religious group activities beyond or in place of those of the institutional church.

Finally, flagellant and other penitential practices continued to form a significant part of the religious devotional rituals among the religious orders and the laity. The popular religious orators António de Sá and Eusébio de Mattos, through dramatic descriptions of the Passion of Jesus and the threat of damnation, exhorted the Catholics to repent; other members of the Orders guided through example. The lay colonists followed their model in their own penitential processions and group services.

These elements of the Luso-Brazilian messianic tradition persisted through this time in forms not unlike those which were originally brought from Portugal. Significant developments may be seen in the increase of lay participation and control over religious activities: the lay ermitão and the lay confrarias became integral and irreplaceable parts of religious devotion, and lay flagellant activity expanded.

In general, however, the structure of religious expression in the Northeast had been established: the rigidity of missionary instruction and the repression by the Inquisition did not allow for radical deviation from the sixteenth-century norm. The later lack of religious instructors, particularly in the backlands, insured the continuation of the above-described elements and thus the Luso-Brazilian messianic tradition in the local communities, along with the laicization of religious functions.

Chapter 7

Brazil: The Late Colonial Period, 1700-1799

The eighteenth century introduced a number of demographic, political and religious changes to Northeastern Brazil. The reigns of João V, José I – with the assistance of the Marquis of Pombal – and Maria I maintained regal absolutism throughout the Portuguese empire, although revolts and conspiracies occurred more frequently. The discovery of gold and diamonds in Minas Gerais in the central interior of Brazil and, later, of gold in Goias and Mato Grosso drew Brazilians and new immigrants to Brazil's interior. Finally, the expulsion of the Jesuits and further decline in the numbers and morality of the remaining clergy and missionaries spurred the continued development of lay religious groups and sectarian beliefs. This chapter will review the messianic beliefs, lay religious activities and penitential practices of the Luso-Brazilians of the Northeast in this period, following a brief outline of the political events of the eighteenth century in Portugal and Brazil.

Historical Circumstances

King Pedro II of Portugal, who ruled until 1706, had launched the absolutist trend of the Portuguese Crown by the end of the preceding century. João V (ruled 1706-1750), whose apparent regal model for monarchy was the French king Louis XIV, continued and supported his predecessor's regalism which reached its climax with José I and his minister, the Marquis of Pombal. This section on the history of Portugal and Brazil in the eighteenth century will discuss the monarchs of Portugal and their eras, together with a brief sketch of contemporary Brazilian events.

In the first years of the eighteenth century, Portugal had reluctantly entered the War of Spanish Succession, allied with the Hapsburgs and England against the Bourbon dynastic family. The expenses of the war moderately diminished the income of the Portuguese empire and, more important, established the pattern for alliances for this and later periods.

João V increasingly delegated governmental authority to his ministers, usually ecclesiastical men, and had appointed three dominant ministries: that of Home Affairs (State), of Foreign Affairs and War, and of Overseas and Marine. These three offices eventually became life-long positions: by 1750 the ministers were replaceable only at death.

King João and most of the Brazilian and Portuguese elite enjoyed the luxuries won from the gold and diamond discoveries of the late seventeenth and earlier eighteenth centuries in Brazil. The "royal fifth"—the tax of twenty percent levied on all gold extracted from the mines—was spent on elaborate constructions such as the grand palace at Mafra and on extravagant feast-day celebrations, the weddings of the royal princesses, and the maintenance of the newly secured patriarchate at a level of luxury equal to that of the Papal Court. A significant portion of the Crown's profit from Brazil during this reign went to British merchants in payment for the manufactured goods and cloth that Portugal could not duplicate. By 1760, however, the output from the mines was dwindling.

José I (1750-1777), son and heir to João V, continued to rely heavily on ministerial control of the functions of the Portuguese government. In 1750 he appointed José Sebastião de Carvalho e Mello, then diplomatic envoy to Vienna, as Minister of State. Carvalho e Mello, later named the Marquis of Pombal, secured in the following decade complete dictatorial powers in the Portuguese Empire, serving as its absolute ruler in all but name until 1777, when José I died.

Pombal had originally gained access to ministerial authority through the Austrian-born Queen of João V. José duly appointed him first Minister of State, then Minister of Foreign Affairs as well. Pombal extended his own power by, in turn, nominating relatives and close allies to all other significant governmental positions. His step to unchecked authority followed the disastrous earthquake in Lisbon in 1755, which leveled much of the center of Lisbon and killed many residents. José turned to Pombal for assistance in dealing with the calamity and eventually surrendered all but the most nominal powers to him. José continued, however, to endorse and sign all of Pombal's actions and edicts through 1777, thus obviating later accusations of usurpation against the Marquis.

The effect of the dictatorship of Pombal was felt in three significant developments in Portugal: first, the suppression and later expulsion of the Jesuits from the Portuguese Empire; second, the suppression of political opposition; and third, economic and educational reforms.[1]

The source of Pombal's obsessive hatred of the Jesuits remains unclear, but it is undeniable that he took every opportunity to block their influence and destroy the Society. He was convinced that the Jesuits were primarily responsible for most of the wrongs of contemporary Portugal – he believed not only that they had obstructed the growth of the Portuguese economy and industries, but also that they were the instigators of most of the opposition to his government, whether in Portugal or in its colonies. Pombal and his allies had also long believed that the Jesuits possessed, along with their actual land holdings in Brazil, secret hoards of gold and silver and were greedily amassing more in order to advance their political schemes.[2]

Pombal met with definite Jesuit resistance in the southern district of Brazil ceded to Spain in 1750, and in Grão-Pará, the northern area of the colony which also underwent a sort of forced secularization under his regime. In 1758 Pombal received at his own request permission from Pope Benedict XIV to reform the entire Jesuit Order in Portugal. During that year, he restricted the Order by degrees: he forbade them to engage in commerce, to preach and to hear confessions, and later exiled their Superior from Lisbon. Following an abortive assassination attempt against King José in which several Jesuits were implicated,[3] Pombal first had the Jesuit Colleges surrounded by troops and later, in 1759, expelled all Jesuits from Portuguese territories.

While Pombal was in power, he imprisoned at best estimate nearly four thousand political enemies[4] and executed Jesuits and nobles alike if suspected of conspiracy. He also initiated numerous reforms of the economic and manufacturing system in Portugal, attempting to model

---

1   Boxer, *Seaborne Empire*, p. 177.
2   No such hoards were found when the Jesuit lands and Houses were seized and searched after 1759.
3   The attempt was actually perpetrated through one of the aristocratic families in Lisbon and was related to an illicit love affair carried on by José. See Livermore, *A New History of Portugal*, pp. 228-231.
4   Boxer, *Seaborne Empire*, p. 190.

it after that of England, and of the education of Portuguese children. Many of his plans, however, were unsystematically conceived and thus short-lived.

Following the death of José I in 1777, his daughter Queen Dona Maria I reigned until 1779. Pombal's power ended completely with José's death, and he spent his remaining years exiled to his estate. Dona Maria began rather circumspectly to undo the worst of Pombal's decrees: she freed the surviving political prisoners and pardoned many nobles implicated in the 1758 assassination attempt. The strain of the monarchy and the morass of the political and economic policies which she inherited eventually proved to be too much for her; she was declared insane in 1792 and replaced by Prince Regent Dom João VI.

Political and, inevitably, religious development in Brazil was drastically affected by the mineral wealth of the Minas Gerais area, which lies to the southwest of Salvador, Bahia. Prospectors moved from all parts of Brazil to the mining district which produced large quantities of gold and diamonds between the years 1699-1750. From one mine alone, nine hundred pounds of gold were extracted. The royal records—from the taxes and confiscations—do not account for the total gold or diamond production because of the widespread and elaborate smuggling operations.

Struggles between Brazilian-born backwoodsmen and incoming Portuguese over control of the gold territory resulted in a limited war there, known as the War of the Emboabas, and were resolved through the establishment of a separately administered state—Minas Gerais—and tightened governmental control. The Diamond District was placed under repressive restrictions in 1740 which barred access to its resources to all but a select few.

Along with the gold and diamond trade, Brazil's other export products continued to be exploited chiefly for the gain of the Portuguese Crown. Conflicts increased, however, between the Brazilian-born colonists, particularly those of mixed background, and the Portuguese newcomers, known as *Reinois*, and further between the *Reinois* and the officials of the remote and oppressive royal government. Several plots and revolts occurred toward the end of the eighteenth century, notably the *Inconfidência Mineira*, an embryonic political scheme against Portuguese rule quickly discovered and defused by the authorities.

The removal of Jesuit missionaries worsened the religious situation throughout Brazil. By the beginning of this period, both foreign visitor and resident alike decried the laxity and immorality of the secular clergy, that is, the priests, as a group; among the religious orders, only the Jesuits and the Capuchins were accorded universal respect. The expulsion of the Jesuits drastically reduced the numbers of missionaries in Brazil and forced the colonists to rely on their own religious practices, on the sporadic visits by Franciscans, or on the function of the less reputable local priest.

In general, Brazil during this time was the scene of considerable growth and confusion. The population reached three million by the end of the century, still concentrated in the northeast coastal plantation regions. Regalism and revolts changed the colony and determined its role and structure in the following century.

Messianic Beliefs

In the eighteenth century in Brazil, the messianic beliefs imported by Portuguese colonists, including Judeo-Christian radical eschatology, other prophetic beliefs, and the legend cycle of Sebastião, and continued by their settled descendants remained a strong unchanging part of Catholicism in the Northeast. The possibility of radical changes in the basic belief structure as it existed at the beginning of this period of religious development was increasingly remote: messianism had become an irreplaceable component element of the rustic or popular Catholicism of the area. While perennially emphasized and thus reinforced by itinerant missionaries or popular religious orators, these messianic beliefs passed from person to person within the family or village in nearly the same form as in the sixteenth century. This section will consider the points of the steady continuance of these beliefs in the eighteenth century in the Northeast, through the preachings of Jesuit Angelo dos Reis and Bento da Trindade, the sermons of the holy missions of the traveling missionaries and through local paths of communication, in *cordel* and cult. These beliefs and their development in this period directly precede the final occurrence of three messianic movements in the following century.

As in the early periods of the history of colonial Brazil, the religious orators of the eighteenth century reiterated the affective motifs and imagery of salvation and damnation, emphasizing the messianic role of Jesus and the desperate straits of their own contemporary situation.

The Jesuit preacher Angelo dos Reis, who had been secretary to António Vieira during the last years of that orator's life, preached and had published several sermons expounding the elements of messianic belief. His sermon on the "Restoration of Bahia," published in 1706, directed the audience to heed the prophecies of the Old Testament, as they would soon come to pass. In that sermon, Reis reminds the listener and reader that Jesus in the few hours before leaving this world, before his Ascension, had promised to come again, to restore all, and that that promise had yet to be fulfilled.[5]

Bento da Trindade, a popular preacher in the latter part of the century, drew the attention of his audience to the inevitability of the Last Days and of the Second Coming of Jesus. Admonishing the sinners, he assures them that "the Sun never illuminated a People so incoherent and so dissolute" as those in Bahia.[6]

Trindade compares Bahia to the whore of Babylon — spoken of in "the Apocalypse of the Evangelist" — who is unsuccessfully "trying to cover her face." Bahia was sunk into the worst of sins, the "abominations of Samaria," the worship of "foreign gods," even in holy places. He warns them that he is speaking frankly, that his warnings were not merely "a figure of speech."[7] Trindade expands his theme by introducing the role of the saving God who will be called upon by the Bahians when they realize that the Last Days are at hand. Jesus would respond then, as the "God who will come personally to free us from the slavery" to evils.[8]

The sermons and writings of António Vieira, still in abundant circulation during this period, kept his particular messianic beliefs before the Brazilian readers and thus part of the messianic tradition. His writings, and others by his Jesuit contemporaries and disciples, were suppressed by Pombal after 1758.

These and other preached and published sermons from the Jesuits and other religious orders in Brazil reinforced the messianic beliefs of earlier periods. Of especial importance in this process, particularly as

---

5   Angelo dos Reis, *Sermam da Restauracam da Bahia, pregado na Se da mesma Cidade* (Lisbon: Miguel Manescal, Impresso do Santo Offício, 1706), pp. 1-3.

6   Bento da Trindade, *Sermão do primeiro dia do Quarenta horas, prégado na Se da Bahia* (Lisbon: Francisco Luis Ameno, 1784), p. 7 (my translation in this and all following quotations).

7   Ibid., p. 9.

8   Ibid., pp. 17-20.

the ranks of missionaries suddenly diminished in the latter half of this century, were the emphatic salvific and messianic preachings of holy missions or *santas missões*. These *missões* had begun with the earlier missionaries but in this period became perhaps the primary vehicle for catechizing and rechristianizing the isolated backlanders and villagers of the Northeast.

In general, throughout the *sertão* or backlands, resident village or parish priests were rare figures; further, as indicated above, those few who lived in the region of Bahia were considered to be religiously and morally lax. The Church attempted to compensate for this lack of religious instruction and guidance by means of sporadic visits by enthusiastic or zealous missionary preachers whose purpose was to bring the wicked back to the right path through the liturgy of the Church. The *santas missões* which these missionaries held in each little town or community were great religious – and social – events, drawing the settlers from the surrounding areas to hear the dramatic and vehemently delivered sermons on salvation and repentance. Because of the scarcity of even these ordained preachers, the intervals between missions were of at least one year, up to at most five years.[9]

For five- to ten-day stays, the missionary, whether Capuchin, Carmelite, Oratorian or Franciscan, lived in the community, heard the confessions of the residents, sanctified makeshift marriage arrangements, baptized infants born since the last mission, said Mass, and delivered warnings to those who remained in an unrepentant state of sinfulness. Certain well-known missionaries, such as Carlos José de Spezia or Appolônia de Todi, drew large crowds, some of which followed them on their journeys to the next town.[10]

The sermons preached during these missions then emphasized the basic themes of salvation: that there was no salvation without repentance of sins, that the end of the world would come without warning

---

9   Thales de Azevedo, *Catholicismo*, pp. 36-37.
10 Hoornaert, "Primeiro período," *História da Igreja no Brasil* 1: 113, 134.

and that Jesus would come again to glorify the good and condemn sinners. Jesuit Gabriel Malagrida, later executed by his enemy Pombal for his undaunted opposition, in his popular *santas missões* in 1730-1745 brought to his listeners the "terrible truths of life: sin, death, hell, Last Judgement, etc."[11] and found many willing to hear him. The Capuchin Vidal de Frascarolla, through his messianic preaching around the year 1785, became known throughout the *sertão* as a great prophet of the future.[12]

These affective themes of missionary sermons recreated the Roman Catholic messianic belief for the *sertanejos*, affirming its primary position in their religious belief structure.

The dwindling numbers of available Roman Catholic clergy and the undiminished strength of the Portuguese Catholicism known to the settlers determined, in this period, the form and continuance of the cult of the saints and similar supportive beliefs of the messianic tradition — such as Sebastianism, belief in heroic legends, and so on — in the religious lives of those in the interior of the Northeast. The gradual loss of institutional religious instruction from the missionaries contributed to two developments in this and later periods: the backlands communities began to be characterized by, first, a sort of religious conservatism and, second, a growing ignorance of Church doctrine and liturgy. On the one hand, the settlers of the Northeast clung to their traditional beliefs including, specifically, the messianic and related beliefs which had become familiar to them as part of their belief structure from the earliest days of the colony. On the other hand, these came to depend on the familial or local cult of the saints, the devotional cult dedicated to a specific supernatural patron, for primary religious expression. Various of their patron saints were inevitably confused with Jesus or an aspect of the Trinity in the songs and prayers of the faithful,

---

11   Paulo Mury, *História de Gabriel Malagrida da Companhia de Jesus*, trans. Camillo Castello Branco (Lisbon: Livraria Editora de Mattos Moreira and Ca., 1875), p. 90.

12   Abelardo Montenegro, *História do fanaticismo religioso no Ceará* (Fortaleza, Brazil: Editora A. Batista Fontenele, 1959), p. 6.

as these figures were understood to be closer or more familiar to the believers.[13]

Sebastianism, as a messianic parallel belief, was not without supporters during this century. It was continually present in the oral legends, songs, and, for those who could read or be read to, the *cordel* pamphlets and almanacs that appeared from time to time in the Northeast. In the interior, away from the more concentrated urban populations, the presence of *cordel* and other literature remained limited, such that legendary material was usually transmitted orally. Messianism and Sebastianism continued in part due to the rigid social formation and subsistence-level lifestyles in the cattle-ranging *sertão*. These legends, prophecies and songs of a better life, describing the promised Messiah who would overturn the world, which were communicated through folk singers or storytellers and reiterated in the dogmatic sermons of the religious missionaries, found eager believers in this region.[14]

In the eighteenth century in Northeastern Brazil, the Portuguese settlers and descendants of earlier immigrants perpetuated the messianic and related beliefs held by the Portuguese of the sixteenth century and the immigrants of that and later centuries, thus continuing this aspect of the messianic tradition.

While the exotic Sebastianist writings of António Vieira continued to circulate and influence the content of messianic beliefs, religious preachers of this period contributed their emphatic declarations on the brevity of temporal life and the imminence of the Second Coming and the messianic age. The Jesuit Angelo dos Reis and later orator Bento da Trindade evoked the dramatic — and popular — imagery of the suffering of Jesus and the corruption of the wayward Brazilians in order to bring their listeners back into the fold of the Church. At the same time, the diminishing of the ranks of the peregrinating missionaries forced the Roman Church to rely heavily on the sporadic visits or *santas*

---

13   Thales de Azevedo, *Catholicismo*, p. 55; [José Possidônio Estrada], *Superstições descubertas, verdades declaradas, & desenganos a toda a gente* (Rio de Janeiro: Typographia de Torres, 1826), pp. 95-96.

14   Records of such legends and prophecies have been collected in contemporary *cordel* writings and in the Manuscript Collection of the Instituto dos Estudos Brasileiros, Universidade de São Paulo, São Paulo.

missões in order to reach their lay members in the interior of the colony. The sermonic style of exaggerated emphasis on the themes of sin and doom versus the Messiah and salvation surfaced in these brief religious events which were intended to replace steady or residential religious instruction, yet served only to reinforce the messianic belief structure of the participants.

The withdrawal of steady evangelization in this region also resulted in the development of dependence on local or familial religious devotional cults, a trend which included the steady development of more communal and public practices related to the saints, ranging from elaborate saint's-day festivals to weekly meetings and processions. Daily prayer services in the family were paralleled by devotions at small outdoor shrines in the village. This effectively extended the cult to the group as a unit, as in like fashion messianic salvation had been extended to the group. This pattern of group involvement was mirrored in the increased lay religious activities discussed in the section below.

Lay Religious Activities

The "golden age" of Brazil, this period during which the colony enjoyed the economic boom from the mining of gold and diamonds, also held the continuance of the growth in numbers and influence of lay religious individuals and independent groups. This section on lay religious activities in the eighteenth century in the Northeast of Brazil will consider this development, including the religious examples of the wandering missionaries, concomitant regulations established by the Church to control lay religious hermits and shrines, the activities of the hermits (*ermitães*) and *beatos* of this period, as well as those of lay religious brotherhoods and *confrarias*.

In the decades preceding the expulsion of the Jesuits from the Portuguese empire, the corps of missionaries had already begun to decrease significantly in number. Following the suppression of the Jesuit order, severe restrictions were placed on the other orders concerning their operations and, particularly, admission of novices. As a result, those few missionaries who traversed the backlands were able to gain considerable influence among the inhabitants and set examples for their own imitation by individuals and groups in their absence.

The most popular of these missionaries was the Jesuit Gabriel Malagrida, who traveled through the Northeast between 1730 and 1750. He walked or traveled by canoe between Salvador, Bahia, and the northern territories. In the various villages and settlements he visited, he established houses or "seminaries" for young men or young women to be guided by the religious principles of the Jesuit order. In 1742, for example, in the village of Iguaraçu in Pernambuco, he founded a house called the "recolhimento do Sagrado Coração" (the retreat of the Sacred Heart) with twenty poor women.[15]

Another important missionary of this time was the Capuchin Anibal de Genova, who worked through Ceará and Pernambuco in 1760-1770. Genova also held *santas missões* of somewhat longer duration than usual in the various villages and small towns he encountered in the backlands, preaching sermons and blessing the people. The regions of Pernambuco which he visited in 1762 had not seen a priest in five to twenty years, nor heard the Mass in that time, for the district bishop, attempting to thwart possible abuses, had prohibited the portable altars necessary for that ritual. At every place that Genova stopped, however, he gathered enormous crowds of local residents as well as of settlers from many miles away who eagerly came to hear religious preaching and participate in the rituals and processions. Genova sympathized with "those poor ones who, abandoning their homes, came with their children in their arms to hear the word of God."[16] Other religious like Malagrida and Genova also worked in the *sertão* with similar purpose and results. These missionaries themselves founded lay religious groups and thereby concrete and approved models for new group formations in this area. Their religious and organizational activities reinforced, at the same time, the example of the wandering penitent which was then mirrored in the similar activities of the lay *ermitães*.

The lay eremetical movement had become such an important part of religious life in the eighteenth century in Brazil that the Roman Church began to seek ways in which to regulate it and, thus, maintain institutional control over this spontaneous phenomenon.

In the Synod of Bahia of 1707, the Archbishop Dom Sebastião Monteiro da Vide introduced, as part of the First Constitutions of the

---

15   Hoornaert, "Primeiro período," *História da Igreja no Brasil*, 1: 112.
16   Fidelis Motta de Primeiro, *Capuchinhos em terras de Santa Cruz* (São Paulo: n.p., 1940), pp. 186-191.

Archbishop of Bahia, special clauses concerning the *ermitão*.[17] Vide, whose diocese then included all of the geographic area under consideration in this book, intended to avert possible abuses of the functions or laws of the Church itself, assuming at the same time that the charismatic lay hermits would be readily absorbed into the institution. The regulations excluded the possibility that the *ermitão*, or the cult shrine itself, might be constituted separately from or in opposition to the Roman Church.[18]

The first points under Title 38 concern the shrines and their caretakers, the *ermitães*:

> In the shrines of our Archbishopric, and principally in those, where there is pilgrimage and devotion, it is necessary to have Hermits [Ermitães] for the Divine cult, and for the cleaning of them. And so that those not be introduced, who should not be admitted, we order that, pertaining to the presentation of others, to be hermits diligent men [be] presented, of convenient age, and good life and habits, and women may not be presented.[19]

The duties of the *ermitães* are specified as well:

> And those Hermits approved, have the care of the guarding and cleaning of the shrines. And if they are located in the countryside, they will not let new things be gathered in them, nor animals, keeping the doors closed when not actually in them, and they will live next to the same Shrines when possible, and maintain its ornaments, and minister to the necessary when Mass is said.[20]

Finally, the comportment and attire of the Hermits is restricted so that Church laws may be observed:

> They will not wear the habits of Religious or Clergy, but may wear long dark robes, or of some other honest color, or other decent clothes. They will not live in said Shrines, but in separate houses. They will not permit that in the

---

17   Azzi, "Eremitas e irmãos," p. 373.

18   Ibid., p. 374.

19   Sebastião Monteiro da Vide, *Constituições primeiras do Arcebispado da Bahia feitas e ordenadas pelo illustissimo e reverendissimo senhor D. Sebastião Monteiro da Vide, 5o. Arcebispo do dito Arcebispado, e do Conselho da Sua Magestade: propostas e aceitas em o Sinodo Diocesano (1707)* (Lisbon: n.p., 1719; reprint ed., São Paulo: Typografia Antônio Louzada Antunes, 1853), p. 232.

20   Ibid.

said Shrines some people sleep, eat, play, play music, or do such things, even if it be under the pretext of pilgrimage; all this they will do under the penalty of being castigated arbitrarily according to their guilt.[21]

Archbishop Vide formulated these regulations in direct response to the religious activity of Francisco Mendonça Mar—Francisco da Soledade—who had founded the grotto-shrine on the São Francisco River in Bahia.[22] Because of the continued surge in the numbers of lay men who adopted the way of life of the *ermitão* in the eighteenth century in Brazil, these regulations were immediately useful. In Minas Gerais, particularly, where the Portuguese government had banned religious orders on suspicion of smuggling operations, *ermitães* filled a significant lacuna in religious leadership and devotional practices.

In the Northeast several of the more influential figures established not only shrines but also religious communities of lay persons. Felix da Costa inaugurated the *ermida* da Nossa Senhora de Conceição, built in 1714 and blessed in 1716, together with the Order of the Conception in 1712.[23] Antônio da Silva Bracarena, a brother of the Third Order of Nossa Senhora de Carmo, founded the shrine of Nossa Senhora da Piedade between 1767 and 1770 and organized a community alongside it.[24] The chapel of São Francisco das Chagas was erected in 1775, and its city of Caninde became a major pilgrimage center of the North and Northeast of Brazil in the eighteenth and nineteenth centuries.[25] Another hermit, Lourenço de Nossa Senhora, established the *ermida* of Nossa Senhora Mãe dos Homens in the Serra of Caraçá in 1770, and the shrine was blessed in 1779.[26]

The number of *ermitães* demanded the increased attention of and regulation by the Roman Church if it was to keep these men—and their lay followers—under their auspices.

In conjunction with the development of the eremetical movement and its regulation and the cotemporal development of the lay community near the shrines, the latter half of the eighteenth century also

---

21   Ibid.
22   See above, Chapter 6.
23   Azzi, "Eremitas e irmãos," p. 380.
24   Ibid., pp. 433-434.
25   Montenegro, *História do fanaticismo religioso*, p. 11.
26   Azzi, "Eremitas e irmãos," p. 435.

saw the appearance of two additional types of religious lay individuals: the *penitente* and the *beato*. The *penitente* or penitent, similar to the members of temporarily organized penitential groups or practitioners of the *encommendação das almas* rituals, had chosen to dedicate his life, or at least a portion of it, to penitential atonement for his sins, particularly if he was guilty of grievous wrongs or for the sins of others. The *penitente*, whether serving a terminal vow or fulfilling a life of dedication, remained unattached to either chapel or shrine and practiced extreme fasts and self-flagellation. These men were not distinguished by any particular mode of dress nor standard behavior. In general, the *penitente* was distinctly removed from institutional as well as from popular religious cult or, conversely, joined with other penitents in a loosely organized group which traversed the backlands practicing penitence.

The *beato*, although apparently known from the earliest period in the colony, did not emerge as a distinct form of lay religiosity until the late eighteenth century. The term, which means "holy man" or "blessed man," had been in origin a primarily derogatory reference used in the sense of "over-zealous hypocrite." It is in this sense that it is used in the *Dialogues* of the orator Amador Arraiz, one of the earliest sources for the term: "You have heard, who is a *beato*, is a great hypocrite, without turning back."[27] Similar usage is found in the writings of António Vieira and other religious preachers. In the latter half of the eighteenth century, however, and particularly after 1780, it was used in an opposite sense to refer to men (or to women: *beata*) devoted to a solitary penitential life of peregrination in the *sertão*.

From the time of the first missionaries in Brazil, especially devout lay men or aspiring novices accompanied the entourage of the Jesuit or Franciscan catechist in his tours of the Brazilindian reductions and villages and the few Portuguese settlements away from the urban centers along the coast. During the later period of the increasing scarcity of members of the religious orders available to bring religious

---

27   Amador Arraiz, *Diálogos de Dom Frei Amador Arraiz* (Coimbra: Diogo Gomez Lourenzo, 1604; reprint ed., Lisbon: Typografia Rollandia, 1846), p. 455. *Beato* was not the term generally used for "blessed" in reference to the saints or in the translation of Jesus' Sermon on the Mount (Mt. 3:3-11); there the appropriate term was *bem-adventurado* or *bendito*.

instruction to the Portuguese descendants in the backlands, the *beatos* followed the earlier example and actually served as replacements for the ordained missionaries. While the *ermitão* was, in the eighteenth century, usually designated as one specifically attached to a shrine or holy locale, the *beato* maintained the role of the wandering holy man. The laity of the backlands had come to rely upon traditional and home-taught religious beliefs and rituals during this period of change; the visit of a wandering *beato*, unschooled as he may have been, provided an additional and valuable source of religious knowledge and acted as arbiter on specific religious problems.

In appearance and activity the *beatos* of the late eighteenth and nineteenth centuries resembled the nonwandering or shrine-attached *ermitão* or hermit. They characteristically wore the dark heavy robe with a large cross of white cloth sewn to front and back or several smaller crosses on different sections of the robe. They carried a crucifix and walking staff and wore a reliquary around the neck together with other scapulars, medals and ribbons. These also made a special vow of chastity and prayed continually as they journeyed across the backlands. Extraordinary penances were not always part of their rituals.[28]

Revered as a religious man of knowledge because of his devotional life, the *beato* was usually welcomed in the ranches and small villages of the *sertão*. The *beato* remained for a short period in each place "to foretell the unknown future, resolve impossible situations, perform miracles and to give to suffering creatures the relief and tranquillity" they desired.[29] For his prayers and healing rituals, the *beato* accepted alms, usually of food or shelter, from his believers. These lay religious men were not, however, universally well received; even in the nineteenth century, they were considered odd in appearance, ostentatious in religious devotion, or ludicrous figures.[30]

The addition of these two further types of lay religious individuals contributed to the development of the eremetical movement as a whole

---

28   Montenegro, *História do fanaticismo religioso*, p. 15; Djacir Menezes, *O Outro Nordeste* (Rio de Janeiro: Livraria José Olympio Editora, 1937), pp. 182-183.

29   Waldemar de Figueiredo Valente, *Misticismo e região: aspectos do sebastianismo nordestino* (Recife, Brazil: Instituto Joaquim Nabuco de Pesquisas Sociais, Ministério da Educação e Cultura, 1963), p. 15.

30   [Estrada], *Superstições*, pp. 37-39.

in the Northeast. More important, however, it was this last figure, the *beato*, who served as the precursor for the messianic leaders of the following century and individually participated in the gathering of the messianic group.

The lay religious groups, including brotherhoods, *confrarias* or more spontaneous religiously oriented associations, shrine communities and penitential groups, also continued to figure strongly in the lay religious activities of the eighteenth century.

The consolidation of the institutionalized lay religious brotherhoods progressed as it had in the seventeenth century, resulting in the ultimate use of the brotherhoods as means for social and religious control over the members by the Roman Church and by Brazilian elites. The brotherhoods of the white elites of the colony benefited from the discovery and mining of gold and diamonds. Several of their important churches, such as the chapel of São Francisco in Salvador and the chapel of the Ordem Terceira da Penitência de São Francisco in Rio de Janeiro and others in Minas Gervais, constructed during the early years of the eighteenth century, received elaborate fixtures of silver and gold as well as extensive gold foil over interior walls.

The Third Orders, that is, those lay groups officially connected with religious orders which continued to emphasize religious devotion and pious activities flourished during this period as well. These groups imitated the life of the ordained friar without requiring abandonment of secular and familial ties and maintained the lay religious ideal in a structured form in a way that the brotherhoods no longer could.

More spontaneous groups had become increasingly popular and acceptable during this period. It was not unusual, therefore, to find a community of men attached to a shrine or *ermida*. These men were dedicated to a life of intense religious devotion, yet their community retained its lay, and thus unique, nature.

In this century, such lay groups formed in conjunction with the *ermida* Nossa Senhora Mãe dos Homens on the Serra do Caraçá and the *ermida* of the Serra of Piedade. These groups, generally under the direction or patronage of the *ermitão* officially in charge of the shrine, looked to the physical care and support of the shrine along with their more spiritual activities.[31]

At the same time, lay religious groups of men or of women were founded with the purpose of complete devotion to religious activities. These were constituted as alternatives to the institutionalized orders which were seen to be diminishing in numbers or in a state of decadence in Brazil. In 1729, for example, a group of lay women founded the convent of the Beatas da Ordem Franciscana in the chapel of Senhor Bom Jesus dos Perdões in a small village to the north of the city of Salvador in the province of Bahia. This group was not recognized by the Church, and for this reason its members were not officially permitted to profess religious vows.[32]

The continuation of the formation of lay religious groups and communities indicates that an alternative was still sought to the institutional religious orders in the Roman Church, as well as to the somewhat restrictive structures of the *irmandades* or brotherhoods. These latter had already in the earlier periods demonstrated a marked tendency toward social and benevolent activities in addition to or in place of religious devotion. Therefore, the laity of Brazil gathered in loosely structured groups, at shrine sites, following the *ermitão* or *beato*, for penitential purposes, or simply for increased involvement in the devotion to one special saint or aspect of God. The vitality of these groups, as well as their functions and structures, persisted in the organization of the three messianic movements of the nineteenth century.

The intensification of lay participation in religious activities in the eighteenth century may be understood in relation to two historical circumstances: first, the declining numbers and thus influence of the religious orders in the Northeast of Brazil in the Pombaline era; and second, the sudden increase in wealth and luxury enjoyed from the profits of mineral exploitation of Minas Gerais, with concomitant extravagance and perceived deterioration of morals. The lay religious individuals and groups responded to the circumstances by providing an alternate yet distinct religious way of life. The participants in these lay

---

31   Riolando Azzi, "Catolicismo popular e autoridade na evolução histórica do Brasil," *Religião e Sociedade* 1 (May 1977): 129.
32   Luís dos Santos Vilhena, *A Bahia no século XVIII*, 3 vols. (Bahia: Editora Itapuã, 1969), 3: 451.

religious activities turned from the vulgarity of the "golden age" in Brazil to penitence and poverty, in solitary or group expression. At the same time they filled the gap in religious leadership and in religious group participation created by the suppression of the Jesuits and other orders.

The shrines established or sanctioned by the Church never lacked for devotees, and the individuals who undertook the religious devotional life were generally encouraged by the Church and respected as genuinely holy men, or women, by the laity in general. The eremetical movement, including the spontaneous groups as well, was the focal point of religious history in the eighteenth century; through the tremendous increase in lay involvement in the cult, the nature of the Roman Catholic Church in the Northeast altered—from one dominated by clerics to one determined by the laity.

The messianic movements of the following period drew on the model of religious leadership, as of the *ermitão* or the *beato*, as well as on the organization structures of the lay religious groups, in their crucial formative stages. The *beatos* and previously established penitential or shrine groups also became attached to the movements, thus supporting their structure and growth.

Penitential Practices

During this time of increased lay religious activities, penitential practices persisted often as an integral part of special lay rituals such as *encommendação das almas* or as the behavioral ideal for the solitary *ermitão* or group of *penitentes*. This section on the configuration of penitential practices in the eighteenth century will consider, first, the continuing missionary example — through word and deed — of extreme penitential practices, including the specific models of Malagrida, Todi and Genova, and, second, the separate practices inaugurated by the laity, the popular lay penitential processions in the Northeast.

The eighteenth century was a period of "reform of the Christian life" in Portugal, stimulated by the founding of the Oratorian Order whose members worked through various provinces there before immigrating to the colony. This group emphasized exterior behavior — rather than

moral rectitude — in religious devotion and fashioned a scheduled system for worship: the members performed one hour of "mental prayer"
in the morning and one half-hour again in the afternoon, accompanied
by public auto-flagellation.[33]

This new enthusiasm for penitence by religious was not universally
accepted; it was also criticized in exhortatory writings such as those of
Jesuit Pedro de Catalayud as self-indulgence or pride. Catalayud wrote
warning of the vanities and passions of the spirit, which included *juízo
proprio*, self-judgement, criticizing those who "have more esteem for
external and noisy virtues which bring them more credit and the
opinion of holiness from the vulgar." He disdained those who "enjoy
counting their penitences and external practices" such as "disciplines
of the blood [flagellation to the point of bleeding], immoderate fasts,
frequent communion...[and] many solitary hours in prayer." He also
instructed his readers that association with those who "live well or
blessedly" did not make one holy as well.[34]

Nevertheless, in the interior of the Northeast, flagellation and other
forms of physical penance remained the major mode for atonement for
sins and for extreme expression of humility and devotion to Jesus and
his missionaries. The participants in the holy missions, or *santas
missões*, regularly included flagellation in the rituals of that intense
religious experience. Excited and dismayed by the vehement and
ominous preachings, the people flagellated themselves with iron-
tipped whips in order to demonstrate their fervor.[35]

The popular missionaries of the eighteenth century also gave ample
and personal support to the continuance of this aspect of the Luso-
Brazilian messianic tradition. Jesuit Gabriel Malagrida followed a pattern in his visits to small *sertanejo* villages which included several
sermons and an effective penitential procession. The first days of his
santa missão were devoted to preaching and hearing confessions.
When his word did not sufficiently move the listeners to repent for their
sins, Malagrida flagellated himself across the back and shoulders with
an iron chain until he fell, exhausted. Such demonstrations were

---

33   Hoornaert, "Terceiro período," *História da Igreja no Brasil* 1: 356-357.
34   Pedro de Catalayud, *Doutrinas práticas, que costuma explicar nas suas
Missoens* (Coimbra: Companhia de Jesus, 1747), p. 43.
35   Moraes, Filho, *Festas*, pp. 140-141.

rewarded by "prodigious conversions" of sinners and imitation of the practice by the laity. The *missão* ended with a penitential procession:

> In front was the cross, then many people in two lines, submitting themselves, for the expiation of sins, to all manner of maceration. Some dragged iron bars, others tied their hands tightly to their backs, others beat their shoulder with bloody disciplines, others wore crowns of thorns on their foreheads, some bound their arms in the shape of the cross to a bar of iron. Others, finally, carried enormous rocks or enormous crosses, all walking barefoot and reciting the psalms of penitence. At the end was Malagrida, barefoot, head crowned with thorns, a rope around his chest, crucifix in hand.[36]

Malagrida especially exerted himself in the attempt to bring to repentance those most entrenched in their evil ways. For these individuals he would again practice flagellation until blood ran on the chapel floor. He also continually warned the settlers of the backlands of the dire results of remorseless sinning; the floods, droughts and epidemics of the region were taken to be proof of his warnings.[37]

Anibal de Genova also regularly included an impressive *procissão de penitência* (penitential procession) in his missionary visits in Pernambuco. He gained followers from "all social categories" through his extraordinary performances.[38]

Appolônio de Todi, who worked in Bahia near the city of Salvador toward the end of the century, not only encouraged penitential practice, but also established a focal shrine for such activity. He founded a "holy mount" in the Serra de Piquaraça along the São Francisco River, converting the steep hill into a religious shrine of the Crucifixion. The path leading up was bordered by chapels for each Station of the Cross, that is, for each significant and stylized event on Jesus' path to his death at Calvary. Todi remained at the mount for part of each year, preaching the importance of Jesus' Passion and the value of the imitation of his suffering.[39]

The practice of self-flagellation among the laity, as noted in the above chapters, was already well established. These continuing

---

36   Mury, *História de Gabriel Malagrida*, pp. 91-92.
37   Ibid., p. 72.
38   Primeiro, *Capuchinhos*, pp. 186-187.
39   Hoornaert, "Primeiro período," *História da Igreja no Brasil*, 1: 113.

examples from the missionaries, the religious representatives of the somewhat remote Roman Catholic institution, supported this lay practice.

Individual *penitentes* and penitential groups independently adopted the rigorous practices of fasts and self-flagellation and centered their lives of religious devotion on these. The *beato*, as the *ermitão* before him, also perpetuated the penitential practices and provided a definite, familiar model for appropriate religious activity. Part of the customary baggage of these wanderers was a cane, piece of reed, rope, thorny branch or iron-tipped whip for self-flagellation. *Beatos* followed a strict schedule, as the missionaries had, for the discipline: flagellation was practiced at night or at sunset and dawn or three times a day, accompanied by the recitation of a special prayer or psalm. Those lay persons who joined the *beato* in his travels, as well as those whom he counseled during his temporary residence in villages, were influenced by his saintly behavior and followed his example in this aspect so that they, too, might be considered holy.

The Processions of Ashes of Recife and Olinda, in Pernambuco, were celebrated events of the religious spirit of the people, although disdained by the elites and eventually banned by the ecclesiastical authorities. This event in Recife of 1720, apparently accompanied by symbolically costumed figures, was commemorated and condemned by the poet and Carmelite, Pacífico de Amaral:

> To the men who reason with science,
> Those who have certainty in speaking,
> These I ask to tell me if it is for the good,
> If penitence touches and provokes,

> To see a crude yokel (the height of dementia!)
> Come running in front of a procession;
> Just as Adam and Eve; more again,
> An angel and Satan in pure essence.

> The first wielding a whip
> To thrash without pain, one after another, the crude ones,
> This he carries in exchange for the fruit.

> And the last thirsty for carnage
> Wishes the infantile mob be immolated,
> But dreads the angel before courage.

And they think that with this laughable scene
They might inculcate penitence in the soul!
Create faith? Oh, no, it is not possible![40]

In Olinda, the neighboring city, a much later description of its Procession of Penitents depicted the parade of nearly two hundred young men and boys, barefoot, wearing only sackcloth or a brief white robe. In their midst also walked twenty or thirty costumed figures who represented "Christian virtues." The procession was led by a fearful figure of death, and some among the young participants also practiced self-flagellation to enhance the penitential message.[41]

Despite limited but significant opposition to and criticism of the phenomenon of auto-flagellation in the Northeast, this and other penitential practices continued to be a vital part of religiosity in this region. Accepted as an appropriate and even superior means to express devotion to the divine cult and sincere repentance for sins, extreme penitence was supported by missionaries such as Malagrida and Genova, by the *beatos* of the backlands, and in the penitential processions of Pernambuco, which were organized and staged by the laity.

The vitality of this practice was related not only to its significance as *imitatio Christi* or as the ideal mode for physical mortification but also to the strength and influence of the groups which focused their structure and rituals — even temporarily — on this activity. It is in this aspect, that is, as an organizational principle, as well as in its aspect as ideal religious behavior that these penitential practices form part of the Luso-Brazilian messianic tradition.

The eighteenth century in the Northeast of Brazil witnessed the distinct trend of increased lay participation in and determination of the Roman Catholic cult, related to and resultant of the suppression of the religious orders there.

Judeo-Christian messianic beliefs, inextricably linked with Portuguese Sebastianism, had been incorporated into the popular religious belief structure of the descendants of the Portuguese settlers. Further emphatic discourses, such as those of Vieira, Bento da

---

40   Costa, "Folk-lore pernambucano," p. 199. My literal translation of this piece does not pretend to capture the poetic imagery and language of this popular poet.

41   Ibid., pp. 199-200.

Trindade and Angelo dos Reis, and the ominous warnings of preachers in *santas missões* reinforced the stability and transmission of these beliefs. The devotional beliefs of the cult of the saints also supported messianism in two ways: first, through its divulgation of messianic-type legends of specific saints, the structural elements of this special belief were repeated and maintained; and, second, the strong independence of the cult lent itself to the continuation of these related beliefs and the rituals linked with them, to the formation of later messianic movements.

In the wake of the expelled Jesuits and in the absence of ordained missionaries, lay religious activities at the individual and group levels flourished during this period. The *ermitães* of localized shrine cults, whose increased numbers and influence resulted in ecclesiastical regulation, and the other solitary religious figures, the *beato* and the *penitente*, followed the example of the lone peregrinating missionary and were received and respected by villagers in the Northeast. At the same time several of the formal brotherhoods developed into primarily social or benevolent groups, while the *Ordens Terceiras*, the Third Orders, and spontaneous shrine communities, penitential and other lay religious groups gained increasing numbers of the devout laity. These latter groups thus secured the function and structure of lay religious association which was adopted by the messianic movements of the following century.

Finally, the practice of self-flagellation and other extreme modes of penitence, crystallizing as they did the perfect act of atonement for sins, were continued through the examples and usages of the missionaries Malagrida, Genova and Todi, the *beatos* of the backlands and the lay penitential processions. This continuance bore the key organizational principles and religious rituals adapted in the messianic movements.

These eighteenth-century manifestations of the three aspects of the Luso-Brazilian messianic tradition, exhibiting slight deviation from the beliefs and practices found in sixteenth-century Portugal, again demonstrate the significance and durability of the messianic tradition. These specific elements, after at least three centuries of development, would contribute to the formulation of the three messianic movements of the nineteenth century.

Chapter 8

Brazil: From Colony to Republic, 1800-1899

The nineteenth century was a period of tremendous change in Brazil. During this time, Brazil hosted the thirteen-year exile of the Portuguese king João VI and became successively a subjugate kingdom, an independent empire and a republic. Concomitantly, religious and ecclesiastical events changed the religious history of Brazil; included among these events were the controversy on the participation of clerics in the Masonic Order, conflict over the dominance of the State over the Church, the revival in evangelization by the Church in the Northeast, and finally three messianic movements, begun in 1817, 1836 and the 1870s.

This chapter on the Luso-Brazilian messianic tradition in the nineteenth century will begin with brief consideration of the significant historical circumstances of the period and elements of the three aspects of the messianic tradition, that is, the messianic beliefs, lay religious activities and penitential practice of the Northeast.

Historical Circumstances

At the beginning of the nineteenth century, Prince-Regent João VI, ruling on behalf of his insane mother, found his Portuguese empire increasingly involved with the European struggles against Napoleon. Portugal had aligned itself with England against France and Spain in an effort to maintain neutrality and determined to refuse any concessions demanded by the Emperor Napoleon. As a result of these policies, Portugal was faced with an invasion of Napoleonic troops in 1806-1807, sent to enforce Napoleon's long-distance edicts. The French army, under General Junot, advanced across Iberia with the intent of conquering and dividing Portugal; as Junot entered Lisbon in 1807, the Portuguese royal family and its entire court disembarked for Brazil.

151

Portugal, with the aid of British marshals and troops, rebelled against the Napoleonic forces, pushing them back city by city. The attempt to retake Iberia was launched in 1810, but by 1811 Generals Wellington and Massena had victoriously ended all battles over Portugal. After these bitter wars, the chaotic economic and social conditions in the homeland and the establishment of an interim revolutionary government did not succeed in recalling João VI until 1821.

Brazil, however, was enjoying its new status as focal point of the Portuguese empire and the booming economic growth precipitated by the presence and power of the king and court. João had finally opened the ports of Brazil, hitherto used only by Portuguese ships, to trade from all nations, lifted the long-standing restrictions on manufacture, encouraged agricultural improvements through special prizes, and allowed the first Brazilian printing press to open. The Court established the Bank of Brazil and in 1814 the National Library was begun and the first newspapers printed. Brazil was raised to the status of kingdom in 1815, thus nominally equal to Portugal. More important, the presence of the royal government unified Brazil and thus advanced the centralization of political authority. Brazilian-born Portuguese began to participate in the royal government, taking high offices; these encouraged the king's prolonged stay in Brazil in order not to lose their new status and benefits.

In 1821, however, João VI bowed to the pressures of English emissaries, Portuguese nationals and the Côrtes and returned to Lisbon, leaving his son and heir Pedro in Brazil. Once he had returned, the Côrtes made unmistakable efforts to reduce the status and freedom of Brazil in the Portuguese empire and immediately demanded Pedro's return as well. Pedro refused and within a year declared Brazil an independent empire under his rule.

The Brazilian constitution of 1824 established four branches of the imperial government: the executive, the legislative, the judiciary and the moderative; the first and the last were invested in the Emperor, giving him undeniable power in his realm. The First Empire under Pedro I was a turbulent period, and Pedro remained involved with disputes in Portugal over succession. When João VI died in 1826, leaving his daughter Maria-Isabel as regent, Pedro I contested his right to the throne with his younger brother Miguel. In 1831, in the face of growing discontent in Brazil over his European concerns, Pedro abdicated his imperial throne in favor of his son Pedro II and left for Europe.

There he fought to secure the Portuguese throne for his daughter Maria da Glória, who later ruled as Maria II of Portugal.

Until the young Pedro reached his majority, however, regencies of three men, later of a single minister, controlled the Brazilian government. Continued anti-Portuguese sentiment and republican rebellions led to Pedro's coronation in 1840, three years earlier than planned.

Pedro II, acclaimed as the first Brazilian-born ruler, was a benevolent but regalistic ruler. Through his own method of appointment of ministers he effectively introduced parliamentary government to his empire. He securely maintained his executive and moderative powers, with the right to call and dissolve the Assembly and to veto all legislation, and regularly installed Assemblies, alternating the dominant political party each session.

The latter half of the nineteenth century saw the new beginnings of republican sentiment in Brazil in reaction to Pedro's unswerving dominance and the influx of ideas from abroad. In 1884, the first republicans held Assembly seats. Pedro's conflicts with the Roman Church, involvement in costly war, controversy over abolition and opposition from the military, together with other significant factors, led to the end of the monarchy and the declaration of the Republic in 1889. Pedro abdicated to the head of the military, General Deodoro, and left Brazil.

During the Second Empire under Pedro II the Brazilian government had attempted to manage rationally the growing demand for the abolition of slavery. In 1850, yielding to pressure from abroad, slave importation from Africa was banned, and in 1871 the Law of the Free Womb promulgated, which determined that all children born to slaves would be free. The government continually encouraged European immigration to make up the diminishing cheap labor force, and private manumission became widespread. In 1885 all slaves over 65 years of age were declared freed, and finally, yielding this time to internal pressures, Pedro's Assembly liberated the remaining slaves in 1888.

The precarious balance between powers of Church and State was not without disruption during this time, although the diminished ranks and wealth of the Brazilian Roman Catholic Church inevitably subordinated it to the more powerful State. Pedro I had assumed the right of the *padroado*, that is, of patronage, and was not challenged in this by Rome; both he and his successor, however, entered into significant disputes with the Papal See.

The first major dispute arose in 1834 over the nominee for the position of Bishop of Rio de Janeiro, António Maria de Mouro. Mouro had advocated slackening of the celibacy requirement for clerics and was therefore opposed by the Vatican. The Brazilian government supported his appointment, but the Pope declined to install him. The issue was settled when Mouro himself withdrew.

The second controversy arose within Brazil over the Masonic Order. In 1864 the Pope had issued an encyclical denouncing that order; the Emperor Pedro II, however, assuming his patronage right, did not approve the official circulation of that encyclical in Brazil. Pedro met with opposition from Brazilian clergy whom he had had educated in Europe in a program to improve the status and quality of the clergy in general; these had returned to Brazil with a European education and ultramontane intent to support papal policies over those of the empire. Bishop Vital Maria Gonçalves de Oliveira of Pernambuco therefore followed the dictates of the anti-Masonic encyclical and called for the expulsion of Masons from religious and social groups, particularly from the brotherhoods. The members of these elite groups protested to the Emperor; Bishop Vital was brought to trial by the Brazilian government in 1874 and found guilty of violations of the criminal code and Constitution. A similar incident with a second cleric followed. Harmony was later restored with a declaration of amnesty by Pedro, but the hierarchy of the Brazilian Church gradually withdrew its political support from the ruler of the Second Empire.

Certain restrictions on the Church were also set by means of Constitutional and additional acts: the Constitution of 1823 allowed religious freedom but designated Roman Catholicism as the state religion, granting the rights of *padroado* (patronage) and *pase* (approval) of pontifical documents to the Emperor. Religious clergy were to be supported from the public treasury and were thus under the direct control of the government. The law enacted in 1828 banned foreign friars and any members of religious orders who owed obedience to superiors not residing in Brazil; new religious orders were prohibited and new novices in the established orders were restricted.[1]

---

1   J. Lloyd Mecham, *Church and State in Latin America* (Chapel Hill: The University of North Carolina Press, 1934), pp. 307-309, 312-313.

The monarchy was overthrown and the Republic installed in a bloodless coup effected by the military in 1889. Church and State were declared separate and, in the hiatus between the coup and the Constitution of 1891, a military dictatorship controlled Brazil. The Constitution was modelled primarily after that of the United States, yet the continuing military control and the persistence of imperial structures in nonurban areas obviated the establishment of completely democratic republicanism in Brazil.

The Luso-Brazilian Messianic Tradition: Three Aspects

Messianic Beliefs

In the beginning of the nineteenth century, those crucial elements of the messianic belief structure were present, perpetuated by the descendants of the Portuguese settlers: belief in the return of Sebastião, in Jesus as the Messiah, in other messiah-like figures such as Arthur, Charlemagne or one of the figures of the cult of the saints. Also recurrent was the belief that the history of Brazil and indeed of each person's life was part of a greater religious drama, that droughts and floods were signs of displeasure from God, and that the Messiah, in whatever incarnate form, would save or recreate Brazil and the Brazilians. The daily communication with the familiar saints of the popular or domestic Catholic cult reinforced this belief structure.

In this section the formative development of messianic beliefs in the nineteenth century will be discussed briefly; the significant beliefs of the messianic movements will be treated separately related to each movement.

At the beginning of this period, the Church recognized that Brazil and specifically the interior was in need of religious instruction and revitalization. Although restricted by diminished numbers and constrictive imperial regulations, the ecclesiastical institution nevertheless began its attempt to bring the word of God, and the Church, to those who had nearly forgotten it. In this move, newly written catechisms were promoted by Brazilian bishops as the principal tools for spreading beliefs and doctrines; ordained missionaries and lay catechists were chosen to teach these catechisms to the lay in small towns and communities.

The most popular catechism of this period was the so-called *Missões Abreviadas* ("Abbreviated Missions") written by the Jesuit Father Manuel José Gonçalves Couto. Couto actually composed two catechisms, the first entitled *Missão Abreviada para despertar os descuidas, convertar os Peccadores e sustentar o Fructo das Missões* ("Abbreviated Mission to awaken the neglected, convert the sinners, and sustain the Fruit of the Missions") and a later *Additamento* ("Addition").[2] These books were eventually published as a unit and enjoyed great popularity — and multiple editions. Couto systematically exhorts the reader or person to be instructed to abide by the laws and doctrines of the Church and, for that end, offers suitable themes for "meditation," recounting lives of the saints, miracle stories, details of the Passion of Jesus, and instructions on significant points of belief. In these texts, Couto emphasizes the dire fate of sinners and the saving role of Jesus the Messiah for all repenters. He warns that the Christians who cannot distinguish truth from heresy or idolatry sacrifice their eternal salvation and are on the path to "eternal torments."[3] His instructions were crucial in this, for "saving your soul is the most important business to be handled in this world." Couto's complicated doctrine concerning sins and Judgement even allowed sin after death, owing to the remaining scandal and bad example set during one's lifetime.[4]

The *Missões* also contained detailed treatment of the doctrine of salvation and the Last Days, with several special meditations on these subjects. The Instruction numbered seventy-seven, for example, was "On the Antichrist and the end of the world"; it offers these ominous thoughts with a doctrinal addition:

> The last times of the world have come, no one can contest this; already nearly everything is contaminated by sin and by evil; we are already living in those dangerous times about which the Sacred Scripture speaks; as soon as the evil reaches its height, the world will end....This is the conviction of many Catholics....[But] it is an article of faith, that first the Antichrist must come.[5]

---

2   Manuel José Gonçalves Couto, *Missão Abreviada*, twelfth ed. (Porto: Sebastião José Pereira, 1884); and *Additamento a Missão Abreviada*, sixth ed. (Porto: Sebastião José Pereira, 1882). The original editions were probably published before 1840.

3   Couto, *Missão Abreviada*, p. 28 (my translation in this and all following quotations).

4   Ibid., pp. 35, 72-73.

5   Ibid., p. 447.

Throughout the *Missões* Couto's concern is to communicate the doctrines and especially the salvific beliefs of the Church by means of effective and dramatic language and images. In light of this, his emphasis on sin and the end of the world, which reinforced the messianic beliefs of the people of the Northeast, is neither unexpected nor unorthodox.

The program of the *santas missões* or holy missions – the sporadic visits by missionaries to individual villages in the interior – had fallen into disuse during the last decade of the eighteenth century but was revived with new enthusiasm in the 1830s. The Dominican Order was at the forefront of this new religious zeal and was joined, particularly during the Second Empire, by Jesuits who were beginning to return surreptitiously to Brazil.[6]

The themes of evangelization in the *santas missões*, as in the earlier periods, dwelt on the rudimentary but critical points of Catholic doctrine. Both sermons and prayers placed emphasis on repentance for sin, the threat of eternal damnation, and the glory of salvation by the Messiah Jesus, particularly for the benefit of those backlanders or *sertanejos* who had never heard these doctrines from an official representative of the Roman Church. The missionaries developed religious programs similar to those of the seventeenth- and eighteenth-century missions: while in each village, they heard confessions, said Mass or led prayer services, baptized the young and consecrated marriages. For their prayer services they used works of catechetics such as that of Manuel Couto and special prayers or songs written for the laity. One such "song" or "holy exercise" refers to the purpose of the *santa missão* itself:

> For us has come the great time
> Of the Holy Mission
> Now we must talk
> Of salvation.

Another indicates the recurrent message from the missionaries:

---

6   Azzi, "Catolicismo popular," p. 143.

> Our eternal destiny
> Is there in glory
> Only the religion of Jesus
> Leads us to victory. [7]

The nineteenth century also saw a rebirth of Sebastianism, both in Portugal and in Brazil. In 1808 during the Napoleonic Wars and again in 1844 and 1860, new editions of the *Trovas* of Bandarra were published in Europe and transmitted to Brazil.

The foreign travelers in Brazil, authors of the effusive travel journals describing the wonders or oddities of that tropical land, remarked and recorded the belief in Sebastianism present in the nineteenth century. A French traveler in the 1830s wrote in explanation of Sebastianist belief to his readers at home:

> On the Sect of the Sebastianists. At once and a propos of the saint venerated by the inhabitants of Rio [de Janeiro], we have named the young king who founded [that] city and who was religiously placed under his protection…Who would believe that in the nineteenth century one would see renewed, in Brazil and in Portugal, the bizarre myth which accorded a sort of immortality to King Arthur, and…that in diverse periods one might wait for him as a sort of messiah. This is what is happening, however, in our days for the King Dom Sebastião; and the sect, being numerous, is no less extravagant. [8]

A well-known British writer added, a decade later:

> In various parts of Brazil, I meet with many individuals belonging to that remarkable sect called Sebastianists; they take this appellation from their belief in the return to earth of King Dom Sebastian, who fell in the celebrated battle of Alcazarquebir, while leading on his army against the Moors. Those who profess this belief, are said to be more numerous in Brazil than in

---

7   *Cânticos e piedosos exercícios para uso das santas missões compilados por um Missionário Franciscano* (Petrópolis: Editora Vozes Ltda., 1946), p. 3.

8   Ferdinand Dénis, *Brésil* (Paris: Firmin Didot Frères, Ed., 1837), pp. 130-131.

Portugal: on his return, they say, that Brazil will enjoy the most perfect state of happiness, and all that our millenarians anticipate, will be fully realized.[9]

Sebastianism was used as a thematic background in a satirical play which was composed by the Brazilian author Manoel de Araújo Porto Alegre in 1853, although apparently not performed. The play was entitled, "The Sebastianist," and while the plot revolved around a young man's unrequited love for an elusive young woman named Sebastiana, the author also took the opportunity to ridicule the widespread belief in the return of Sebastião, referring, for example, to Bandarra as the dragon guarding the house of the young woman in question.[10] By 1850 there was also a large body of prophetic tracts and poems associated with the *Trovas*, some attributed, albeit falsely, to Bandarra. These works appeared gathered in volumes of collections of wonder stories or prophetic stories and were listed and briefly quoted in works which vehemently criticized the continued belief in Sebastianism.[11]

Apart from this clamorous revitalization, Sebastianism had also remained an integral element in the religious beliefs in the backlands of the Northeast. The backlands tradition of Sebastianism, or *sebastianismo caboclo*, was integrated with stories of saints and miracles, prophecies announcing the end of the world, and messianic-like themes of the popular literature, the *cordel*. The literary cycle or *ciclo* of Sebastianism was related to a "messianic cycle" of apocalyptic elements, including numerological calculations of the crucial dates of Sebastião's arrival in years numbered 55, 66 or 88, or 60, 70 and 80.[12]

---

9   George Gardner, *Travels in the Interior of Brazil* (London: Reeves Brothers, 1846; condensed reprint ed., New York: AMS Press, 1970), p. 218.

10   Manoel de Araújo Porto Alegre, "O Sebastianista" (Rio de Janeiro, 1853), Ms., Coleção Araújo Porto Alegre, Instituto Histórico e Geográfico Brasileiro; Act 1 (second version). Two incomplete versions of this play are extant in the Coleção.

11   Such volumes are contained in the Manuscript Collection of the Instituto de Estudos Brasileiros, Universidade de São Paulo, from a private Paulista collector. One example of the highly critical works is that of José Agostalo de Macedo, *Os Sebastianistas* (Lisbon: António Rodrigues Galhardo, 1810).

12   Carlos Alberto Azevedo, *O Heróico e o messiânico na literatura de cordel*, Coleção Cadernos de Sociologia de Literatura, no. 1 (Recife: Edicordel/Edições, 1972), pp. 10, 18, 21-22.

This aspect of the Luso-Brazilian messianic tradition, comprising the messianic and Sebastianist beliefs of the residents in the Northeast together with the religious lessons learned from the circulated teaching catechisms such as the *Missões Abreviadas* and from the sermons of missionaries in the *santas missões*, was, however, most vividly and violently expressed in the messianic movements of this period. These are considered separately below.

Lay Religious Activities

The lay religious activities in the Northeast of Brazil in the nineteenth century continued the forms and functions of lay groups and lay religious individuals, begun and developed in earlier periods. The lay religious brotherhoods or *irmandades*, for example, although they had become stratified and institutionalized by this period, had nonetheless contributed an accepted and adaptable socio-religious structure to the formation of lay religious groups in general in Brazil. In this section the continuing crisis of the lack of suitable clergy in the backlands will be considered, together with the developments of the nineteenth century related to this: the emergence of the religious leader Father Ibiapina, an acknowledged role model for lay religious men, and the growth in the phenomenon of the *beato*, including the appearance of several well-known individuals such as Beato Zé Lourenço and Antônio Maciel.

The decline of the religious orders in Brazil, having reached its extreme in the last decades of the eighteenth century, reversed slightly during the first half of the nineteenth century. The Papal Nuncios to Brazil during this time made especial mention of the dearth of priests, the endemic lack of seminarians to replace the diminished numbers, and the shockingly open immorality of parish clerics. Nuncio Caleppi, in Brazil between 1808 and 1817, reported that the lack of seminarians had forced the schools to graduate the few maleducated students they possessed with only brief lessons in grammar and a single course in morals to administer the sacraments. Pietro Ostrini, the Nuncio in the following decade, wrote to Rome that the worst example was being set by ignorant priests who "lived publicly with concubines, surrounded by children." Their village parishioners showed these no respect whatever and broke with the Church.[13]

Related to the general decline of the religious orders was the cotemporal decline in religious confraternities or *confraries*, those lay groups instituted and directed by members of religious orders. The laity turned increasingly to noninstitutional groups, such as the shrine-associated groups, the *penitentes*, and to the communities of the messianic movements.

One significant missionary figure remains in the chronicles of this period, however, owing to his zealous effort to restore Roman Catholicism in belief and ritual practice in the Northeast. Ibiapina (1806-1883) first trained as an attorney but entered a seminary and emerged as a missionary in 1853. Struggling against what he saw as the abandonment of the *sertanejos* (the backlanders) by the Church, Ibiapina traveled extensively through the area, initiating reconstructive work on churches and seminaries and evangelizing the inhabitants. He was a dedicated and devout preacher and a singular ascetic; he brought many back to the Catholic cult by his own example. Ibiapina also established sisterhoods and houses for unmarried and widowed women, similar to the houses of charity of the beguines in sixteenth-century Portugal; the residents of these houses adopted the dress and activities of nuns, calling themselves *beatas*.[14] Following the ideal example of Padre Ibiapina and of other ordained and lay religious figures, the *beato*, or holy man, had become a recognizable and revered person in the *sertão* or backlands. The chroniclers of the history and customs of the Northeast in the nineteenth century specified his characteristics and sharply distinguished the true or sincere *beato* from the hypocritical or power-hungry impostors. The *beato* was then a

---

13   Hildebrando Accioly, *Os Primeiros núncios no Brasil* (São Paulo: Instituto Progresso Editorial, 1949), pp. 24, 79-80. Cf. Gardner, *Travels*, p. 187.

14   Celso Mariz, *Ibiapina: um apóstolo do Nordeste* (João Pessoa, Paraíba, Brazil: A União, 1942), pp. 53, 90; Della Cava, *Miracle at Joaseiro*, p. 18.

celibate fellow, who makes vows of chastity (real or apparent), who lives on charity...He passes the day praying in churches, visiting the sick, burying the dead, teaching prayers to the believers, all in accordance with the concepts of the catechism![15]

This religious devotee wore the dark robe and various distinguishing accoutrements of the missionary or lay hermit, including innumerable holy objects about his neck and shoulders, such as scapulars, ribbons, medals and the reliquary called, in this period, the *mostra*.[16]

In the latter half of this century several renowned *beatos* made their presence felt in the religious events of the Northeast. One of these was Antônio Maciel, who began preaching in the *sertão* around 1872; later known as Antônio Conselheiro ("the Counselor"), he was the leader of the messianic movement at Canudos, Bahia. Another was the *beato* José Lourenço, known as Zé Lourenço, an esteemed black lay religious figure especially famed for his devotional and penitential practices. In the late 1890s he joined Maciel at Canudos as well.[17]

The lay religious activities of this period, supported by the dynamic example of the peregrinating missionary Ibiapina, indicate that although the laity of the Northeast were distant from the regulated institutions of the Roman Church, they still continued to join and maintain lay religious groups and support the figure of the lay religious *beato* in their stead. This lay support was manifested in the eager participation in the messianic movements.

Penitential Practices

The penitential practices, including self-flagellation, among laity and religious in the Northeast continued unabated in popularity. In this section the ongoing approval for this practice from the ecclesiastical institution, particularly in the *Missões Abreviadas*, as well as the active support by the laity in penitential groups, will be discussed.

---

15   Antônio Xavier de Oliveira, *Beatos e cangaceiros* (Rio de Janeiro: n.p., 1920), p. 39.
16   Alceu Maynard Araújo, *Folclore nacional*, 3 vols., second ed. (São Paulo: Edições Melhoramentos, 1953), 3: 300.
17   Aglae Lima de Oliveira, *Lampião, cangaço e Nordeste*, third ed. (Rio de Janeiro: Edições O Cruzeiro, 1970), p. 79.

The *santas missões*, still occasionally held in the *sertão*, placed considerable emphasis on penitence, particularly in physical expression, as part of its own special rituals and of normal Catholic behavior in repentance for sins. The penitential processions inaugurated by the missionaries were often continued by the laity in the months and years following the visit of the missionary, during Lent or in response to harsh droughts or sudden floods.

The popular catechism of the region, the *Missões Abreviadas* of Manuel Couto, vigorously supported penitence through physical mortification, as by self-flagellation. Couto explains that "only by the road of mortification and penitence" could one go to Heaven and urges all sinners to suffer as Jesus had, in an allegorical Meditation:

> Oh stop, cruel executioners! Stop tormenting Jesus Christ, who is holy and innocent; do you not see many and great sinners, and so criminal? So torment these, who are guilty; these are the ones who merit whipping.[18]

Although Couto assured the penitents that they need not practice those extreme measures which might damage their health, he nevertheless cites, in the lengthy hagiographic chapters, the extraordinary penitential practices of "some saints." He included as saintly examples S. Luiz Gonzago, who "very much loved mortifications," S. Francisco Xavier, who would "discipline himself with such rigor that blood ran from his body," Santa Thereza de Jesus, who "took rigorous disciplines," S. Domingos, who "practiced three [sessions of] disciplines each night" and so on.[19] It was these latter examples which were followed by the more assiduous among his readers and those instructed.

The practice of *encommendação das almas* persisted in the São Francisco River valley, there known as *alimentação das almas*, the "feeding of the souls." This practice of flagellation, held on Fridays at midnight, was accompanied by a mournful prayer for the dead in Purgatory, a *lamentação*. The ritual also included other prayers and litanies and served, until the present day, not only to save the souls

18 Couto, *Missão Abreviada*, pp. 100, 126.
19 Ibid., pp. 583, 594, 600, 624. The numerous examples of flagellant saints continues through page 680. The reader is reminded that "mortification" refers to physical abuse through fasting and public displays and "disciplines" are whippings.

already in Purgatory, but also to prevent one's own sojourn there after death.

In the region around Crato, the capital of Ceará, flagellation was reported to have "nearly an obligatory character." It was practiced regularly during Lent from 1857 through 1890.[20] The practice of flagellation, despite regular but mild repressive moves from the ecclesiastical authorities, had not ceased in the Northeast but had rather grown to the proportion that several bands of flagellants or *penitentes* circulated through the region, especially near Cariri, the São Francisco River valley. Adopting this extreme mode of penitence, the members of the groups were repenting for their own sins and for the sins of the community in the face of what they believed to be the imminent end of the world. These groups met in the isolated cemeteries of the *sertão* before crosses erected at crossroads or near small shrines or roadside chapels to pray and flagellate themselves or each other with leather whips tipped with tin or iron. They also appeared in regions beset by sudden natural crises, such as droughts, which phenomena were often interpreted as signs of disapproval from God, or as omens of the approaching cataclysm.[21]

The *penitentes* chanted or prayed during their rituals and produced songs such as the following from the end of the nineteenth century:

> Oh! my mother,
> Oh! what pain in my heart!
> The whip cuts, cuts
> On the backs of the penitents
> As Jesus was cut
> At the hour of communion!
>
> Oh! my mother,
> Oh! what pain in my heart!
> Inside paradise
> God will grant me pardon.

---

20   Araújo, *Folclore nacional*, 3: 28-31; Montenegro, *História do fanaticismo religioso*, p. 14.

21   Cesar, *Crendices do Nordeste*, pp. 133-134.

The brother says that it does not hurt
But he is one who feels the pain,
The whip cuts, cuts
on the back of the sinner![22]

One group of penitents located in the Cariri region was called the "Sociedade dos Serenos" ("Society of the Serene Ones") or the "Chios," apparently inaugurated in response to a prophecy of the end of the world made by a missionary in 1850. These held their rituals at night, meeting to pray or chant and flagellate; as they walked through the backlands, they also wore hairshirts and thorns. When they failed to survive on alms, however, they began to rob villagers and were expelled from the province.[23]

This widespread penitential activity among the laity, supported by the writings and teachings of the Roman Catholic missionaries, was clearly related to repeated sermons and prophetic warnings of the imminence of the end of the world. As such and as spontaneous lay activity in group formation, this third aspect of the Luso-Brazilian messianic tradition contributed to the development of the Northeastern messianic movements.

In this period in Brazil these three aspects of the messianic tradition, that is, the messianic beliefs, lay religious activities and penitential practices, continued strongly, bearing the religious elements and structures first glimpsed in sixteenth-century Portugal and developed in colonial Brazil. This complex messianic tradition, essentially grounded in the "popular" religious practices of the *sertanejos*, came to fruition in the appearance of the three messianic movements in Serra do Rodeador, Pedra Bonita, and Canudos. Each movement will be considered separately and particular emphasis drawn to those elements of the persistent tradition recurrently discussed in the above chapters.

---

22   Ibid., p. 135.
23   Otacélio Anselmo, *Padre Cícero, mito e realidade* (Rio de Janeiro: Editora Civilização Brasileira, 1968), p. 9. Euclides da Cunha, *Os Sertões*, p. 117, offers a considerably less sympathetic description.

Serra do Rodeador: 1819-1820

In 1817 in Recife, Pernambuco, an abortive attempt at an urban republican revolution had been staged by Roman Catholic priests and Masons. Two years later, however, a rather different movement was launched through the interior of Pernambuco and Alagoas to the South; this was the first messianic movement in the Northeast, centered later at the Serra do Rodeador.

Silvestre José do Santos had been a soldier in the Twelfth Battalion of the Militia, but toward the end of 1817 this intensely religious man began to travel through the backlands of Alagoas, preaching on the imminence of the end of the world to the *sertanejos* there.[24] He rapidly gathered a group of believers and settled temporarily in Lages do Canhoto but was expelled by local authorities because of his prophecies and religious doctrines.

In 1819 Silvestre established a village community in Southern Pernambuco on a hill called Rodeador near a large rock. There he first erected a chapel or hut for prayers and sermons and collected a following of from two to four hundred *sertanejos*, including women and children. Silvestre, called the Prophet and Mestre (Master) Quiou, relied upon another former soldier, Manoel Gomes das Virgens, as his auxiliary. Together they expounded and interpreted the doctrine and led the sect until its violent suppression in 1820.

The chapel at Rodeador had been constructed next to a holy or enchanted stone or boulder from which Silvestre and his aide were said to hear the voice of a female Saint, the Santa Milagrosa, or Miraculous Saint of the Rock. The voice revealed to them that King Sebastião and his army would emerge from the enchanted rock at the very place marked by a cross and would make Silvestre and Manoel princes of his new Realm and their followers wealthy nobles. The site was christened the City of Terrestrial Paradise and was also referred to as "the place of the miracle" or "the place of the enchantment."

---

24   The history of Silvestre and his group is derived from René Ribeiro, "O Episódio da Serra do Rodeador (1817-20): um movimento milenar e sebastianista," *Revista de Antropologia* 8 (December 1960): 133-144; Costa, "Folk-lore pernambucano," pp. 33-35; and Queiroz, *O Messianismo*, pp. 220-222.

With the aid of his second-in-command, Silvestre organized his followers rigidly and instructed them in the proper behavior and attitude to be maintained in preparation for the arrival of Sebastião. He structured the group as an *irmandade*, or brotherhood, such that all participants were called "brother" or "sister," and added significant points of military discipline and training as well. The two leaders, called "Procuradores de Jesus Christo" ("Proctors of Jesus Christ"), controlled the social and religious aspects of the group as a whole. Immediately subordinate to them was a Board of twelve men, the "learned ones," and other individuals with special titles and duties: these latter included a military commandant in charge of daily drills and marches, captains, ensigns, and male "Proctors of the honesty of men" and female "Proctors of the honesty of women" to prevent any religious or moral laxity in the group. The majority of the followers were "the learners"; when these numbered over one thousand, the New Age with Sebastião would be inaugurated.

The specially built chapel next to the Holy Rock of the Saint contained figures of Bom Jesus, of Our Lady of the Conception, and of many different locally popular saints. Each day the entire group gathered before the chapel to pray, sing, and listen to the sermons preached by Silvestre himself, often including new revelations from the Saint. Prayers included the common litanies, the rosary, the Office of our Lady and other customary recitations familiar to the people of the backlands from the rituals of the cult of the saints; special prayers were added by Silvestre or by one of his designated agents. Following night rituals, a large portion of the group, including many women, would practice the penitential rituals of rhythmic chanting and self-flagellation in order to perfect their own religious devotion to the sect and the Saint. Although reported to be illiterate, Silvestre was nonetheless knowledgeable of religious doctrine and rituals and was known to be an impressive orator. He preached each day on the coming reappearance of King Sebastião and on the necessity of devotion to Jesus. He promised fortunes and happiness to the devotees upon the arrival of King Sebastião and planned to conquer Jerusalem and all those people who opposed the sacred plan consecrated by the law of God. In case of battle, Silvestre assured his listeners that Sebastião would miraculously render them invisible to their enemies.

At the beginnings of the formation of his group, he had made a practice of sending the new adepts to the local priests for Mass and confession; as their numbers grew, however, he initiated a form of group confession made directly to the Saint of the Rock. Silvestre himself directed the required penance for the sins confessed. Through this act, he divested the group of all relations with the institutional Church but took no aggressive or hostile actions against either the priests or the Church.

One integral part of the religious rituals established in the group was an initiation ceremony for all men of the brotherhood. Each brother confessed his sins to the Saint of the Rock, and a special penance and absolution were given him by a daughter of one of the twelve "learned ones." Following absolution he was lifted by two brothers with un-sheathed swords before the altar of the chapel; there he solemnly swore to guard the secret of the *irmandade* and to fight to the death in defense of Jesus Christ and King Sebastião. Except for the young woman as-sisting in part of the ceremony, women were banned from viewing or participating in this ritual.

As Silvestre established himself at Rodeador, his fame as a prophet and healer – although there are no extant accounts of cures – spread through the vicinity. He and his lieutenant also sent specially chosen emissaries to proselytize in nearby communities and to invite all to live at the Serra do Rodeador and defend the cause of the true faith and religion of Jesus Christ and King Sebastião. Attracted to the life of cenobitic austerity and religious devotion with Silvestre were ranch workers, artisans, even deserters from the militia with their entire families. They gathered near Silvestre in order to communicate more closely with the saints and with Jesus, to express their devotion to the traditional religious cult and to achieve the ends of terrestrial salvation repeatedly promised in the religious teachings of the Church. Unable to participate fully in the rituals of the institutional Church in their own villages or to expect a proper religious burial because of their poverty (and, thus, lack of contributions to the local cleric), they readily turned to the familiar and evocative message of Silvestre's messianic move-ment. The brotherhood at Rodeador subsisted on communally shared donations from the members themselves, from supporters outside Rodeador and on produce raised on plots near the "place of enchant-ment."

Silvestre resisted the arguments of the parish priests who sought to dissuade him from his sacred purpose, separate the group and thus reintegrate the participants with the Roman Church. He was, however, unable to resist the repressive reaction of the harsh governor of the province of Pernambuco, Luis do Rêgo Barreto. Barreto viewed the

messianic group as a militaristic revolt against his authority and government and sent militia troops to suppress the group. In October 1820
the troops attacked the community and massacred most of the men and
many of the women there. Silvestre escaped the armed attack, but the
survivors, the wounded men, women and children, were taken to prison
for a short time and later released to their villages.

This messianic movement at Serra do Rodeador, Pernambuco, in
1819-1820 drew upon the established elements of the Luso-Brazilian
messianic tradition of the Northeast. The movement led by Silvestre
José dos Santos was founded on the messianic-type beliefs in the
miraculous return of D. Sebastião, a legend begun in 1578. The legendary motif which placed Sebastião under a secret enchantment connected with a particular location is related to the Arthurian legend of
the enchanted isle, as well as to the themes present in the Portuguese
myth of the *Encoberto*. The members also appealed to faith in Jesus
and employed aspects of the domestic cult of the saints in their rituals
in the chapel and in the relationship with the Saint of the Rock. The
designation of the rock as a holy site was similar to the establishment
of shrine sites near unusual rock formations in Brazil and to the devotion, which had been transplanted from Europe, to the aspect of Mary
as Nossa Senhora da Penha, "Our Lady of the Rock."

The movement itself was a lay religious group and led by a lay
religious leader similar in function and role to the ordained missionaries who had crossed the *sertão* and gathered lay followers. The
laity of the *sertão* had come together around Silvestre as around the
true representative of the Church and of Sebastião. The development
of the leader's role, similar to that in parallel movements such as those
messianic groups occurring in later years in Brazil, involved his increasing assumption of religious power and authority in the group. Acting
at first as a lay replacement for the absent or unacceptable missionary
or priest, Silvestre later took over priestly functions as preacher and
confessor. The distinction between ordained priest and lay religious
leader in messianic movements characteristically blurs; in some movements, such as that at Canudos, the leader may actually come to assume the role of the Messiah as well.

Penitential practices were also incorporated into the religious rituals
of the group at Rodeador, serving as a focal rite following daily prayers
and, thus, as an organizational principle for group cohesion.

In the messianic movement at Serra do Rodeador as well as in the
following two messianic movements were present elements of belief

and practice which were not integral to the Luso-Brazilian messianic tradition in the constitutive form discussed through this study. These religious beliefs and practices were, however, derived from other facets of the Roman Catholic religion or folk customs familiar to the people of the Northeast. At Serra do Rodeador several apparently foreign elements may be understood in terms of other, nonmessianic traditions. The initiation ceremony over which Silvestre presided had structural connections with similar rituals of entrance into the Brazilian Military Orders, which were prestigious social fraternities, or other brotherhoods. The use of swords in the ceremony supports such derivation; similar origin may be suggested for the titles of the "Proctors." The practice of communal confession, however, has no clear corollary in northeastern religious rituals; it may have been developed from the practice of universal or plenary indulgences at religious festivals or from the concept of group salvation of the messianic movement itself.

The three continuing aspects of the Luso-Brazilian messianic tradition, that is, the messianic beliefs, lay religious activities and penitential practices derived from the parallel and related beliefs and practices in Portugal and colonial Brazil, dominated the formation of this and of the two following messianic movements in the Northeast.

Pedra Bonita: 1836-1838

During the year 1836 a resident of Pernambuco, João Antônio dos Santos, began traveling through the Flores district with two large gemstones which he exhibited to the local residents.[25] João Antônio prophesied that the end of the world was imminent: that Sebastião and his court and army, temporarily under a powerful enchantment, were soon to break the enchantment and emerge to rule the world. João himself knew the secret of the enchantment and any followers who would support him would share in the power and wealth of the new kingdom. João preached this Sebastianist belief, inspired by a

25   The primary source for the history of Pedra Bonita is by Antônio Áttico de Souza Leite, "Memoria sobre a Pedra Bonita ou Reino encantado na comarca de Villa Bella, província de Pernambuco," *Revista do Instituto Archeológico e Geográphico de Pernambuco* 9 (1903-1904): 218-249. A derivative account appears in Queiroz, *O Messianismo*, pp. 222-224.

pamphlet he carried about with him which contained one of the legends then in vogue recounting the mysterious disappearance of Sebastião in Africa and his imminently expected resurrection.[26] João particularly emphasized the lines of the pamphlet's poem on the legend which indicated that the enchantment of Sebastião would end when "João married Maria"; when he himself contrived to marry a local girl named Maria, he gained renewed enthusiasm and increased numbers of followers and believers.

On the strength of these predictions and his personal religious fervor, João gathered a group of disciples and received loans of money, food and cattle. All of the loans were to be repaid twice over when the Kingdom was established.

This Sebastianist sect had been launched in the period of the strong influence of a new vicar for the three local districts. This vicar, learning of the new dissent group, requested that a renowned missionary be sent to the locale to hold a *santa missão* in order to dissuade João and his followers. The missionary succeeded in breaking up the nascent sect; João gave up his preaching and disappeared from Pernambuco.

Two years later João Ferreira, brother-in-law of João Antônio dos Santos, began to renew the same Sebastianist group in the same district. He too began to preach, predicting the end of the world and upcoming arrival of King Sebastião. Quickly gathering a large number of followers from the *sertão*, João Ferreira established his community at Pedra Bonita near a huge extraordinary rock formation, then designated the Rock of the Kingdom. The formation included two large upright boulders which were said to be the two towers of the royal cathedral and other large rocks and several caves; one large subterranean cave, used as a refectory room by the group, was called the Holy House, the *Santa Casa*, while another higher cave was the *santuário*, or chapel for prayers.

João dominated the group, holding sway as King, and introduced members of his family, including his father and brothers, as elites in his court hierarchy. One of these, Manoel Vieira, officiated as priest for the community, serving under the name Frei Simão; his name was apparently taken from the recently deceased Franciscan *capellão*, or

---

26   Leite, "Memoria sobre a Pedra Bonita," p. 221.

chaplain, of a nearby village. The community eventually numbered two or three hundred by local estimate and consisted mainly of ranch workers, cattle herders and sharecropping farmers who joined with their entire families. These individuals, generally of the lower social levels and of mixed Portuguese and Brazilindian descent, abandoned their work and homes to live in the community under João and pray with him for the resurrection of Sebastião.

As the king of his group, João wore a crown apparently constructed of vines. He preached to his followers daily from a high rock ledge, revealing the secrets of the enchantment of Sebastião to his disciples and leading them in the recitation of the familiar litanies, prayers and songs that made up their rituals. The members of the group also participated in two special rituals, each held frequently, each related to the arrival of Sebastião. The first involved the drinking of *vinho encantado*, enchanted wine, by the participants. The drink was a locally known intoxicant made from bark or root and under its influence João and his disciples envisioned King Sebastião, his court, his treasure, and their own future happiness in his terrestrial paradise. The second common ritual in the group was the marriage feast: João had initiated the practice of polygyny among his followers and urged marriages to be arranged before the breaking of the royal enchantment. João also reserved the right of the first night with each of the brides.

Because of the imminence of Sebastião's Kingdom, all personal vanity and hygiene was forbidden, including washing and cleaning. The members of the group were at first sustained by contributions but later took to scavenging fruit and meat from local ranches.

João predicted that the enchantment of the Kingdom and court of Sebastião would be broken only with the shedding of blood: after one hundred innocents were sacrificed, Sebastião would emerge from hiding. In May of 1838, João sought to hasten this event and began to berate his followers as weaklings and unbelievers. He insisted that one particular rock of the Pedra Bonita formation, called the rock of sacrifice, must be covered with blood of willing victims in order that the prophecy might be fulfilled. He assured them that all those sacrificed would be resurrected pure white, wealthy, powerful, young, and in the glorious army of King Sebastião. Under his influence the sacrifices began on May 14 with the voluntary deaths of his father and several other adults and the slaughter of children by their parents. The blood-letting continued until May 17, when João himself was killed and violently dismembered, in response to a new revelation that Sebastião required his death as well. The rock was then covered with the blood of thirty children, twelve men, eleven women and fourteen dogs; their bodies had been arranged on the ground around the rock formation. A large number of the group, however, had fled in order to avoid their own slaughter.

The new leader of the group, Pedro Antônio, decided to lead the remaining believers away from the decaying bodies to a nearby grove, where they could await Sebastião. There, while constructing temporary shelter, the group was attacked by members of an expeditionary force of cavalry and local ranchers. These had been sent by the police commissioner of the district who had received reports from those who had deserted the group during the earlier sacrifices. The remaining Sebastianists fought eagerly, believing that victory or a victorious resurrection awaited them and expecting to be joined in battle by Sebastião himself. The women and children who did not engage in the battle prayed and chanted loudly to Sebastião and to the saints. The expeditionary force won after only a brief fight; the surviving men were taken to prison and the women and children released to return to their villages.

After the battle, missionaries and local officials visited Pedra Bonita and wrote detailed descriptions of the bodies found there. The area is today considered to be haunted.

The district of Pedra Bonita was thus actually the site of two consecutive messianic movements: the first led by João Antônio dos Santos and aborted through ecclesiastical intervention, the second under the leadership of his brother-in-law, João Ferreira. As a whole, however, the movement at Pedra Bonita participated in the Luso-Brazilian messianic tradition and closely paralleled the movement of Serra do Rodeador in its specific, Sebastianist beliefs.

The messianic beliefs of the group centered at the rocks of Pedra Bonita had been derived from the local Pernambucano legends of Sebastião and his army; the first leader, João Antônio dos Santos, had as his own constant and reliable source a *cordel* pamphlet on this special legend. The two lay leaders, João Antônio and João Ferreira, drew their authority from the established role model of the lay religious leader or prophet-missionary; their followers gathered around them in the same manner as religious groups which were attached to pilgrimage shrines or individual *ermitães* or *beatos*.

Although the historical sources provide rather elaborate detailing of the rituals of the *vinho encantado* and marriages at Pedra Bonita, they are reticent on the subject of the other religious beliefs and practices of the movement. References are made, however, to the "common prayers," that is, the *benditos*, litanies and chants of the prayer rituals, and to the vehement sermons of João Ferreira, apparently patterned after the sermons on penitential and eschatological themes delivered by itinerant missionaries during *santas missões*. The focusing of the community at the rock formation at Pedra Bonita as at Serra do Rodeador recalled shrine and Marian devotion centers on rocks or ridges. The crown worn by João Ferreira may be linked both to the royal crown of the returning Sebastião and to the crown of thorns worn by Jesus.

Other elements present in the beliefs of this messianic movement are, as was the case at Serra do Rodeador, derived from nonmessianic religious or folk customs. Since the complete text of the *cordel* pamphlet used by João Antônio dos Santos is not extant, the range of assimilated belief contained in that Sebastianist poem is not known. For this reason, the source of the prophecy of João's marrying Maria may not be accurately ascertained; however, the prophecy is probably a late addition to the body of prophecies which the Sebastianist cycle incorporated. The *vinho encantado* used in the central ritual of the messianic group was a locally created intoxicant called *jurema* and has been connected with native religious ceremonies and with later Afro-Brazilian *candomblé* rituals. It has also been used as an aphrodisiac for magical purposes.

The most striking ritual of the group, their final self-sacrifice to break the enchantment of Sebastião, has been related both to the enigmatic legendary poems on the King and to the doctrines taught by missionaries, such as resurrection after death into the Celestial Kingdom of Paradise. Another contributive source, albeit remote, of the motif of the slaughter of the innocents may have been the biblical story of Herod's slaughter of the children (Mt. 2:16-18), available to the backlanders in the paraphrastic versions of the Bible.

The recognizable aspects of the Luso-Brazilian messianic tradition, that is, the messianic beliefs, lay religious activities and penitential practices which were elaborated in the messianic movements of Serra do Rodeador and Pedra Bonita, appear in further development in the later movement at Canudos.

Canudos: 1873-1897

The most widely known and studied of the modern Brazilian religious events is the messianic movement led by Antônio Maciel and established at Canudos, Bahia.[27]

Antônio Vicente Mendes Maciel, born into one of the two feuding families of the *sertão* of Ceará, had been unsuccessfully destined by his father for a career as a cleric in the Roman Church; owing to that, he received sufficient education to read and write and thus gain employment as a clerk in a small town in his province. After a series of upheavals in his personal life, Antônio abandoned the town around 1869 and devoted himself to a rigorously ascetic religious life, following the established examples of the missionaries and ambulatory *beatos*. He had as his personal role model the missionary Ibiapina, who had known the Maciel family.

As a religious pilgrim, Antônio crossed Ceará and Bahia in the years 1869-1872, coming again into towns in 1873 as a *beato* himself. Antônio dressed in a long blue tunic like the robe of the friars and let his hair and beard grow long. He was completely devoted to the religious life and to penitence; his solitary hours were spent reading books on the saints and other devotional works, and his penitential fervor and fasting had left him emaciated. He lived by begging, and the historical sources concur in the legendary report that he only accepted what was necessary for each day's sustenance.

In each town that Antônio visited, particularly those without resident clergy, he was welcomed by the laity; under his guidance, they prayed litanies and novenas, held penitential processions, rebuilt rundown chapels and cemeteries and inaugurated houses of charity for women. Antônio began to gain renown as a fiery and influential preacher: he warned the *sertanejos* of the consequence of their evil ways and induced them to burn or destroy those objects which were contrary to religion and morality. He assumed the pulpit of local churches at the invitation of the clergy who recognized his efficacy and

27 Chief sources for the history of this movement include Cunha, *Os Sertões*, translated as *Rebellion in the Backlands*, an unfortunately biased source; Abelardo Montenegro, *Antônio Conselheiro* (Fortaleza, Brazil: A. Batista Fontenelle, 1954); and José Calasans Brandão da Silva, *O Ciclo folclórico do Bom Jesus Conselheiro* (Bahia: Typografia Beneditina Ltda., 1950). Cf. Queiroz, *O Messianismo*, pp. 225-228.

popularity. Antônio characteristically employed simple but persuasive language to convey his developing message on the fate of sinners and the imminence of the end of the world. While the basis of his sermons was the recognizable Catholic eschatology of the missionaries, he also began to include in his predictions the promised return of King Sebastão to Brazil in fulfillment of the prophecy of the *Trovas* of Bandarra. Further, he spoke against unnecessary luxury and personal vanity, especially of women, and exhorted them to cut their hair and burn their fancier clothes.

Antônio relied upon two literary sources for the doctrine of his sermons: the *Missões Abreviadas*, that is, the catechism written by Manuel Couto, and the *Horas Marianas*, the office of Mary, which comprised prayers to this saint, probably compiled by a Franciscan monk. He also drew upon the wealth of messianic beliefs and legends which the popular Catholicism of the backlands preserved, combining these with his own interpretations of religious doctrines and historical events and further prophecies.

By 1876, Antônio had gathered a small following in his pilgrim's path from town to town. At each stop he made, people came from nearby villages and settlements in order to participate in his holy mission, his *santa missão*: they traveled to hear his sermons, pray with him, and consult with "Brother Antônio." Rituals were held in a chapel or church, if such existed, or before his own *oratório*, a portable wooden shrine which enclosed an image of Jesus crucified. As his prestige as a holy man grew, he was called Antônio Conselheiro, "the Counselor," and Santo Antônio Apparecido, "Saint Anthony on earth." His beliefs and behavior led his followers to regard him as a representative of God. During this period, a popular poem on his life and works emerged and was documented in 1879:

> From heaven came a light
> That Jesus Christ sent
> Saint Anthony on earth
> Free us from punishments!
> Who hears and does not learn
> Who knows and does not teach

On the Judgement Day
His soul will suffer![28]

During the months of June through August of 1872, Antônio was detained by the police in a small town in Bahia for having suggested disrespect to the local vicar. He was sent to Salvador and thence to Fortaleza, Ceará, was temporarily imprisoned and then released.

In the following years, Antônio continued his religious ascetic life, leading his lay group on his pilgrimage through the *sertão*. Ecclesiastical authorities, who had once condoned and even supported his activities, began to condemn his beliefs and discourage his followers. In 1882, the Archbishop of Bahia recommended to the parishes under his authority that they not invite Antônio to speak nor allow him access to church facilities. In 1887 the same Archbishop circulated another warning: that Antônio had been preaching subversive doctrines contrary to religion and the State and would agitate against duly constituted authority.[29]

Antônio settled his messianic group in the abandoned community called Canudos; they rebuilt the existing structures and added numerous shacks to house the growing numbers of members. In Canudos, Antônio remained the undeniable leader and religious authority. He himself continued to live as a penitent, spending long contemplative hours alone and eating very little.

The news of the settlement spread quickly in the backlands and men, women and children began to abandon their homes to join the holy community, to live in tents or under trees, in order to be near Antônio and under his religious rule. Each family was allowed a private space and a strip of farm land for a garden and was expected to give one-half of their possessions to the community and to share their produce. Contributions were also received from supporters in other villages; these sustained Antônio and the poorer members.

The focus of religious devotion at the settlement was the *santuário* or chapel which held the many statues and paintings of saints brought by the followers to Canudos. Antônio himself directed daily prayer

---

28 Sylvio Romero, *Cantos populares do Brasil* (Rio de Janeiro: Livraria Clássica de Alves and Cia., 1897), pp. vi-vii.
29 Montenegro, *Antônio Conselheiro*, pp. 24-25.

services of litanies, the rosary and the traditional ritual, of the cult of
the saints, of kissing the various images of the saints. He was assisted
in these by his twelve appointed apostles. Antônio also encouraged extreme penitential practices, particularly prolonged fasts, to the members of the group in order to prepare for the coming world changes. In
his frequent sermons he emphasized the imminence of the end of the
world, Judgement Day and the coming of Sebastião. He preached
against republicanism and, following the establishment of the Brazilian
Republic, denounced the new government as the reign of the
Antichrist. Poems written at Canudos by one of his followers detail his
beliefs:

> Dom Pedro the Second left
> For the kingdom of Lisbon
> The monarchy was ended
> Brazil became lost.
>
> Guaranteed by the law
> Are those evil ones
> We have the law of God
> They have the law of the dog!
>
> Disgraced are those:
> Establishing the election
> Destroying the law of God
> Upholding the law of the dog!
>
> Marriage is made
> Only to delude the people
> They will marry everyone
> In civil matrimony!
>
> Dom Sebastião is coming
> With a great regiment
> Ending the civil
> And establishing [true] marriage!
>
>
> The Anti-Christ was born
> To govern Brazil
> But here is one Counselor
> To free us from him!
> Coming to visit us
> Our king Dom Sebastião

Pity the poor fellow
Who is under the law of the dog![30]

In his sermons, Antônio offered significant and symbolic predictions for the future:

> In 1896 a thousand flocks must run from the beach to the backlands; then the backlands will become beach and the beach will become the backlands. In 1897 there will be much pasturage and few trails, and only one shepherd and only one flock. In 1898 there will be many hats and few heads. In 1899 the waters will turn to blood and the planet will appear at sunrise with the ray of the sun, the bough will find itself in the sky. There will be a great rain of stars, and then will come the end of the world. In 1900 the lights will be turned out. God said in the Gospel: I have a flock who walks outside of the sheepfold, and it is necessary that it be reunited because there is only one shepherd and only one flock![31]

He went on to describe the destruction of the world through war and the final triumphal return of Sebastião:

> In truth I say to you, when nations battle nations, Brazil with Brazil, England with England, Prussia with Prussia, Dom Sebastião will come out of the waves of the sea with his entire army. Since the beginning of the world he and his army have been enchanted, and will restore it with war. And when the enchantment was cast, he struck his sword into a rock up to its hilt, and said: Farewell, world! For a thousand and many to two thousand you will not come! On that day when he emerges with his army he will take all with the edge of the sword from this role [sic] of the Republic. The end of this war will be ended in the Holy House in Rome and the blood will go even to that great assembly.[32]

Antônio was vehemently opposed to the new tax laws and district reorganization which they entailed, as well as to other administrative results of the new Republic. It was his unabated support for the return of monarchy to control of Brazil which served as a primary reason for later governmental suppression of the "revolutionary" sect.

---

30   Cunha, *Os Sertões*, pp. 183-184; cf. *Rebellion*, pp. 163-164. As these lines indicate, Antônio was particularly opposed to the effects of the separation of Church and State, one of which was the establishment of civil marriage.

31   Cunha, *Os Sertões*, pp. 150-151; cf. *Rebellion*, p. 135. These and other predictions were found recorded on paper following the decimation of the community in 1897.

32   Cunha, *Os Sertões*, p. 151; cf. *Rebellion*, p. 136.

In 1895 two missionaries journeyed with a local vicar to the site of
Canudos in an attempt to break up the growing group around Antônio
Conselheiro and discourage that *beato* from his independent religious
and political stance. They remained in Canudos for four days perform-
ing marriage ceremonies, baptisms and hearing confessions of his followers; they failed, however, in their entreaties to Antônio and,
encountering hostility in the movement, left the area.

Antônio's fame and the account of his prophecies spread through
Bahia and Ceará as his community at Canudos expanded. New poems
appeared, attesting to his saintliness:

> Who wants a holy remedy
> Relief for everything
> Look for the Counselor
> Who is there in Canudos

and to his developing religious role:

> The sun has now risen
> In its full splendor
> Antônio has replaced Jesus
> And will free us from punishment.[33]

The messianic community drawn to the religious life directed by
Antônio also attracted other inhabitants of the *sertão*: the *jagunços* and
cangaceiros, notorious bandits and thieves of the Northeast. The addition of these members precipitated the eventual destruction of
Canudos and of the messianic movement. Antônio had been considered a threat to Church and State since 1872; his outlaw followers
and their raids on neighboring villages, combined with his own
conservative beliefs, brought the repressive attacks from state and
federal militia.

Thus, in 1896, the military campaigns against Canudos began, following an attack from Canudos on a local merchant. The first three
campaigns launched failed because they underestimated the numbers
and fervor of not only the bandits, but also the entire community under

---

33   Montenegro, *Antônio Conselheiro*, p. 60; and Silva, *O Ciclo folclórico*, p.
37. The remarkable line, "Antônio has replaced Jesus" (*"Antônio substitue Jesus"*),
indicates the significant position of Conselheiro in the religious beliefs of his
followers.

Antônio. One estimate had placed the population at four thousand; these were eager to enter the battle with the forces of the Anti-Christ and defend Antônio/Jesus the Counselor in the final battle. In 1897, however, a well-planned attack with bombings destroyed Canudos and slaughtered most of the inhabitants. Most of the survivors fled under attack, but three hundred older people, women and children were left to surrender. Antônio Conselheiro was found in his sanctuary, already dead of prolonged fasting.

The messianic movement at Canudos was the largest and most influential of Brazilian history. It drew participants from over a hundred miles away and had a lasting impact on that region of Bahia. Antônio Conselheiro, who was Saint Anthony on earth and, later, Good Jesus, is still considered a holy figure in the Northeast.

Antônio Maciel early assumed the dress and behavior of the *beato* and was recognized and welcomed as such by the backlanders wherever he ventured in Ceará, Bahia and Alagoas. In each town he visited he led prayers and penitential services, ministered to the sick and dying, gave religious counsel to the residents and preached on the coming of the end of the world. In these activities, Antônio continued the unbroken chain of the role of religious itinerants which had begun with the first missionaries in Brazil. This *beato* collected a following of lay adepts even in his early journeying between 1873 and 1880. When he established his religious center at Canudos, the messianic movement grew quickly—in numbers and influence. Several of the contemporary historians reported that the Conselheiro even affected local election results.

The messianic movement at Canudos brought together the three distinctive threads of the Luso-Brazilian messianic tradition in forms remarkably similar to those of sixteenth-century Portugal. Antônio and his followers believed in the return of King Sebastião, which belief had merged with beliefs in the Second Coming of Jesus, the end of the world from the canonical book Revelation, the battle with the Anti-Christ and the legend of Arthur. The prophetic themes which appeared in Antônio's predictions—the one flock out of many, the falling of the stars, sudden darkness and the internal wars which would set brother against brother—were drawn from the canonical Gospels. The image of the sword in the stone, however, is Arthurian in origin. The legends of Antônio himself were affiliated with the beliefs of the cult of the saints: he assumed the mythic role of Santo Antônio, one of the popular and therefore powerful saints of the region. From that role, and in a progression parallel to the displacement of Jesus by the saints, and of the ordained priest by the *beato* in the practice of the backlands, Antônio substituted for the messianic figure for the participants in the messianic movement.[34]

The group configuration at Canudos, structured such that Antônio dominated the group with twelve disciples immediately under him and the remainder of the community subordinate, reflected the forms of other lay religious groups such as the *irmandades* and shrine-attached groups. The spontaneous development of the movement, on the other hand, was related to that of the loosely structured or temporary devotional groups. Other groups migrated to Canudos to join the messianic movement and a number of well-known *beatos*, such as Zé Lourenço, also devoted themselves to the life under Antônio Conselheiro. Finally, Antônio incorporated extraordinary penitential practices into the rituals of his following, including self-flagellation and fasting, and it was determined that he himself died after a long period of rigid fasting.

The *jagunços* and *cangaceiros* who joined Antônio at Canudos were part of the historical upsurge of bandits and banditry in the Northeast after 1850. Some of these outlaws achieved local status as folk heroes, defiant of the remote monarchical or republican government, involved with the endemic feuding of the powerful Northeastern families; others were simply robbers and thieves.

---

34   Antônio Conselheiro's assumption of this role and his adherence to the prophetic Sebastianist beliefs are historically determined, despite the claims to the contrary by José Carlos de Ataliba Nogueira, *Antônio Conselheiro e Canudos: revisão historico*, second ed. (São Paulo: Editora Nacional, 1978). On the basis of a series of sermons attributed to the hand of Conselheiro, Nogueiro proposed that Antônio was a well-intentioned preacher with quite ordinary beliefs who had been maligned and persecuted by the ecclesiastical authorities because of his popularity. Nogueira verifies the authenticity of his documents based on the similarity of the script to that of two unpublished samples of Antônio's signature; Nogueira, however, fails to note that the few writers in the Brazil of that era utilized a standardized script for documents and that individual handwriting style is a relatively recent phenomenon. If the writing could be accurately assigned to a specific hand, it would not necessarily be that of the author: these "Predicas" or Sermons bear resemblances in style to that of the *Missões Abreviadas* and in content to the Office of Mary. This work and that of Edmundo Moniz, *A Guerra social de Canudos* (Rio de Janeiro: Editora Civilização Brasileira S. A., 1978), are clearly intended as attacks on the writing of Euclides da Cunha, rather than as original scholarship.

While Brazilian historians generally link the appearance and growth of the movement at Canudos with the upsurge of republicanism, it is clear that this messianic movement partakes of the Luso-Brazilian messianic tradition with its array of related elements and is significantly more than a minor local reaction to political events. Opposition to the Republic was a commonplace in that region. Antônio, however, had begun his devotion to the solitary religious life in 1869 and drew to himself the *sertanejos* who, familiar with the myths of the messiah and the lay religious structures and models, intended to begin a more intensely religious life and secure for themselves part of the promised glory.

The nineteenth century in Northeastern Brazil saw the continuation of the elements of the Luso-Brazilian messianic tradition transmitted through three centuries and their manifestation in three distinct messianic movements. Each of these movements, that at Serra do Rodeador in 1817-1819, at Pedra Bonita in 1836-1838 and at Canudos in 1882-1896, incorporated and developed the messianic beliefs, lay religious activities and penitential practices which that messianic tradition comprised.

Primary among the messianic and related beliefs of these three groups was the myth of the return of King Sebastião. For each group, Sebastião's return marked the end of this world and the beginning of a better one, invested with the power, glory and wealth of the legends of the royal court and of the Catholic image of Paradise. The belief structure of Judeo-Christian messianism, focused in Roman Catholic Brazil on the figure of Jesus, and the supportive beliefs of the cult of the saints, which assigned messianic-like roles to certain saints, were also apparent in each group's beliefs and contributed to the acceptability and stability of the Sebastianist myths.

The three groups formed as lay religious organizations, employing social relation structures established in the *irmandades*, *confrarias* and more spontaneous shrine-attached groups. The leaders in each messianic movement based their authority and religious behavior on the models of the ordained missionaries and lay religious individuals such as the *ermitão* and the *beato*.

Part of the religious rituals of each of the three movements were the penitential practices adopted by the Portuguese and Brazilian religious and laity as means for atonement for sins. Fasting and other physical penances were practiced in all three; self-flagellation was included as a special ritual at Serra do Rodeador and Canudos. These penitential practices, aside from their use as effective self-inflicted punishment for sins, also served as organizational motifs for the groups, as foci for devotional activities in group practice.

In this century, the three constitutive elements of the Luso-Brazilian messianic tradition continued and were vividly presented in the three extraordinary movements. This tradition did not, however, end with the nineteenth century or perish with the last survivors of Canudos. The Luso-Brazilian messianic tradition remains an integral part of the religiosity of the inhabitants of northeastern Brazil as well as other regions and continues to give impetus to new developments and to new movements avowing these special beliefs and practices.

Chapter 9

Summary and Conclusions

The purpose of this thesis has been to trace the appearance and development of the Luso-Brazilian messianic tradition in its three aspects of messianic and related religious beliefs, lay religious activities and penitential practices, including self-flagellation. The historical study of this tradition took as its beginning the sixteenth century in Portugal and moved thence through colonial and postcolonial Brazil to the explosive messianic movements of the nineteenth century. The intent of this endeavor has been to test the hypothesis that, prior to the formation of the messianic movements, there existed an established, available religious tradition of messianic beliefs and integrally connected practices and group relational structures from which the content and form of the eventual messianic movements were drawn.

The history of the Luso-Brazilian messianic tradition began for the purposes of this study in sixteenth-century Portugal at the time of the waning of power of the great Portuguese Empire. Portugal, diminutive in size in comparison to its Brazilian colony, nevertheless dominated and determined the political and religious development of Brazil through 1821.

The belief structure of messianism was firmly rooted in that early period in Portugal. Contributory elements of the belief structure were the beliefs of Judeo-Christian religions in a messiah, Portuguese legendary myths of the *Encoberto* or Hidden King, João Prestes and the tragic king Sebastião. The introduction of the *Trovas* of Bandarra during the 1540s and the strong presence of the cult of the saints gave a substantial impetus to the continuation of these elements.

The lay religious activities in groups and individual modes drew upon the organizational and behavioral patterns of the institutional orders of the Roman Catholic Church. In that early period, lay religious associations such as brotherhoods, Third Orders, beguine communities and less structured groups were available to those Portuguese who sought to express their religious devotion without permanently withdrawing from the secular way of life. During this time a small number of solitary shrine hermits and pilgrims also temporarily assumed a religious life like that of the eremetical orders.

Penitential practices, including self-flagellation, were widely accepted as appropriate physical atonement for sins among the religious orders, particularly among the Jesuits. During the sixteenth century these focal ritual practices were also adopted by the laity in groups under their own control or that of the Jesuit Order, thus establishing in a concrete form the organizational structures relevant to the messianic tradition.

In the sixteenth century in Brazil (1549-1599), a small number of these elements had been transplanted from Portugal and gave early indication of their later flourishing.

The catechistic and sermonic teachings of the religious orders who sent missionaries to Brazil emphasized the crucial Christian salvific beliefs which supported messianism, and teachers such as Jesuit José de Anchieta communicated these dramatically. *Cordel* literature and popular oral tradition served to transmit the continuing belief in Sebastianism.

A small number of lay religious brotherhoods were begun in this century in Brazil, perpetuating the structural model for group religious activities separate from the institutional forms of the Roman Catholic Church. At the same time, flagellant practices were introduced by the Jesuit and Franciscan missionaries in controlled group settings. The immigrant laity followed their example separately and added the usage of self-flagellation to the Portuguese customary ritual of *encommendação das almas*, mirroring with this exceptional focal ritual the structures of the other lay associations.

In the seventeenth century in Brazil, during which period the Portuguese throne was restored from Spanish control and gold was discovered in the colony, the Luso-Brazilian messianic tradition increased considerably in content and influence.

The dramatic baroque sermons of the neo-Sebastianist (or Johannist) António Vieira and of his religious contemporaries, as well as the special teachings of the holy missions or *santas missões*, not only reinforced the continuing belief in messianism and related myths but also supported the acceptability of the entire messianic belief structure through their institutional connections. Circulating pamphlets of popular romances transmitted the parallel legends of messiah-like heroes, and the cult of the saints transplanted from Portugal, in its practice of devotion and ritual dedicated to particular holy figures, echoed the content and form of the messianic beliefs as well.

The lay religious activities, including the group forms of the lay brotherhoods and confraternities, continued to grow in the seventeenth century. The first Brazilian appearance of the lay *ermitão*, or hermit, who took the itinerant missionary as the model for his solitary devotional life was recorded in the latter half of this century. These lay activities perpetuated the religious social formation structures from Portugal, thus providing an alternative means for the individual or group expression of religious sentiments.

In this period penitential practices, particularly self-flagellation, were emphasized through the teachings and example of several noted religious figures such as Eusébio de Mattos. Penitential processions were initiated among the laity, led or organized by missionaries, and groups of lay penitents temporarily adopted the practice of self-flagellation for remission of sins or during Lent. Through these examples and forms the practice of penitence remained an accepted part of religious ritual in the Northeast and an organizational principle for religious group formation.

In the eighteenth century in Brazil, in the era of the exploitation of the gold and diamond mines and of the Pombaline dictatorship, the messianic and related beliefs of the Luso-Brazilian messianic tradition continued strongly. Taught by preachers such as Angelo dos Reis, together with missionaries in *santas missões* and sustained in popular Sebastianist tracts and in the belief system of the expanding cult of the saints, the messianic and messianic-type legends familiar in earlier periods formed, by this period, an integral and even dominant part of the religious belief system of the settlers in the Northeast of Brazil.

Although the lay brotherhoods had become rather constrictive social associations, the other lay religious groups, confraternities, Third Orders and shrine-associated groups increased in numbers and strength in the absence of Jesuit and other religious orders. The lay *ermitão* and lay *beato*, in their role and function in the religious community and as solitary religious exemplars, filled the considerable gap in leadership and teaching left in the wake of the suppressed orders. These lay religious activities in the Northeast began to change and determine the nature of Roman Catholicism there, effectively reconstituting it as a lay-dominated cult.

Penitential practices, exemplified by the religious models of ordained missionaries and lay religious figures, persisted in group practice as an appropriate means for penance for one's sins and the sins of
others. As such, and therefore as part of the Luso-Brazilian messianic
tradition, these practices continued as the focal points for group associations.

In the nineteenth century in Brazil, the final time-period of this historical study, sweeping political changes took the colonial territory to
its new status in 1889 of Republic. At the same time, the three aspects
of the Luso-Brazilian messianic tradition in the Northeast continued
unabated as part of Brazilian culture.

The messianic beliefs and particularly Sebastianism spread through
the instruments of catechetics such as the text of Couto's important
Missões Abreviadas, through the salvific motifs of the newly resumed
practice of *santas missões* and through the heroic legend cycles of the
cordel. The cult of the saints, comprising messianic-like hagiographic
legends and key rituals, also contributed through this time to the continuance of the tradition.

Lay religious activities perpetuated the social structures for group
and individual relations and behavior. While again the lay brotherhoods had ceased to figure as effective noninstitutional religious
groups, less structured religious associations such as confraternities,
shrine communities and temporary groups — including those assembled for penitential practices — assumed and continued that crucial function. At the same time, *ermitães* or shrine-linked hermits and
the wandering *beatos* imitated and replaced the ordained missionaries.
These latter individuals, with the exception of such as Padre Ibiapina,
neglected the religious education of the backlanders.

Finally, the penitential practices, especially the extraordinary mode
of self-flagellation, found renewed reinforcement in sermonic themes
and the teachings of the *Missões Abreviadas*. The laity took up these
practices enthusiastically, particularly in penitential groups which,
temporarily or for long periods, devoted themselves to self-inflicted
punishment for their own and others' sins. In this way these practices
continued to serve as organizational principles as part of the Luso-
Brazilian messianic tradition.

The three messianic movements of the nineteenth century, at Serra
do Rodeador in 1819-1820, Pedra Bonita in 1836-1838, and Canudos
in 1882-1897, drew upon this continuing tradition of religious elements.
They held these beliefs, rituals and organizational dynamics in

common: (1) messianic beliefs, emphatically including the imminence of the end of the world and the need to prepare for Judgement Day, as well as Sebastianist beliefs, combined with parallel popular legends and myths and rituals derived from the cult of the saints; (2) lay religious organizational structures based on the Brazilian religious brotherhoods and confraternities together with the assumption by the leader of the role and function exemplified by the *beato*; and (3) penitential practices, including flagellant activity at Serra do Rodeador and Canudos, which served as focal behavioral and ritual patterns for group consolidation.

This summary demonstrates the presence of elements of the three aspects of the Luso-Brazilian messianic tradition in the continuum from sixteenth-century Portugal through nineteenth-century Brazil. Yet each aspect or category of elements of that tradition exhibited independently certain trends of development and underwent changes in the four centuries of transmission. In order to illustrate these trends, each aspect will be considered in turn and the development over time indicated.

The core belief of messianism of the Judeo-Christian religious system, that is, the belief in the coming or return of the Messiah and in the related circumstances of the Last Days and the final Judgement, served as the foundation for this first aspect of the messianic tradition. With continual emphasis from the preachers and catechists, this basic belief persisted through the entire span of history under study, although the Portuguese Jewish influence slackened sharply after transmission to the interior of Brazil. It provided, however, the central officially approved belief structure upon which the parallel legends grew and merged.

The Portuguese legends of João Prestes, Afonso Henriques and the *Encoberto* which were separately influential elements of the messianic tradition of sixteenth-century Portugal waned in importance as time passed. Their mythic symbols and structures were generally absorbed by the Sebastianist legend cycle. Belief in the return of Sebastião, which had begun in the years immediately following his death in 1578, underwent several changes. Through the time of the "Spanish captivity" it was a widely accepted belief, assumed by ecclesiastical or political elites and rural residents alike. The myth was readily appropriated during the Restoration and reign of João IV as supportive of João's claim to the Portuguese throne. Afterwards, however, Sebastianist beliefs in Brazil lost their general acceptability among members of the governmental and ecclesiastical hierarchy; they became, however, integral to the religious belief system of the descendants of the Portuguese settlers in the Northeast and continued as such through the nineteenth century. Other legendary material, including Arthurian legends which were already known in sixteenth-century Portugal and transmitted by *cordel* to Brazil, the legend of the life of Charlemagne which was introduced later, and the heroic tales of Portuguese folklore and Brazilian *cordel* literature also merged with the Judeo-Christian messianism and the Sebastianist cycle. The result of this merging is evident in the predictions of the end of the world in the sermons of Antônio Conselheiro at Canudos: he predicted the stormy Last Days, based on Christian canonical beliefs, incorporated recognizable elements of the Arthurian legend, and focused upon Sebastião himself as the messianic hero.

The cult of the saints, usually unacknowledged in Brazilian studies because of its inaccurately ascribed status as "popular" or "folk" religion, contributed to the pattern of messianic beliefs as well. The hagiographic legends of its saints contained messianic or salvific motifs, and the rituals centered on the images of the saints persisted even in the communities of the messianic movements of the nineteenth century. In sixteenth-century Portugal, devotion to the cult of the saints was expressed on two levels: first, in village-wide devotion to a designated patron saint, and second, in individual devotion, particularly at special shrine sites or tombs of martyrs and local holy figures. In early colonial Brazil the lack of established shrines and the customary village community caused a diffusion of the devotion to the saints: it appeared primarily as a domestic practice, separate in each family. The trend toward public or communal devotion recommenced in the eighteenth and nineteenth centuries, and the cult of the saints, with prayer rituals of commonly known litanies, novenas and chants, became the primary means of religious expression for the *sertanejos* of the Northeast. This was especially the case in the absence of the institutional rituals of the Roman Catholic Church during the Pombaline suppression of missionary orders. The common communal presence of the practices of the cult of the saints was demonstrated in the gathering of the saints' images in the chapel of each of the three messianic movements and in their usage of the rituals and prayers.

As a continuing part of the messianic tradition, the thread of messianic beliefs developed through this extensive time period by absorbing and merging the established Portuguese legendary beliefs with parallel content and structure in the religious doctrinal and practical beliefs. This is not to say, however, that the diversity of elements present in the sixteenth century fused into an undiversified whole; on the contrary, many variant motifs and patterns remained throughout. Through this tradition, rather, a recognized structure of belief emerged based on the messianic mythic pattern of dismal world situation/sudden reversal by supernatural agent/glorious paradise on earth. This structure proved adaptable to heroic legends and other religious stories as well and was supported by parallel structures in European myths and the cult of the saints.

The aspect of lay religious activities generally exhibited a tendency toward increased numbers of participants and enhanced influence through the four centuries considered in this study.

The social groups developed in separate patterns. The *irmandades* or brotherhoods which had been uniquely founded in Portugal as religious rather than purely trade-related associations shifted definitely toward emphasis on social-charitable activities by the eighteenth century in Brazil. Although they had been extensively popular in Portugal, the brotherhoods did not secure a footing in the religious establishment of early colonial Brazil until well into the seventeenth century. With the incoming wealth of the mineral deposits of that colony, the Brazilian *irmandades* turned increasingly from solely religious purposes, obviating at the same time their function as available social formations for lay religious participation, secular alternatives to the religious orders. They had, however, contributed in two ways to the advancement of lay religious groups in general: first, as they had been approved and accepted means of religious expression from their first appearance, the brotherhoods thereby encouraged similar imitative groups, usually less rigidly conceived; and second, the internal structure of the brotherhoods, consisting of an administrative board of officers with designated duties governing the subordinate body of members, became a permanent element in the messianic tradition and was adapted to the formation of most other lay religious groups.

The Third Orders, those lay religious associations specifically attached to monastic orders, and confraternities retained their primarily religious ends, although these groups, as the brotherhoods, did not appear strongly in Brazil until the seventeenth century. The shrine-associated groups and beguine-type associations which had been neither securely established nor long tolerated in Portugal flourished after a century's hiatus with the erecting of shrine sites in Brazil. It is with these latter, spontaneously assembled, distinctly noninstitutional religious groups that the lay religious activities gained influence and numbers. These represented, particularly in times of diminished communication with the Church or of closure of religious orders to new novices, appropriate alternative means for the backlanders for intensive group participation in the religious cult.

The lay religious individuals, particularly after the end of the seventeenth century, were an astonishingly powerful factor in the religiosity of the Northeast. Figures like the *ermitão* and the *beato* had existed in Portugal of the sixteenth century, but these remained for the most part subordinate to the dictates of the Church, operating in designated offices and with limited power. The *ermitão* in Brazil, at first only loosely associated with a specific *ermida* or shrine, eventually became closely tied to shrine functions; his power was involved with the power of the shrine and, after the mid-eighteenth century, was under the regulating authority of the Roman Church. The *beato*, appearing after 1750, assumed a much freer role, accepting the function of the (then-missing) religious missionary, local priest and lay *ermitão* in his ministrations to his lay following. These two lay figures stimulated lay religious group formation as well: the *ermitão* gathered a shrine association of lay pilgrims under his direction, while the *beato* was usually joined by a small band of devotees on his travels.

The aspect of lay religious activities, in group and individual form, represented the clear trend toward lay dominance of religious devotions in the Northeast, to the extreme of substitution for the absent guidance and operations of the Church. The lay holy men and lay religious groups existed as alternatives to established or institutionally produced religious leaders and associations and, as such, continued and kept available for later formation of the messianic movements crucial social relational structures. Without the significant religious leadership role of the *beato* and the acceptable social pattern of the lay religious groups, the messianic movements could not have formed; they would have lacked the necessary organizational principles and focal religious leaders.

The persistence of penitential practices from Portugal to republican Brazil similarly contributed to the Luso-Brazilian messianic tradition with a trend of development analagous to that of the lay religious activities.

In the sixteenth century in Portugal, the extreme penitential practices which included self-flagellation appeared under the control of the religious orders, particularly the Jesuits. At that time, individual practice was undertaken by the Jesuits and lay penitential participation was under their direction. In Brazil, the example and influence from Jesuit and Franciscan missionaries perpetuated this pattern; in addition, independent lay practice of penitences in the *encommendação das almas* and Lenten or supplicant processions appropriated and significantly expanded the use of rigorous fasting and self-flagellation as lay religious ritual activity. In the late eighteenth century and through the nineteenth century, penitential groups circulated in the Northeast and, like their remote medieval antecedents, contributed to the growth of the messianic movements.

These penitential practices were most important to the messianic tradition as organizational or focal rituals in the group-formation process, as part of the dynamics for spontaneous association. Their increasingly lay nature substantiated, in a separate form, the trend of lay religious ascendency in the Northeast, and their group base for these activities mirrored the collective salvific perspective of the messianic beliefs.

While each of these three aspects of the Luso-Brazilian messianic tradition may be followed in its own trend of development, these aspects are not completely separable from one another, but are interconnected and interwoven in their historical occurrence. Messianism pervaded the religious beliefs of the Northeast, thus affecting the religious ends of the lay religious groups and individuals as well as the foundational beliefs of the penitential and flagellant groups. The religious benefits to be derived from increased religious devotion, shrine rituals, eremetic practices and flagellation were understood in the context of individual and group salvation and were thus informed by the messianic mythic structure. From a different perspective, the lay religious activities were continually linked with the other aspects of the messianic tradition. The rituals of the cult of the saints, particularly when expressed in group devotion, were themselves part of the lay religious trend, as were the penitential groups of the eighteenth century and the practice of *encommendação das almas*.

The general increase in the laicization of Roman Catholicism in the Northeast, together with the religious crisis triggered by the reduction and suppression of Brazilian monastic and secular orders, played significant roles as additional religious historical factors in the shaping of the Luso-Brazilian messianic tradition.

This reconstructive study of religion and history has demonstrated the existence and effect of the Luso-Brazilian messianic tradition, an intricate and complex trajectory of religious elements comprising three distinguishable and traceable tracks. That tradition antedated the appearance of the Brazilian messianic movements, underlay their beliefs and group structures and gave rise to their development. It persisted, in a certain sense, with its own history and pattern of change, part of religiosity in Portugal and Brazil, independent of nonreligious factors.

This model for the study of messianic movements, which essentially grounds the movements in a preexistent and developing religious messianic tradition of beliefs and related practices, has proven successful in this single historical study of Luso-Brazilian messianism. Through this study, messianic movements have been shown to be not freak occurrences or epiphenomenal in relation to the religious context, but rather founded in a religious tradition of considerable complexity and strength. Further, this perspective has suggested a depth of religiosity in these messianic movements, owing to their integration with the broader religious tradition, and thus has served to advance the understanding of this mode of religious expression. This model for historical study which emphasizes the foundation of religious tradition in this way may be suitable for application to the interpretation of other messianic movements as, again, part of the religious messianic tradition from which they emerge. From this perspective, which gives precedence to persisting religious factors in the development of religious movements, messianic movements may be seen to be integrated with a profound religious base, rather than existing in isolation. Factors usually ignored, such as parallel religious legends, supportive religious practices and essential group formations, are part of this perspective as well, for these substantiate the religious history and illustrate the connection of the messianic movement with its religious context.

This model for study, which relies on neither broad lateral comparisons nor a myopically limited field for investigation, but which expands the interpretation of messianic movements to include the supportive religious tradition from which they emerged, is therefore appropriate as a hermeneutic tool in the study of messianism and millenarianism in the diverse geographic and historical circumstances in which they have occurred.

Bibliography

Accioly, Hildebrando. *Os Primeiros núncios no Brasil.* São Paulo: Instituto Progresso Editorial, 1949.

Albuquerque, Ulysses Lins de. *Um Sertanejo e o sertão.* Rio de Janeiro: Livraria José Olympia Editora, 1957.

Almeida, Fortunado de. *História da Igreja em Portugal.* 4 vols. Coimbra: Imprensa Acadêmica, 1910-1922.

Alvarez, Eduardo. *Memoria açerca da batalha de Alcacer-Quibir.* Lisbon: Imprensa Nacional, 1892.

Alves, Joaquim. "Juazeiro, cidade mística." *Revista do Instituto do Ceará* 62 (1948): 16-32.

Alves, Marieta. *História da veneravel Ordem Terceira da Penitência do Seráfico Padre São Francisco da congregação da Bahia.* Bahia, Brazil: n.p., 1948.

Amarel, R. Joviano. *Os Prêtos do Rosário de São Paulo: subsídios históricos.* São Paulo: Edições Alvárico, 1953.

Ameal, João. *Santos portugueses.* Porto: Livraria Tavares Martins, 1957.

Anchieta, José de. *Na vila de Vitória e Na visitação de Santa Isabel.* Edited by M. de L. de Paula Martins. Documentação Linguística, no. 3. São Paulo: Museu Paulista, 1950.

_____. "Sermão do Padre Jozé d'Anchieta: In die convertionis S. Pauli, 1568, Piratininga." *Revista do Instituto Histórico e Geográfico Brasileiro* 54, Pt. 2 (1891): 109-130.

Anselmo, Otacélio. *Padre Cícero, mito e realidade.* Rio de Janeiro: Editora Civilização Brasileira, 1968.

António das Chagas. *Escola de Penitência, e flagello de viciosos costumes, Que consta de Sermoens Apostolicas do Muito Veneravel Padre António das Chagas.* Edited by Manoel da Conceicam. Lisbon: António Rodriques Galhardo, 1763.

Aragão, Pedro Moniz de. "Canudos e os monarquistas." *Revista do Instituto Histórico e Geográfico Brasileiro* 237, Pt. 1 (1957): 85-131.

Araújo, Alceu Maynard. *Folclore nacional.* 3 vols. Second edition. São Paulo: Edições Melhoramentos, 1964-1967.

Arraiz, Amador. *Dialogos de Dom Frey Amador Arraiz*. Coimbra: Diogo Gomes Lourenzo, 1604; reprint edition, Lisbon: Typografia Rollandia, 1846.

Audrim, José M. *Entre sertanejos e índios do norte: o bispo-missionário Dom Domingos Carrerot, O.P.* Rio de Janeiro: Livraria Agir Editora, 1946.

Azevedo, Carlos Alberto. *O Heróico e o messiânico na literatura de cordel*. Coleção Cadernos de Sociologia da Literatura, no. 1. Recife, Brazil: Edicordel/Edições, 1972.

Azevedo, João Lúcio de. *A Evolução do sebastianismo*. Second edition. Lisbon: Livraria Clássica Editora, 1947.

_____. *História de António Vieira*. 2 vols. Second edition. Lisbon: Livraria Clássica Editora de A. M. Texeira & Ca., 1931.

Azevedo, Thales de. *O Catholicismo no Brasil*. Rio de Janeiro: Ministério da Educação e Cultura, 1955.

Azzi, Riolando. "Catolicismo popular e autoridade na evolução histórico do Brasil." *Religião e Sociedade* 1 (1977): 125-156.

_____. "Eremitas e irmãos: uma forma da vida religiosa no Brasil antigo." *Convergência* 94 (1976): 370-383.

_____. "As Romarias no Brasil." *Religiosidade popular na América Latina, Revista de Cultura Vozes* 73 (1979): 39-54.

Baena, Antônio Nicolau Monteiro. *Bosquejo chronológico da Veneravel Ordem Terceira de São Francisco da Penitência do Gram-Pará*. Pará, Brazil: Commércio do Pará, 1878.

[Bandarra, Gonçalo Annes.] *Trovas do Bandarra*. Porto: Imprensa Popular de J. L. de Sousa, 1866.

Barata, Mário. *Igreja da Ordem Terceira da Penitência do Rio de Janeiro*. Rio de Janeiro: Livraria Agir Editora, 1975.

Barkun, Michael. *Disaster and the Millennium*. New Haven, Connecticut: Yale University Press, 1974.

Barroso, Gustavo. *A Margem da história do Ceará*. Ceará, Brazil: Imprensa Universitaria do Ceará, 1962.

Bastide, Roger. *Sociologia do folclore brasileiro*. São Paulo: Anhambi, 1959.

Batista, Sebastião Nunes, ed. *Antologia da literatura de cordel*. Natal, Brazil: Fundação José Augusto, 1977.

Beltrão, Luiz. *Comunição e folclore*. São Paulo: Edições Melhoramentos, 1971.

Bertram, James G. [William M. Cooper]. *Flagellation and the Flagellants*. New revised and corrected edition. London: W. Reeves, [1904].

Boxer, C. R. *The Dutch in Brazil: 1624-1654*. Hamden, Connecticut: Archon Books, 1973.

_____. *The Golden Age of Brazil: 1695-1750*. Berkeley: University of California Press, 1962.

_____. *The Portuguese Seaborne Empire: 1415-1825*. New York: A. A. Knopf, 1969.

Braga, Theophilo. *O Povo portuguêz nos seus costumes, crenças e tradições*. 2 vols. Lisbon: Livraria Ferreira Editora, 1885.

Brooks, Mary Elizabeth. *A King for Portugal*. Madison: University of Wisconsin Press, 1964.

Brown, Peter L. *The Cult of the Saints: Its Rise and Function in Latin Christianity*. Chicago: University of Chicago Press, 1981.

Burns, E. Bradford. *A History of Brazil*. New York: Columbia University Press, 1970.

Burridge, Kenelm. *Mambu*. New York: Harper and Row, 1960.

_____. *New Heaven, New Earth*. New York: Schocken Books, 1969.

Calatayud, Pedro de, Padre. *Doutrinas practicas, que costuma explicar nas suas Missoens*. Coimbra: Companhia de Jesus, 1747.

Caldas, José António. *Notícia geral de toda esta capitânia da Bahia desde o seu descobrimento ate o presente ano de 1759*. Lisbon: n.p., [1760].

Camargo, Paulo da Silveiro. *História ecclesiástica do Brasil*. Petrópolis: Editora Vozes Ltda., 1955.

Campos, Renato Carneiro. *Ideologia do poetas populares do Nordeste*. Second edition. Recife, Brazil: Instituto Joaquim Nabuco de Pesquisas Sociais, Ministério da Educação e Cultura, 1977.

Cânticos e piedosos exercícios para uso das santas missões complilados por um Missionário Franciscano. Petrópolis: Editora Vozes Ltda., 1946.

Cantril, Hudley. *The Psychology of Social Movements*. New York: John Wiley and Sons, Inc., 1963.

Cardim, Fernão. *Tratados da terra e gente do Brasil*. Second edition. São Paulo: Companhia Editora Nacional, 1939.

Cardoso, Jorge. *Agiologia lusitano dos sanctos*. 4 vols. Lisbon: Officina Craesbeekiana, 1652.

Cardozo, Manuel S. "The Lay Brotherhoods of Colonial Bahia." *The Catholic Historical Review* 33 (1947): 12-30.

Carrato, José Ferreira. *As Minas Gerais e os primórdios de Caraçá*. São Paulo: Companhia Editora Nacional, 1963.

Cascudo, Luis da Câmara. *Coisas que o povo diz*. Rio de Janeiro: Block Editores S. A., 1968.

_____. *Folclore do Brasil*. Rio de Janeiro: Editora Fundo de Cultura, 1967.

Castro, Joam [João] de. *Paraphrase et concordançia de alguas propheçias de Bandarra, çapateiro de Trancoso*. [Paris]: n.p., 1603; facsimile edition, Porto: Officina Typographica de A. F. Vasconcelos, 1901.

Castro, Luiz Christiano de. *A Catechese dos Indios: inefficacia e perigo das missões leigas, necessidade da catechese religiosa*. Rio de Janeiro: Typographia da Patria Brazileira, 1910.

Cesar, Getúlio. *Crendices do Nordeste*. Rio de Janeiro: Irmãos Pongetti Editores, 1941.

Christian, William A., Jr. *Local Religion in Sixteenth Century Spain*. Princeton, New Jersey: Princeton University Press, 1981.

Cidade, Hernani. *A Literatura autonomista sob os Filipes*. Lisbon: Ed. Livraria Sa da Costa, n.d.

Clastres, Hélène. *Terra sem mal*. Translated by Renato Janine Ribeiro. São Paulo: Editora Brasiliense S. A., 1978.

Cohn, Norman. *The Pursuit of the Millennium*. Second revised edition. London: Oxford University Press, 1961.

Costa, Francisco August Pereira da. "Folk-lore pernambucano." *Revista do Instituto Histórico e Geográfico Brasileiro* 70, Part 2 (1907): 5-641.

Coutinho, Afrânio. *An Introduction to Literature in Brazil*. Translated by Gregory Rabassa. New York: Columbia University Press, 1969.

Couto, Manoel José Gonçalves. *Missão Abreviada para despertar os descuidados, convertar os Peccadores e sustentar o Fructo das missões*. Twelfth edition. Porto: Sebastião José Pereira, 1884.

_____. *Additamento à Missão Abreviada*. Sixth edition. Porto: Sebastião José Pereira, 1882.

Cunha, Euclides da. *Os Sertões*. Fifth edition. Rio de Janeiro: Tecnoprint Gráfica Editora, 1967.

_____. *Rebellion in the Backlands*. Translated by Samuel Putnam. Chicago: University of Chicago Press, Phoenix Books, 1944.

d'Abbeville, Claude. *História da missão dos padres capuchinhos na Ilha do Maranhão e terras circumvizinhas*. Paris, n.p., 1614; reprint edition, São Paulo: Editora da Universidade de São Paulo, 1975.

d'Assumpção, Lino. *Os Jesuítas: o catolicismo no século XVI.* Lisbon: Guillard, Aillaud e Ca., 1888.

Delahaye, Hippolyte. *Les Origines du Culte des Martyrs.* Second revised edition. Brussels: Société des Bollandistes, 1933.

_____. *Sanctus: Essai sur le Culte des saints dans l'antiquité.* Brussels: Société des Bollandistes, 1927.

Della Cava, Ralph. "Brazilian Messianism and National Institutions: A Reappraisal of Canudos and Joaseiro." *Hispanic-American Historical Review* 48 (1968): 402-420.

_____. *Miracle at Joaseiro.* New York: Columbia University Press, 1970.

Dénis, Ferdinand. *Brésil.* Paris: Firmin Didot Frères, Ed., 1837.

Dias, Carlos Manheiro, gen. ed. *História da colonização portuguesa do Brasil.* 3 vols. Porto: Litografia Nacional, 1924. Vol. 3, Chapter 8: "A Instituição do govêrno geral," by Pedro de Azevedo.

Dias, Jaime Lopes. *Etnografia da Beira.* 9 vols. Lisbon: Livraria Ferin, Ltda., 1926-1963.

Dias, José Sebastião da Silva. *Correntes de sentimento religioso em Portugal, séculos XVI a XVIII.* 2 vols. Coimbra: Universidade de Coimbra, 1960.

Diégues, Manuel, Júnior. *Literatura de cordel.* Cadernos de Folclore, no. 2. Rio de Janeiro: Ministério da Educação e Cultura, 1975.

Encyclopedia Britannica, eleventh edition. S.v. "Flagellants."

Encyclopedia of the Social Sciences. S.v. "Messianism," by Hans Kohn.

Ertle-Wahlen, Brigitte. "Sobre as causas de movimentos messiânicos em populações tribais." *Revista de Antropologia* 17 (1969): 1-16.

Estevão, Tomas. *Doutrina cristã em lingua Concani (1622).* Edited by Mariano Saldanha. Lisbon: Agência Geral das Colônias, 1945.

[Estrada, José Possidônio.] *Superstições descubertas, verdades declaradas, & desenganos a toda a gente.* Rio de Janeiro: Typographia de Torres, 1826.

Ewbank, Thomas. *Life in Brazil.* New York: Harper and Bros., Publishers, 1856.

Facó, Rui. *Cangaceiros e fanáticos.* Rio de Janeiro: Editora Civilização Brasileira, 1963.

Falcão, Edgard de Cerqueira. *Encantos tradicionais da Bahia.* São Paulo: Livraria Martins, 1943.

Fernandes, Gonçalves. *O Folclore mágico do Nordeste*. Rio de Janeiro: Editora Civilização Brasileira, 1938.

Figueiredo, José de, Filho. "Casa de Caridade de Crato, fruto do apostolado multiforme do Pe. Ibiapina." *A Província* (Crato) 3 (1955): 14-25.

Fleury, Claude. *Pequeno cathecismo histórico*. Second edition. Rio de Janeiro: Typografia Nacional, 1856.

Fonseca, António Belard de. *Dom Sebastião*. 2 vols. Lisbon: n.p., 1978.

Fonseca, António Monteiro da, ed. *Sobre o sebastianismo: um curioso documento de começo do século XVIII*. Coimbra: Coimbra Editora, Ltda., 1959.

Franco, António. *Imagem da virtude em o noviciado da Companhia de Jesu no real collégio de Coimbra*. Évora: Officina da Universidade, 1719.

Freyre, Gilberto. *The Mansions and the Shanties*. Translated by Harriet de Onis. New York: A. A. Knopf, 1963.

Friedland, William H. "For a Sociological Concept of Charisma." *Social Forces* 3 (1964): 18-26.

Fuchs, Stephen. *Rebellious Prophets*. New York: Asia Publishing House, 1965.

Fülöp-Miller, René. *Leaders, Dreamers and Rebels*. New York: Viking Press, 1935.

Furtado, Celso. *The Economic Growth of Brazil*. Berkeley: University of California Press, 1963.

Galvão, Eduardo. *Santos e visagens*. Second edition. São Paulo: Companhia Editora Nacional, 1955.

Gardner, George. *Travels in the Interior of Brazil*. London: Reeves Brothers, 1846; condensed reprint edition, New York: AMS Press, 1970.

Graham, Thomas Richard. *The Jesuit António Vieira and his Plans for the Economic Rehabilitation of Seventeenth-Century Portugal*. Coleção Monografias, no. 1. São Paulo: Secretaria de Cultura, Ciência e Tecnologia, Departamento de Arte e Ciências Humanas; Divisão de Arquivo do Estado, 1978.

Grainha, E. Borges. *Histoire de la Compagnie de Jesus en Portugal*. Lisbon: Imprimerie Nationale, 1915.

Greenleaf, Richard E., ed. *The Roman Catholic Church in Colonial Latin America*. New York: A. A. Knopf, 1971.

Gross, Sue Anderson. "Religious Sectarianism in the *sertão* of Northeastern Brazil 1815-1966." *Journal of Inter-American Studies* 10 (1968): 369-383.

Guimarães, Alba Maria Zaluar. "Os Homens de Deus." Master's Thesis, Programa de Pos-graduação em Antropologia Social, Museu Nacional, Rio de Janeiro, 1974.

_____. "Os Movimentos 'messiânicos' brasileiros: uma leitura." *Boletim Informativo e Bibliográfico de Ciências Sociais* 6 (1979): 9-21.

_____. Review of *Milagre em Joaseiro*, by Ralph Della Cava, in *Religião e Sociedade* 4 (1979): 17-21.

Haring, C. H. *Empire in Brazil*. Second edition. New York: W. W. Norton and Co., Inc., The Norton Library, 1968.

Harris, Marvin. *Town and Country in Brazil*. New York: Columbia University Press, 1956.

Hessel, Lothar, and Raeders, Georges. *O Teatro jesuítico no Brasil*. Porto Alegre, Brazil: Editora da Universidade Federal do Rio Grande do Sul, 1972.

Hobsbawm, E. J. *Primitive Rebels*. New York: W. W. Norton and Co., Inc., 1959.

Hollander, E. P. *Leaders, Groups and Influence*. New York: Oxford University Press, 1964.

Hoornaert, Eduardo; Azzi, Riolando; Grijp, Klaus vander; and Brod, Benno. *História da Igreja no Brasil*. 2 vols. Petrópolis: Editora Vozes Ltda., 1977-.

Instituto de Teologia do Recife. *A Fé popular no Nordeste*. Salvador, Bahia: Editora Beneditina Ltda., 1965.

Jarvie, I. C. *The Revolution in Anthropology*. Chicago: Henry Regnery Co., 1967.

Jorge, Marcos. *Doutrina Christã*. Revised by Inácio Martins. Lisbon: Geraldo da Vinha, 1624.

Kanter, Rosabeth Moss. *Commitment and Community*. Cambridge, Massachusetts: Harvard University Press, 1962.

Kidder, David P. *Sketches of Residence and Travel in Brazil*. 2 vols. London: Wiley and Putnam, 1845.

Kidder, David P., and Fletcher, J. C. *Brazil and the Brazilians*. Philadelphia: Childs and Peterson, 1857.

Koser, Constantino. *Planos de sermões*. Separata Selecta, no. 8. Rio de Janeiro: Revista Eclesiástica Brasileira, 1956.

Koshiyama, Alice Mitika. *Análize de conteúdo da literatura de cordel: presença dos valores religiosas*. São Paulo: Escola de Comunicação e Artes, Universidade de São Paulo, 1972.

Koster, Henry. *Travels in Brazil*. Revised edition. Carbondale: Southern Illinois University Press, 1966.

LaBarre, Weston. "Materials for a History of Studies of Crisis Cults: A Bibliographic Essay." *Current Anthropology* 12 (February 1971): 3-44.

Lanternari, Vittorio. "Messianism: Its Historical Origin and Morphology." *History of Religions* 2 (1962): 52-72.

_____. *The Religions of the Oppressed*. Translated by Lisa Sergio. London: MacGibbon and Kee, 1963.

Lapa, José Roberto do Amaral, ed. *Livro da visitação do Santo Offício da Inquisição ao estado do Grão-Pará: 1763-1769*. Petrópolis: Editora Vozes Ltda., 1978.

Lawrence, Peter. *Road Belong Cargo*. Manchester: Manchester University Press, 1964.

Leacock, Seth, and Leacock, Ruth. *Spirits of the Deep*. Garden City, New Jersey: Doubleday Natural History Press, 1972.

Leão, Duarte Nunez do. *Descripção do reino do Portugal*. Lisbon: Jorge Rodriguez, 1610.

Leite, Antônio Áttico de Souza. "Memoria sobre a Pedra Bonita ou Reino encantado na comarca de Villa Bella, província de Pernambuco." *Revista do Instituto Archeológico e Geográphico de Pernambuco* 11 (1903-1904): 218-249.

Leite, Serafim. *Artes e ofícios dos Jesuítas no Brasil: 1549-1760*. Lisbon: Edicões "Broteria," 1953.

_____. *História da Companhia de Jesus no Brasil*. 10 vols. Lisbon: Livraria Portugalia, 1938-1950.

Leite, Serafim, ed. *Cartas dos primeiros Jesuítas do Brasil*. 3 vols. São Paulo: Commissão do IV Centenário da Cidade de São Paulo, 1956-1958.

Lessa, William A., and Vogt, Evon Z. *Reader in Comparative Religion: An Anthropological Approach*. Second edition. New York: Harper and Row, 1965.

Lewy, Guenther. *Religion and Revolution*. New York: Oxford University Press, 1974.

Livermore, H. V. *A New History of Portugal*. Cambridge, England: Cambridge University Press, 1966.

Lobo, A. de Sousa Silva Costa. *Origens do sebastianismo: história e perfiguração dramática*. Lisbon: Livraria Moderna Editora, 1909.

Loyola, Ignatius. *The Spiritual Exercises of St. Ignatius*. Translated by Anthony Mottola. New York: Doubleday and Company, Inc., Image Books, 1964.

Mariz, Celso. *Ibiapina: um apóstolo do Nordeste*. João Pessoa, Paraíba, Brazil: A União, 1942.

Marques, A. H. de Oliveira. *Daily Life in Portugal in the Late Middle Ages*. Translated by S. S. Wyatt. Madison, Wisconsin: University of Wisconsin Press, 1971.

Martins, Mário. "O Penitencial de Martim Perez, em mediêvo-português." *Lusitania Sacra* 2 (1957): 57-110.

_____. *Peregrinações e livros de milagres na nossa Idade Média*. Second edition. Lisbon: Edições "Broteria," 1957.

Martins, Valdomiro Pires, ed. *Catecismo Romano: versão fiel da edição autêntica de 1566*. Petrópolis: Editora Vozes Ltda., 1962.

Massina, Nestor. *A Igreja em Brabecena*. Rio de Janeiro: Serlico Gráfico do IBGE, 1952.

Mattos, Eusébio de. *Ecce Homo: Praticas prégadas no Collegio da Bahia às sestas feiras à noite, mostrando se em todas o Ecce Homo*. Lisbon, Ioam da Costa, 1677.

_____. *Sermoens do P. Mestre Eusébio de Mattos*. Lisbon: Miguel Deslandes, 1694.

Mattoso, José. "Eremitas portugueses no século XII." *Lusitania Sacra* 9 (1970-1971): 7-40.

Mecham, J. Lloyd. *Church and State in Latin America*. Chapel Hill: The University of North Carolina Press, 1934.

Meihy, José Carlos Sebe Bom. "A Presença do Brasil na Companhia de Jesus: 1549-1649." Ph.D. Dissertation, Universidade de São Paulo, 1975.

Mendoça, Heitor Furtado de. *Primeira visitação do Santo Ofício às partes do Brasil: confissões da Bahia, 1591-1592*. Rio de Janeiro: F. Briguet & Ca., 1935.

_____. *Primeira visitação do Santo Ofício às partes do Brasil: denunciações da Bahia, 1591-1593*. São Paulo: Editora Paulo Prado, 1925.

Menezes, Djacir. *O Outro Nordeste*. Rio de Janeiro: Livraria José Olympio Editora, 1937.

Moniz, Edmundo. *A Guerra social de Canudos*. Rio de Janeiro: Editora Civilização Brasileira S. A., 1978.

Montenegro, Abelardo F. *Antônio Conselheiro*. Fortaleza, Brazil: A. Batista Fontenele, 1954.

_____. *História do fanaticismo religioso no Ceará*. Fortaleza, Brazil: Editora A. Batista Fontenele, 1959.

Montenegro, João Alfredo de Sousa. *Evolução do catolicismo no Brasil*. Petrópolis: Editora Vozes Ltda., 1972.

Moraes, Mello, Filho. *Festas e tradições populares do Brasil*. São Paulo: n.p., 1846; reprint edition, São Paulo: Editora da Universidade de São Paulo, 1979.

Moraes, Rubens Borba de. *Livros e bibliotecas no Brasil colonial*. São Paulo: Secretaria da Cultura, Ciência e Tecnologia do Estado de São Paulo, 1979.

Morais, José Xavier Pessoa de. *Tradição e transformação do Brasil*. Rio de Janeiro: Editora Leitura S. A., 1969.

Mury, Paulo. *História de Gabriel Malagrida da Companhia de Jesus*. Translated by Camillo Castello Branco. Lisbon: Livraria Editora de Mattos Moreira & Ca., 1875.

Naquin, Susan. *Millenarian Rebellion in China*. New Haven, Connecticut: Yale University Press, 1976.

Nóbrega, Manuel da. *Cartas do Brasil e mais escritos*. Edited by Serafim Leite. Coimbra: University of Coimbra, 1955.

_____. *Dialogo da Conversão do Gentio*. Edited by Mecenas Dourado. Rio de Janeiro: Tecnoprint Gráfica S. A., 1968.

Nogueira, José Carlos de Ataliba. *Antônio Conselheiro e Canudos: revisão histórico*. Second edition. São Paulo: Editora Nacional, 1978.

Novaes, R. P. Americo de. "Methodo de ensino e de catechese dos Índios usado pelos Jesuítas e por Anchieta." In *Terceiro Centenário do veneravel Joseph de Anchieta*, pp. 140-188. Lisbon: Aillaud & Ca., 1900.

Oliveira, Aglae Lima de. *Lampião, cangaço e Nordeste*. Third edition. Rio de Janeiro: Edições O Cruzeiro, 1970.

Oliveira, Antônio Xavier de. *Beatos e cangaceiros*. Rio de Janeiro: n.p., 1920.

Omegna, Nelson. *Diabolização dos Judeus*. Rio de Janeiro: Distribuidora Record, 1969.

Ott, Carlos B. *Formação e evolução étnica da cidade do Salvador: o folclore bahiano*. 2 vols. Salvador, Bahia: Tipografia Manu Editora Ltda., 1955.

Overmeyer, Daniel L. *Folk Buddhist Religion: Dissenting Sects in Late Traditional China*. Cambridge, Massachusetts: Harvard University Press, 1976.

Pierson, Donald. *O Homem no valé do São Francisco*. Rio de Janeiro: Ministério do Interior, 1972.

Pimental, Antônio José de Mesquita. *Cartilha ou compêndio da doutrina christã*. Rio de Janeiro: Agostinho Gonçalves Guimarães e Ca., 1877.

Pinto, José Wanderley de A. "Costumes monásticas na Bahia: frades no século XVIII." *Revista do Instituto Geográphico e Histórico da Bahia* 46 (1920): 169-181.

_____. "Costumes monásticas na Bahia: freiras e recolhidas." *Revista do Instituto Geográphico e Histórico da Bahia* 44 (1918): 123-138.

Pires, Antônio. "Carta que o Pe. Antônio Pires escreveu do Brasil, da capitânia de Pernambuco, aos irmãos da Companhia, de 2 de Agosto de 1551." *Revista do Instituto Histórico e Geográfico Brasileiro* 7 (1844): 95-103.

Pires, Antônio Machado. *D. Sebastião e o Encoberto*. Lisbon: Fundação Calousta Gulbenkian, 1971.

Pires, P. Heliodoro. *Temas de história eclesiástica do Brasil*. São Paulo: São Paulo Editora, 1946.

Pita, Sebastião de Rocha. *História da América portuguesa*. Lisbon: n.p., 1730; reprint edition, São Paulo: Editora da Universidade de São Paulo, 1976.

Prado, Caio, Júnior. *Formação do Brasil contemporâneo: colônia*. Seventh edition. São Paulo: Editora Brasiliense, 1963.

Preto-Rodas, Richard A. "Anchieta and Vieira: Drama as Sermon, Sermon as Drama." *Luso-Brazilian Review* 7 (1970): 96-103.

Primeiro, Fidelis Motta de. *Capuchinhos em terras de Santa Cruz*. São Paulo: n.p., 1940.

Querino, Manuel. *A Bahia de outr'ora*. Second edition. Bahia, Salvador: Livraria Econômica, 1922.

Queiroz, Maria Isaura Pereira de. *O Campesinato brasileiro: ensaios sobre civilização e grupos rústicos no Brasil*. Second edition. Petrópolis: Editora Vozes Ltda., 1976.

_____. "O Catolicismo rústico no Brasil." *Revista do Instituto de Estudos Brasileiros* 5 (1968): 103-123.

_____. "Classifications des méssianismes brésiliens." *Archives de Sociologie des Réligions* 5 (1958): 111-120.

_____. *O Messianismo: no Brasil e no mundo*. Second revised edition. São Paulo: Alfa-Omega, 1976.

_____. "Mouvements méssianiques et dévélopment économique au Brésil." *Archives de Sociologie des Réligions* 16 (1963): 109-121.

_____. "O movimento messiânico do Contestado." *Revista Brasileira de Estudos Políticos* 9 (July 1960): 118-139.

Ramos, Jovelino P. "Interpretando o fenômeno Canudos." *Luso-Brazilian Review* 11 (1974): 65-83.

Reis, Angelo dos. *Sermam da Restauraçam da Bahia, prégado na Sé da mesma Cidade.* Lisbon: Miguel Manescal, Impressor do Santo Offício, 1706.

Ribeiro, René. "O Episódio da Serra do Rodeador (1817-20): um movimento milenar e sebastianista." *Revista de Antropologia* 8 (December 1960): 133-144.

Rio de Janeiro. Arquivo Nacional. Seção Histórico. Documentos sobre a Extinção dos Jesuítas; Brasil e Portugal, 1773-1801.

Rio de Janeiro. Biblioteca Nacional. Seção dos Manuscritos.

Rio de Janeiro. Instituto Histórico e Geográfico Brasileiro. Coleção Araújo Porto Alegre.

Rodrigues, Francisco. *História da Companhia de Jesus na Assistência de Portugal.* 4 vols. Porto: "Apostolado de Imprensa" Empresa Editora, 1931-1950.

Rodrigues, Pedro. "Vida do Padre José de Anchieta." *Annaes da Bibliotheca Nacional,* Rio de Janeiro 19 (1897): 1-49.

Rodrigues, Raimundo Nina. *A Loucura epidêmica de Canudos: Antônio Conselheiro e os jagunços.* Rio de Janeiro: Sociedade "Revista Brasileira," 1897.

Rodriguez, Carmen Garcia. *El Culto de los santos en la Espana romana y visigoda.* Madrid: Consejo Superior de Investigaciones Ciêntificas, 1966.

Romero, Sylvio. *Cantos populares do Brasil.* Rio de Janeiro: Livraria Clássica de Alves & Ca., 1897.

Rower, Basílio. *Páginas da história franciscana no Brasil.* Rio de Janeiro: Editora Vozes Ltda., 1957.

Russell-Wood, A. J. R. *Fidalgos and Philanthropists: The Santa Casa da Miséricordia of Bahia, 1550-1755.* London: Macmillan, 1968.

Sá, António de. *Sermam do Dia de Cinza que pregou o P. António de Saa da Companhia de Jesu.* Coimbra: Rodrigo de Carvalho Coutinho, 1673.

Sampaio, José Pereira de. *O Encoberto.* Porto: Livraria Moreira Editora, 1904.

São Paulo. Arquivo da Cúria da Sé de São Paulo. Livros do Tombo.

São Paulo. Instituto Histórico e Geográphico de São Paulo. Arquivo Histórico. Manuscript Collection.

São Paulo. Universidade de São Paulo. Arquivo do Instituto dos Estudos Brasileiros. Codice 15.

São Paulo. Universidade de São Paulo. Arquivo do Instituto dos Estudos Brasileiros. "Compêndio de profecias traslados em o anno de 1810."

São Paulo. Universidade de São Paulo. Arquivo do Instituto dos Estudos Brasileiros. "Dialogo portuguêz de anônimo utupiense, que trata da Philozophia do Encoberto." [Brazil], 1659.

Saraiva, António José. *História da cultura em Portugal*. 3 vols. Lisbon: Jornal do Foro, 1950-1962.

_____. *Inquisição e cristãos-novos*. Fourth edition. Porto: Editorial Inova Ltda., 1969.

Scarano, Julita. *Devoção e escravidão*. Second edition. São Paulo: Companhia Editora Nacional, 1978.

Seguro, Turíbio Vilanova. *Bom Jesus da Lapa*. Third edition. São Paulo: Gráfica São José, 1948.

Shils, Edward. "Charisma, Order and Status." *American Sociological Review* 30 (April 1965): 199-213.

Silva, Fernando Altenfelder. "As Lamentações e os grupos de flagelantes do São Francisco." *Sociologia* 24 (March 1962): 15-28.

Silva, Innocêncio Francisco da. *Diccionário bibliográphico portuguêz*. 7 vols. Lisbon: Imprensa Nacional, 1859.

Silva, José Calasans Brandão da. *O Ciclo folclórico do Bom Jesus Conselheiro*. Bahia: Typografia Beneditina Ltda., 1950.

_____. *No Tempo de Antônio Conselheiro*. Bahia: Publicações da Universidade da Bahia, 1959.

Siqueira, Sônia A. *A Inquisição portuguesa e a sociedade colonial*. São Paulo: Editora Ática, 1978.

Soares, José Carlos de Macedo. *Fontes da história da igreja católica no Brasil*. Rio de Janeiro: Imprensa da Instituto Histórico e Geográfico Brasileiro, 1954.

Sousa, Gabriel Soares de. *Tratado descriptivo do Brasil em 1587*. Third edition. Rio de Janeiro: Companhia Editora Nacional, 1938.

Souza, Joaquim Silvério de. *Sítios e personagens*. São Paulo: Typographia Salesiania, 1897.

Spix, Johann Baptist von, and Martius, Karl von. *Através da Bahia*. Third edition. Translated by Manoel A. P. da Silva and Paulo Wolf. São Paulo: Companhia Editora Nacional, 1938.

Stavenhagen, Rodolfo. "Seven Erroneous Theses about Latin America." *New University Thought* 4 (1966-1967): 25-37.

Telles, Balthazar. *Chrônica da Companhia de Jesu da Provincia de Portugal*. 2 vols. Lisbon: Paulo Craesbeeck, 1645-1647.

Teixeira, Marcos. "Livro da Denunciações qu se fizerão na Visitação do Santo Ofício a Cidade do Salvador da Bahia de Todos os Santos do Estado do Brasil, no Anno de 1618." *Annaes da Biblioteca Nacional do Rio de Janeiro* 49 (1927): 75-198.

Thrupp, Sylvia, ed. *Millennial Dreams in Action*. The Hague: Mouton and Co., 1962.

Trindade, Bento da. *Sermão do primeiro dia de Quarenta horas, pregado na Se da Bahia*. Lisbon: Francisco Luiz Ameno, 1784.

Valente, Waldemar de Figueiredo. *Misticismo e região: aspectos do sebastianismo nordestino*. Recife, Brazil: Instituto Joaquim Nabuco de Pesquisas Sociais, Ministério da Educação e Cultura, 1963.

Varnhagen, F. A. de, ed. "Excerptos de várias listas de condemnados pela Inquisição da Lisboa, desde o anno de 1711 ao de 1767." *Revista do Instituto Histórico e Geográfico Brasileiro* 7 (1845): 54-86.

Vasconcellos, Simão de. *Chrônica da Companhia de Jesu do estado do Brasil*. Second edition. 2 vols. Lisbon: A. J. Fernandez Lopes, 1865.

_____. *Vida do veneravel Padre José de Anchieta*. 2 vols. Lisbon: Oficina de João da Costa, 1672; reprint edition, Rio de Janeiro: Imprensa Nacional, 1943.

Velloso, J. M. de Queiroz. *D. Sebastião*. Second edition. Lisbon: Empresa Nacional de Publicidade, 1935.

Vide, Sebastião Monteiro da. *Constituições primeiras do Arcebispado da Bahia feitas e ordenadas pelo illustrissimo e reverendissimo senhor D. Sebastião Monteiro da Vide, 5o. Arcebispo do dito Arcebispado, e do Conselho da Sua Magestade, propostas e aceitas em o Sinodo Diocesano (1707)*. Lisbon: n.p., 1719; reprint edition, São Paulo: Typographia Antônio Louzado Antunes, 1853.

Vieira, António. *Cartas*. 4 vols. Lisbon: J. M. C. Seabra & T. Q. Antunes, 1855.

_____. *Cartas do Padre António Vieira*. Second edition. Edited by João Lúcio de Azevedo. Lisbon: Imprensa Nacional, 1970.

_____. *Obras escolhidas*. Edited by António Sergio and Hernani Cidade. 12 vols. Lisbon: Livraria Sá da Costa Editora, 1951-1954.

_____. *Por Brasil e Portugal*. Edited by Pedro Calmon. São Paulo: Companhia Editora Nacional, 1930.

Vieira, Hérmes. *História das missões*. São Paulo: Officinas Gráphicas da "Ave Maria," 1938.

Vilhena, Luís dos Santos. *A Bahia no século XVIII*. 3 vols. Bahia: Editora Itapuã, 1969.

Wallis, Wilson D. *Messiahs: Christian and Pagan*. Boston: The Gorham Press, 1918.

Walzer, Michael. *The Revolution of the Saints: A Study in the Origins of Radical Politics*. Cambridge, Massachusetts: Harvard University Press, 1965.

Warren, Donald, Jr. "Portuguese Roots of Brazilian Spiritism." *Luso-Brazilian Review* 5 (1968): 3-34.

Willeke, Venâncio. *Franciscanos na história do Brasil*. Petrópolis: Editora Vozes Ltda., 1977.

Willems, Emilio. *Followers of the New Faith*. Nashville, Tennessee: Vanderbilt University Press, 1967.

Wilson, Bryan R. *Magic and the Millennium*. London: Heineman, 1973.

Worseley, Peter. *The Trumpet Shall Sound*. New York: Schocken Books, 1968.

Xidieh, Oswaldo Elias. *Semana santa caboclo*. São Paulo: Instituto de Estudos Brasileiros, 1972.